THE LEADERSHIP MOMENT

THE LEADERSHIP MOMENT

*Nine True Stories of Triumph and Disaster
and Their Lessons for Us All*

MICHAEL USEEM

THREE RIVERS PRESS

NEW YORK

Published by Three Rivers Press, New York, New York.
Member of the Crown Publishing Group.

Random House, Inc. New York, Toronto, London, Sydney, Auckland
www.randomhouse.com

THREE RIVERS PRESS is a registered trademark and the Three Rivers
Press colophon is a trademark of Random House, Inc.

Originally published in hardcover by Times Books in 1998.

Printed in the United States of America

Library of Congress Cataloging-in-Publication Data
Useem, Michael.
The leadership moment: nine true stories of triumph and disaster
and their lessons for us all / by Michael Useem.
Includes bibliographical references and index.
1. Leadership—Case studies. 2. Elite (Social sciences)—Case studies.
3. Executive ability—Case studies. I. Title.
HM141.U83   1998
303.3'4—dc21   98-11282

ISBN 0-8129-3230-7

30 29 28 27 26 25 24 23

Foreword

What a delight to come upon Michael Useem's fascinating and seminal book. What a sublime pleasure to read a book about my favorite topic that is artfully and compellingly written, in which the lessons are profound and the spellbinding narratives are about people playing for mortal stakes and not mind-numbing case studies about "empowerment" or "process re-engineering." (There should be lifetime term limits on how often business books use those words.) Aside from its clarity and elegance, there are at least three reasons why this book, of the seven hundred or so of its type published within the past year, is exemplary. (There are more than three, but my aim is to make sure that my foreword is not longer than any of the following chapters.)

First, there is the selection of cases: nine fascinating narratives, from Roy Vagelos's decision while he was CEO at Merck to develop a cure for river blindness on behalf of millions of Africans to Arlene Blum's leadership of a group of committed women climbers to the peak of Annapurna. It wouldn't surprise me if the history of science rests on the exquisite selection of a few cases. Think about Darwin's Galapagos journey, the Hawthorne experiment, Freud's six cases, Erikson's biographies of Gandhi and Luther, William H. Whyte's two "street corner gangs," and so on. Exemplary scholars not only know the "whys" and "hows" of their subjects, they know the "wheres," too: where to look. Useem knows where to look. The stories he recounts are about real people, not stick figures, facing excruciatingly tough decisions, where real danger lurks and many possibilities exist, where the conditions are labile, and action has to be taken. One of the most fascinating stories, bordering on the Sophoclean, tells how John Gutfreund, the so-called "King of Wall Street," failed to take action and was "resigned" from his own creation, Salomon Inc., which then had to be rescued by the redoubtable Warren Buffett.

Second, the cases deal with what in theater would be called "turning points": those propitious moments where a particular action (or inaction, à la Gutfreund) could lead to colossal damage. Like a good historian, Useem gets all around the subject and the protagonist, and gives the reader a prismatic, you-are-there view of the action. Each chapter was suspenseful and I raced to the end with ambivalence, wanting to know how it turned out, but not wanting it to end—the feeling you get when you're reading a terrific novel. But this is about real people facing dramatic, life-challenging, morally consequential events fraught with risk and danger.

Finally, number three. The principles Useem draws from his narratives are universal. They are not specific to industry, to consulting, or to high-tech ventures, but can be applied to the management of artistic enterprises, PTAs, corporate America, and the International Monetary Fund. The lessons we learn from this book are eternal and universal because they have everything to do with the human spirit and with such old fashioned verities as integrity, bravery, commitment, and downright common sense.

As you can sense, I loved this book. It's one helluva read.

—Warren Bennis
University Professor
University of Southern California

Contents

Introduction:
The Leadership Moment

"To be courageous . . . is an opportunity that sooner or later is presented to all of us."

—John F. Kennedy, *Profiles in Courage*

W E ALL NEED to be ready for those moments when our leadership is on the line and the fate or fortune of others depends on what we do. Perhaps only a few people will be touched by the decisions that we make at such critical moments; perhaps many will. But either way, we need to be prepared if we are to seize the opportunity.

It is my view that one of the most effective ways of preparing for such challenges is by looking at what others have done when their own leadership was on the line. By examining their experience and asking what they did and what they could have done, and by wondering what you would have done yourself, you can better anticipate what you should do when faced with your own leadership challenges.

This book presents accounts of nine such experiences. We witness people at extraordinary moments. We examine how they guided their crew, company, or country through the climactic events that followed. Each account is about an individual who faced a turning point—and how that person led when it counted most.

3

The purpose is to help you and your associates face your own critical challenges, to triumph when your own leadership is put to the test. The book is also intended to help you better ready yourself for everyday tests of leadership when your actions, whether large or small, will shape the future of others.

Leadership has acquired nearly as many incarnations as there are analysts and consultants. For historian James MacGregor Burns, leadership is a calling. For Peter Drucker, leaders are those whose followers "do the right thing." For Abraham Lincoln, leadership appealed to the "better angels of our nature."[1]

A precise definition is not essential here; indeed, it may be impossible to arrive at one. But I take leadership to signify the act of making a difference. Leadership entails changing a failed strategy or revamping a languishing organization. It requires us to make an active choice among plausible alternatives, and it depends on bringing others along, on mobilizing them to get the job done. Leadership is at its best when the vision is strategic, the voice persuasive, the results tangible.

Leadership on the Line

OUR FOCUS IS on exceptionally difficult decisions—those fateful moments when our goals are at stake and it is uncertain if we will achieve them, and when the outcome depends on mobilizing others to realize success. The more extraordinary the stakes, the more profound the outcome, the more searing the stress, the more such events stand out.

Think back on your own experiences at work and in your community over the years. Ask which few still seem truly singular, unforgettable events. In some cases, you may have felt you were a different person afterward. In others, you may wish you had done something very differently. For most, you may ever after feel elated or despondent when you recall your actions. The glow of pride lingers—or the cringe of remorse. You may still be awed by the number of people who joined you in doing what was right. Or you may be dogged by the missed opportunities that might have guided those around you to a safer harbor.

Consider an opportunity facing mountaineer Peter Hillary, whose father, Sir Edmund Hillary, had made the famous first ascent of Mount Everest in 1953, and who himself had scaled Everest in 1990. Four years later, Hillary and seven fellow climbers were nearing the summit of K-2, the world's second highest mountain, when deteriorating weather convinced him that the entire party should turn back. He failed to persuade the others, however, and so descended alone while they pushed on toward the summit. None of the other seven ever returned. Today, Hillary says, the decisions he made at that critical junction—his own determination to turn back, his inability to convince his fellow climbers—still haunt his waking moments: "You get the opportunity to reenact in your mind those closing scenes again and again and again."[2]

One of my own early moments still serves as a point of continuing reflection. A college friend and I—twenty-two-year-olds in Europe for the summer—had just climbed Monte Rosa, a long but not technically difficult feat. We set out from Zermatt, Switzerland, on a rainy August day to scale a nearby peak called the Dom. At 14,942 feet, it is the highest summit wholly within Switzerland—higher than the Matterhorn or the Jungfrau, though not quite as high as Monte Rosa on the Swiss-Italian border or Mont Blanc on the French-Italian border. Refusing to be deterred by worsening weather, we clambered aboard a cogwheel train in Zermatt for a ride down a valley to the tiny village of Randa at the base of the Dom.

From there at noon we moved quickly up a steep forested trail, lamenting the continuous rainfall and limited views. As we climbed out of the valley, the rain intensified and the temperature dropped as the sky darkened. Our rain gear soon proved inadequate in the downpour, and by 6 P.M. we were very wet, very tired, and very alarmed about the remaining distance to a high hut staffed by the Swiss Alpine Club. Our plan had been to overnight there and set out at 3 A.M. for the Dom's magnificent icy summit. But the precipitation had turned to snow, the trail to the refuge had long ago crossed the timber line, and the path was increasingly difficult to follow.

By 8 P.M., the elements were ominous. We were now hours above the protective comfort of the valley with half a foot of fresh snow obliterating the trail. Darkness fell, we were drenched to the bone, and there was no sign of any hut. The adrenaline of controlled panic pushed us forward as fast as we could move. But still no sign. By 9 P.M., we began searching for crevices in the rocky canyon up which we were climbing. We had brought neither tent nor sleeping bags, convinced that the Dom hut would provide all the warm shelter we needed. Now we hoped to spot a protected bivouac site that would allow us to survive the night.

A futile half-hour search left us even more desperate and hopelessly lost when suddenly we spotted a tiny light at a great distance. It was a miraculous moment, for surely the light marked the Dom refuge. An hour later the hut keeper and his guest climbers opened the door and welcomed two bedraggled stragglers, blanketed with snow from head to toe. The guests had all turned in for the night, but the hut keeper, to our ever-lasting gratitude, had placed a kerosene lamp outside the hut's door just in case a beacon might be needed by any unlucky souls caught in the worsening storm.

What did we do right? Very little, though perseverance in the face of rapidly worsening weather did prove essential.

What was our biggest mistake? Several vie for the designation. Among our greatest was the failure to anticipate or prepare for the new conditions that emerged. Equally important was our failure to mobilize people whose assistance we needed. The hut keeper's display of the lamp proved fortuitous, but a local guide would have known the way under any conditions. How much better if we had followed that path of prudence from the begin-ning, instead of relying on blind luck and the hut keeper's good-will.

What do we wish we had done ahead of time? Better reconnaissance tops the list. We wish we had known more about the approaching storm, the time required to reach the hut under the best of conditions—an optimistic estimate had led to a late start—and the topography around the hut, which would have helped us locate the refuge even with an obliterated trail.

What is the most enduring lesson for my actions now? I study far more avidly and prepare far more carefully before moving onto unknown terrain. Such lessons remain a powerful influence years later on my actions with groups and organizations for which I carry any responsibility. And I wonder, even now, about the consequences if the hut keeper had not displayed the lamp.

Leading in a More Turbulent Era

LEADERSHIP DECISIONS AND the development of good leaders are important in any age, but the changing face of business and government makes both more important today than perhaps they have ever been before.

The decentralization of private companies, public agencies, and even community groups has spread the responsibility for decision making more broadly at the same time that it has created greater accountability for each individual decision made. Such corporate restructuring and reengineering—and its public variant, "reinventing government"—puts a premium on leadership not just at the top, where it has always mattered, but throughout an organization. Raymond Smith, chief executive officer of Bell Atlantic Corporation, forced his firm through a wrenching remake on its way to a 1997 merger with NYNEX Corporation. To get there, he offered this formula: "We have to change everything in our organization. We have to transform everybody from a bureaucrat to an owner." For Smith, the company's future depended upon "making everybody into a strategic thinker."[3]

Companies and investors are also more globalized, with ever-greater portions of business coming from Canada, Chile, or

China. Cross-border alliances, international mutual funds, and foreign direct investments are outstripping purely domestic growth. In 1996, McDonald's Corporation opened nine new restaurants per day—six of those outside the United States. Managing your way through a world of diverse dialects and conflicting customs requires a nimbleness seldom expected in the past.[4]

Finally, managers everywhere face more turbulent times as they negotiate their way through a world of greater ambiguity and less certainty. In a study of chief executives at forty-eight firms among the Fortune 500 largest U.S. manufacturers, Wharton Professor Robert House asked two executives at each of the companies to assess the extent to which their own CEOs (1) were visionary, (2) showed confidence in themselves and others, (3) communicated high expectations, (4) personally exemplified the firm's values, and (5) demonstrated determination and courage. House then compared firms that experienced dynamic and uncertain environments with those whose contexts were more predictable. His finding: CEOs made a significant difference to profit margins for companies facing a world of change and uncertainty but far less for firms not so challenged.[5]

No wonder we remember wartime prime ministers and presidents better than peacetime leaders. Leadership matters most when it is least clear what course should be followed. Our own turbulent times make this an opportune time to examine what others have done when their leadership has been on the line.

A Plan of Action

THIS BOOK OFFERS nine accounts of leaders facing critical moments. Each is shaped around the experience of one person encountering circumstances that would test leadership to its utmost. Taken together, these stories map a broad terrain, from strategic vision and persuasive communication to team building and fast action. The nine episodes:

- Roy Vagelos ends river blindness in Africa.
- Wagner Dodge outruns a Montana forest fire.
- Eugene Kranz returns the Apollo 13 astronauts to Earth.
- Arlene Blum ascends Annapurna.
- Joshua Lawrence Chamberlain commands on the Gettysburg battlefield.
- Clifton Wharton restructures a pension giant.
- John Gutfreund loses control of Salomon Inc.
- Nancy Barry builds a bank for Third World women.
- Alfredo Cristiani cracks El Salvador's killing cycle.

Out of each of these stories emerges a set of guiding principles that can be remembered and used in everyday management, whether in a company or community. Collectively, these stories and the principles drawn from them offer a threefold prescription: prepare yourself, prepare your colleagues, prepare your organization.

The decisions and actions of those above, beside, and below you matter more when your organization faces challenge or requires redirection. Yet these are the very moments when developing leadership is least practical. Periods of normalcy—when strategies are working and results are flowing—are the times to develop leadership even though its need is least evident.

Leading under fire is when the flame burns brightest, when we can see what makes a difference. It is by examining these defining events of the past, I believe, that we can best understand and remember what we will need for our own leadership in the future.

❦

CHAPTER 1

Roy Vagelos Attacks River Blindness

"The drug was needed only by people who couldn't afford it."

O NE DAY IN NOVEMBER 1988, a chief and fourteen elders—all male, mostly in their fifties and sixties—welcomed a visitor to the village of Sikoroni in Mali, West Africa. Several were led to the gathering, held under a veranda, by young boys pulling the ends of their walking sticks. Of the fourteen, twelve arrived with lifeless eyes, victims of one of the world's most dread diseases, river blindness. Among the 20 million people afflicted worldwide, a third of a million are completely blind. In some regions of Africa, villagers assume that growing old means becoming blind. But many never reach that state: river blindness can cut life expectancy by a third or more.

The disease is spread by tiny, humpbacked blackflies that breed in fast-moving streams. In much the same way that mosquitoes transmit malaria, the flies pick up the larvae of a parasite known as *Onchocerca* when they bite those already suffering from river blindness. Later, when they bite the uninfected, the flies leave some of the larvae behind. The baby parasites rapidly multiply and spread through the recipient's body, lengthening to as much as two feet and living for as long as fourteen years. Their prodigious offspring—as many as 200 million micro-worms inhabit some victims—spread through the skin, causing

Children guiding blind adults in the village of Sikoroni, Mali

severe itching, and into the eye, where the result is progressive blindness. The chief of Sikoroni village has some vision remaining, but the mottled skin on his legs indicates that blindness is only a matter of time. "Before you have white hair," he says, "it is normal to become blind."

The banks of the West African rivers on which the carriers breed should provide ideal farmlands in an otherwise water-deprived region between the Sahara Desert to the north and the rain forests to the south. Instead, they are regions of human devastation, the African equivalent of American ghost towns. Entire communities have migrated to drier lands, abandoning their ancient villages and fertile valleys. River blindness is a scourge not only of human health but also of economic development.

Until the late 1970s, public officials combatted the disease by targeting the insects' breeding grounds with pesticides, but the grounds were too numerous and too unpredictable for complete control. Exotic drug treatments were available, but they required medical supervision and could not be massively applied. River blindness persisted worldwide.

And then, in 1978, a potential solution emerged unexpectedly—not in West Africa but in a New Jersey laboratory. William C. Campbell, a research scientist at Merck & Company, one of the nation's leading pharmaceutical firms, specialized in drug treatments for parasitic worms in livestock. His team was developing what would later be marketed as ivermectin, a potent agent with virtually no side effects, when Campbell realized that it might also be effective against a strain of horse worms that are biological cousins of the human parasites that cause river blindness.

Appreciating the human potential for the animal treatment, Campbell asked P. Roy Vagelos, his laboratory director, for approval to develop a form of the drug for human use. Such an undertaking would require several years of costly research in Merck's labs followed by extensive testing in African villages. In all, the price tag for development was likely to run into the millions of dollars; and even if Campbell was correct in his conjectures, there was virtually no prospect of paying customers on the horizon: most river blindness victims were without the means to acquire any drug.

Dr. Vagelos, former chair of the department of biological chemistry at the School of Medicine of Washington University, is a physician and biochemist who joined Merck in 1975 as senior vice president of research. His investigation of the link between cholesterol and heart disease had led to the development of a major cholesterol-lowering drug, Mevacor, that had been credited with lowering heart attack rates by 40 percent. But Vagelos was also an executive of the company, responsible for judicious use of its investors' equity, and now he was being faced with a corporate conundrum of the most difficult sort: if

P. Roy Vagelos

he approved Campbell's request, he might be committing Merck and its shareholders to underwriting a product of no commercial value; if he denied Campbell's request, he might short-circuit a drug that could lift a plague from the lives of millions of poor people.

River Blindness

RIVER BLINDNESS WAS first medically identified in 1893, but its association with the species of flies that flourish in fast-moving water—*Simulium damnosum*—was not understood until 1926. Later, as the British and French West African colonies were winning independence in the 1960s and their populations were burgeoning, the devastating effects of the disease emerged as one of the region's premier curses. By the 1970s, according to the World Health Organization (WHO), 85 million people were at risk in thirty-five developing countries, mainly in Africa—from Ethiopia to Nigeria and Angola to Malawi—but also in Latin America, including Brazil, Guatemala, and Mexico. Eighteen million people already carried the parasites, and more than a million had suffered visual impairment. In endemic areas, half of the residents would be expected to become blind before death. Two drugs—diethylcarbamazine and suramin—could be used to treat those infected, but their administration was arduous and their side effects were sometimes lethal.

"When I was born, my sight was normal," recalled a seventy-one-year-old man in the village of Bayong in western Cameroon, southeast of Nigeria and just above the equator. "It all started one day when my eyes became watery and sticky. Then I began seeing faintly. Eventually I could not see at all. I was eight." Near the Nkam River, four out of five people were infected. Grotesque nodules of worms bulging through the skin and patchy loss of pigmentation—"leopard" skin—were common sights. More than a million of Cameroon's 6.5 million people were estimated to carry the parasite, and 3 million more were at risk.

The massive scale of the affliction called for an attack on the disease before it struck, and WHO took the offensive, establishing its Onchocerciasis Control Program in 1974 in Ouagadougou, the capital of what is today Burkina Faso, to combat the carriers across the region. Pesticides had long been used to decimate everything from malarial mosquitoes to fruit flies, and the program targeted the blackflies' breeding grounds with toxic chemicals. Focusing on the more than twelve thousand miles of the Volta and Niger Rivers in Benin, Burkina

Faso, Ghana, Ivory Coast, Mali, Niger, and Togo, the program used fleets of trucks, airplanes, and helicopters to spray. In 1986, the application was extended to the neighboring nations of Guinea, Guinea-Bissau, Senegal, and Sierra Leone.

There was no prospect of eradicating the flies themselves— their niche in nature was too secure—but if their numbers could be reduced in the worst areas, what is known as an "inflection point" might be reached. With too few flies to carry sufficient larvae among villagers, active cases might subside, and, as they declined, the remaining flies would have fewer sources from which to draw and then redistribute the larvae. If the vicious circle of parasite transmission could be broken long enough, most fly bites should become harmless and the disease would ebb.

Insect control, however, is a daunting task. Because of the region's vastness, program managers had to pinpoint the areas where the flies were breeding most actively. Adult females deposit two hundred to eight hundred eggs at a time on water bodies, and eggs successfully adhering to rocks or sticks just below the surface will survive and hatch within two days—if they can draw ample oxygen from fast-flowing water. (The supply of oxygen is critical: river blindness was rare in Gambia, for example, where the main waterways become languid as they near the sea.) Once the eggs hatch, the fly larvae consume tiny nutrients in the water for five to eight days, and that is the time to strike: the larvae ingest not just the water but whatever toxins have been added to it.

But the right microconditions for the egg hatching changed constantly with the rains and river flows, and a comprehensive control system would require hundreds of human "captures." These "vector collectors," or "fly boys," position themselves on riverbanks and expose their legs as bait. When flies take the bait, they are scooped into test tubes and their parasitic cargoes assayed to determine whether the insecticide is working and where more is needed.

Alternative methods of collecting the flies do not work well, placing a premium on the collectors, who run the risk of contracting the very disease they are working to prevent. The strategy itself also contains an Achilles' heel: rapidly reproducing insects tend to build resistance to chemical sprays. Most die in the lethal mix, but a few survive, and their offspring, quick to reproduce in large numbers, enjoy the same protective genetics that spared their parents. Moreover, the insecticide often decimates the blackfly's natural enemies, and in the absence of predators, the insect populations sometimes come back with a vengeance. Even worse, parasite-bearing flies can travel fifty miles a day or more with a good tailwind, and they sometimes suddenly reinfest a region that seemingly had been freed.

Still, this labor-intensive method reduced the incidence of river blindness, and the United Nations and other donors invested millions of dollars to make it work. Their generous backing allowed WHO to attack breeding grounds across a region twice the size of France.

Discovering a Cure

DURING THE 1970S, Merck's chief executive officer, Henry W. Gadsden, and his successor, John J. Horan, were worried about the firm's unstable growth. Two prescription drugs—Indocin for rheumatoid arthritis and Aldomet for high blood pressure—had been blockbusters, but their seventeen-year patent protection was about to expire. To refill the pipeline, the company counted on its amply funded, well-staffed scientific enterprise, Merck Sharp & Dohme Research Laboratories. Under Roy Vagelos's direction, the lab consumed almost a billion dollars between 1975 and 1978, much of it going to highly paid scientists who were encouraged to pursue their instincts, publish their results, and view their studies as a means of mitigating human suffering. The investment was working: Vagelos and his staff developed a powerful antibiotic and successful products to treat arthritis and glaucoma. Their achievements built on an honored tradition dating to the 1930s that included the synthesis of vitamin B12 and the creation of cortisone.

Each success, though, was extraordinarily expensive in both cash and time. Just to bring a single drug to market required on average $200 million and twelve years. To cull the few most promising prospects for such an investment from among the thousands proposed, Vagelos conducted rigorous reviews and then presented the best to a committee of scientific advisers. The advisers determined which of the proposed products would be most likely to succeed in development and then in the marketplace. It was here that treatments for rare diseases often fell by the wayside: with few patients who would be willing to pay for a given treatment, the high cost of manufacturing it would make it uneconomical. Because of the risks attending such decisions, pharmaceutical companies rely on tough-minded research managers such as Vagelos to ensure that only winners are picked.

Such rigor at the back end of product development was balanced by license at the front. To cultivate the biochemical candidates for development, creative talents such as William Campbell were given free rein at Merck. In that tradition, Campbell and his research team gathered bacteria from around the world, hoping that some naturally occurring microbe would prove effective against the parasitic worms afflicting their laboratory test mice. By 1975, their collection stood at about 100,000 varieties of bacteria. Some 40,000 of these microorganisms had already been tested for antiparasitic powers, but only one—retrieved from a golf course near the Japanese city of Ito—had yielded any results. But those results had been dramatic.

The first evidence came from a single infected mouse fed a broth containing the bacterium: it ate little, but it was almost immediately worm-free. Other mice soon displayed the same remarkable recovery. "I remember the feeling of excitement in the group," Campbell recalled. "Not only was a new product showing activity against the worms," but it was effective "in extremely small amounts, and it was not harming the mice at all." The research team discovered that it also served as a nerve poison against parasites in sheep, pigs, and dogs. Dogs are often infected with heartworms, and as Campbell examined those tested with the drug, the impact was "breathtaking."

The Merck group used its discovery to create a drug later named ivermectin, and in 1978 the U.S. Department of Agriculture approved its sale as Ivomec. The drug in its many applications—against ear mites in cats and heartworms in dogs, among others—would become the world's leading health care product for animals in the 1980s and Merck's second biggest moneymaker ever. By 1992, sales of ivermectin reached $500 million a year and continued growing by 15 percent annually. By 1997, revenue from the drug was near $1 billion. But all that is for later.

In 1978, as Campbell conducted further studies of ivermectin's clinical properties, he noticed that it was effective against an obscure horse parasite, *Onchocerca cervicalis*. While this worm does little damage to its hosts and was of scant clinical interest, Campbell recognized that it was biologically akin to *Onchocerca volvulus*, the parasitic cause of river blindness. He shared ivermectin with an Australian researcher, who soon reported the drug's success in treating cattle. With this drug's proven success in two distinct animal species, Campbell believed that, time and money permitting, he might be able to create a form for humans. He wrote his supervisor a memo on May 9, 1977, suggesting that human application might be possible. The memo was forwarded to Roy Vagelos, who sent a personal note to Campbell, urging him to continue his work and acquire all the data he could on human application. Having come from three levels up the hierarchy, Vagelos's memo fortified Campbell's focus on this compelling objective.

By 1979, Campbell was convinced he had the necessary scientific evidence to continue, and he and his boss, Jerry Birnbaum, were whisked by company helicopter to the laboratory's research management council—the preeminent decision-making forum on drug development, chaired by Roy

Vagelos—to make their case. The council was known for its tough-mindedness, but Campbell and Birnbaum were convincing, and the group was persuaded even though the drug being proposed was an almost certain money loser.

"We knew that it was going to be a borderline economically viable project at the start," Vagelos recalls, and not just because the potential customer base was drawn from the world's most impoverished people. Attempting to apply an antiparasitic drug to another species frequently fails. Worse, if the human application had unanticipated side effects, it could jeopardize sales of the animal product, as customers wondered whether toxic reactions in people might be experienced by animals as well. Those responsible for developing and marketing animal health care products with ivermectin told Vagelos it would be a mistake to continue.

But not to proceed would dismay Campbell and his researchers, convinced as they were that they might be on the verge of a scientific breakthrough against a disease that was the curse of millions. For Vagelos to block them, even knowing the financial drain, would have contradicted the company axiom that health precedes wealth. A green light would also strengthen the firm's premier position in parasitology.

"Emotionally, you become very involved in what you can accomplish," Vagelos explains, "so we could hardly wait to start these experiments." With Vagelos's go-ahead, Campbell built on the microbiology and chemical identification work of an entire Merck team that included Mohammed A. Aziz, a tropical disease expert and director of clinical research. In January 1980, Vagelos approved the drug's first clinical trials in West Africa.

The field testing itself would prove no easy task, since it would require tight administration of the drug and precise data from its users. For assistance, Merck turned to WHO, which was already spraying for river blindness but was ready for anything less burdensome. The director of the WHO program, Brian Duke, responded skeptically. "Initially, when Merck came to us and said it had this fancy new drug," he recalled, "my reaction was 'We've got several drugs, and they all incite violent reactions.' " Still, the prospect of an easily administered medication proved too alluring to pass up, and in February 1981 WHO donated scientists and facilities at the University of Dakar in Senegal to conduct the field tests.

Merck's Aziz and the university's Michel LaRivière moved cautiously at first. They initially administered tiny doses, and LaRivière stayed with the patients through the night to monitor their reactions. Within a few weeks, skin snips from the patients' hip areas revealed a remarkable clearing: virtually no parasites remained. By the end of the year—and many patients later—Aziz and LaRivière were more confident: the human guinea pigs had experienced few adverse effects, and a small dose was all they required to radically reduce their microworm count for months or more. The scientific community, however, was far from convinced by what seemed an almost magical cure. A former WHO official, André Rougemont, now a scientist at the University of Geneva, cautioned in late 1982 that Aziz and his colleagues were being "over-optimistic." Rougemont's letter to *The Lancet*, the leading British medical journal, warned that ivermectin "brings no really new or interesting feature to the treatment" of river blindness. A group of WHO officials visited Merck headquarters to review the data, and they suggested that the river blindness victims in the clinical test had had only mild cases. They also warned that dangerous toxicity was sure to be encountered when applied to larger populations, and even one fatality in 25,000 applications can be enough to doom a product.

Stung by the skepticism, Aziz and his colleagues ran extensive new tests. In 1983–1984, they conducted trials in Ghana, Liberia, Mali, and Senegal, and in 1985–1986 they carried out even larger experiments with 1,200 patients in Ghana and Liberia. The tests confirmed the remarkable early findings and allowed a fine-tuning of the regimen required. The researchers discovered that, ingested as a pill, the drug killed most microworms, inhibited adult worms from producing offspring, and drove parasites from the skin, leaving few for biting flies to transmit. The effects were not always enduring or complete, but when taken as a single dose once a year—just one or two small pills annually—the medication inhibited both the spread of parasites and progressive blindness. It could not be used with pregnant women, the severely ill, or preschoolers, but it worked with most others, and adverse reactions included only a low-grade fever and lymph-node tenderness. What's more, the immediate relief was tangible. For some, the skin infection had been akin to a lifelong case of poison ivy; with a single dose of Mectizan, they were free of severe itching for the first time in years. A study of the drug's impact in Liberia in the late 1980s reported that "Ivermectin could have a revolutionary impact on the transmission of onchocerciasis."[1]

Delivering a Product

SO STRIKING WERE the human benefits and so modest the medical downsides that Roy Vagelos sought commercial approval in 1987. By now the company decision was entirely his to make. Though Vagelos says he "never had the yearning to run a large corporation," in 1985 the Merck board had promoted him to chief executive officer.

In deciding whether to manufacture a drug that will never sell and will likely cost more than $3 a tablet to produce and distribute, the fifty-eight-year-old Vagelos drew on a company history almost unique to American business. While Japanese *keiretsu* such as Sumitomo trace their roots back centuries, few U.S. firms can boast a history of more than decades. Merck, however, traces its lineage to 1668, when Friedrich Jacob Merck acquired an apothecary in the German town of Darmstadt. In 1891, what by then had become a thriving family company dispatched its eldest son, age twenty-four, to open a business in the United States. He and his son, George W. Merck, transformed the American branch into an independent drug developer and manufacturer. Merck and Company found great success during the 1940s in developing penicillin and strepto-mycin, and by 1978 the company was employing 28,000 around the world, selling more than $2 billion worth of products annu-ally, and earning more than $300 million. Its success had long been guided by a culture that put patients and customers first, company and stockholders second.

Ten years after Campbell first recognized ivermectin's human potential, Merck requested regulatory approval from the French Directorate of Pharmacy and Drugs. France had a spe-cial interest in river blindness: some human carriers of the par-asites reside in that country, having arrived with the illness from Chad and other former French colonies in Africa. The French Directorate was also the agency to which West Africa turned for guidance, and in October 1987 the directorate authorized com-mercial production.

Merck labeled its creation "Mectizan," but its jubilation over government approval was short-lived since the company now faced the daunting task of delivering the drug it had taken a decade to produce. Market research had already confirmed the obvious: the West African victims were too poor to pay for the drug and too isolated to reach easily. First-year costs alone were expected to be $2 million, and that was just to begin mov-ing the product through the distribution pipeline. The annual cost could exceed $20 million before the disease was con-trolled.

In anticipation of French government approval, Vagelos sought public underwriting of Mectizan's production and distri-bution. He approached the U.S. Agency for International Development, which has a mandate to provide social and eco-nomic assistance to the developing world. "This is an opportu-nity to plant the U.S. flag in West Africa at almost no cost," he pleaded. Administrator M. Peter McPherson responded with a line that Vagelos would hear repeatedly in the months ahead: "We don't have any money."

Vagelos canvassed other potential donors, including international development agencies, private foundations, European governments, and African nations. Former U.S. Secretary of State Henry Kissinger, now a Merck consultant, opened doors for Vagelos around the world. "I was doing more for this than I'd done for any other drug," Vagelos remembered, but all to no avail. The pharmaceutical industry refers to drugs with uneconomic markets as "orphans." Nobody, it seemed, wanted this one.

WHO's Brian Duke publicly urged Merck simply to give away the drug. At first Vagelos was dismayed by Duke's comments. "That's not the way you do things in a commercial organization," he said. "You don't start out by thinking you're going to give something away." Inside the company, however, Mohammed Aziz was urging the same costly course of donation; doing so, he believed, was a matter of professional calling.

Though Merck's culture made health its first priority, simply giving away the drug—and even arranging for its distribution— would have been without precedent. Yet in the absence of other sponsors, Mectizan would remain a laboratory curiosity. "We could get no one else to buy it," Vagelos recalled. "We faced the possibility that we had a miraculous drug that would sit on a shelf."

Finally, Vagelos decided to give away the drug to all who need it forever—and to ensure it was delivered before the microworms could take their devastating toll. "Sometimes in your life," he says, "you've got to take a leadership position and make a decision." At press conferences in Paris and Washington on October 21, 1987, Vagelos and other Merck officers described a "unique situation in which the drug was needed only by people who couldn't afford it."

Distribution of the product presented its own set of dilemmas: without pharmacies, health care professionals, or even roads to reach the millions of villagers who need Mectizan, the free supplies would languish in storehouses. For Merck to become directly responsible for moving the drug into the bush, however, required capacities it did not possess. It would also require approval by government, which might find it awkward for a multinational corporation to be rendering humanitarian assistance. The solution: Merck formed the Mectizan Expert Committee, a group of public health experts, to formulate guidelines, select suitable parties for distribution, and compile medical records. Chaired by William H. Foege, executive director of the Carter Center and former director of the U.S. Centers for Disease Control, the committee moved the drug to more than a million people within two years. In 1991, the U.S. Agency for International Development, which had earlier denied Vagelos's request for backing, provided $2.5 million for distribution assistance.

As news of the drug's miraculous qualities spread across the back country of West Africa, people walked through the night to villages where it was rumored that the drug would be dispensed. In 1989, William Campbell visited one such village in northern Togo. After a nine-hour auto trip, he arrived on a designated treatment day. He saw a line snaking past a record keeper, who noted whether each female recipient was the first, second, or later wife of the male head of household, and where the children fell in that order. The recipients were weighed, screened for pregnancy, and then handed the tablets and a bowl of water. The parents of many of the children were already blind, a fate their offspring would now escape. Some had risen in the middle of the night and walked for miles to reach the village in time.

"This is great!" one village chief told Campbell. "Now go back and find the cause of death." Another chief of several villages reported that he had been ousted from two of them because he had been unable to bring in the treatment. "We had begun with a smear in a bottle" a decade earlier, Campbell remembers, and now "to see these little white tablets given to people" and the great excitement they created was "an absolutely unforgettable moment of my professional life."

Public Health or Investor Value?

ROY VAGELOS UNDERSTOOD full well that Mectizan was less a commercial product than a philanthropic commitment of long standing. The drug kills the microworms but not the adults, and though it interrupts their reproduction, it does not totally control it. Ridding the body completely of onchocercae requires annual dosages for up to fourteen years, and given that 18 million people were hosts to the parasite and another 80 million were at risk, Vagelos was also under no illusion that it would somehow look cost-free to Merck shareholders. By 1997, a decade after his decision to go ahead, the lost income from the drug had reached $200 million or more—an investment that could have brought at least one commercially viable product to market.

Vagelos also worried that free distribution of Mectizan could set a precedent for future donations of medicines for diseases such as malaria and guinea worms, which also affected millions of poor people in developing nations. (Guinea worm disease, carried by tiny fleas in drinking water, also produced human parasites that spread through the body, resulting in blistering of the skin and muscle damage similar to the crippling effects of polio.) If development agencies came to expect free distribution of Third World treatments, it could have the ironic effect of inhibiting research on them. He was concerned, too, about product liability: if even a few patients experienced debilitating reactions, even in the remotest corners of West Africa, trial lawyers could develop a lucrative business.

Vagelos worked for directors who were elected by shareholders to represent their financial interests, and he was surely correct to assume that they wanted as much return as possible on their investment. The company's top twenty-five investors in 1996, as shown in Table 1.1, picked Merck over thousands of other stocks for financial gain, not noblesse oblige. The more than 240,000 individuals and institutions who own Merck stock

TABLE 1.1. LARGEST INVESTORS IN MERCK & CO. AS OF SEPTEMBER 30, 1996

	INSTITUTIONAL INVESTOR	NUMBER OF SHARES
1	BZW Barclays Global Investor	31,082,551
2	Bankers Trust	20,203,763
3	Sarofim, Fayez	20,059,101
4	Alliance Capital Management	19,318,268
5	FMR Corporation (Fidelity)	17,454,217
6	State Street Corporation	16,742,638
7	Capital Research and Management	15,335,000
8	College Retirement Equities Fund	11,438,399
9	Mellon Bank	10,293,027
10	J. P. Morgan & Company	10,233,807
11	Investors Research Corporation	10,127,300
12	The Travelers Group Inc.	10,085,418
13	University of California	10,038,215
14	Invesco Capital Management	9,540,340
15	PNC Bank Corporation	8,668,294
16	Chase Manhattan Corporation	8,558,953
17	Northern Trust Corporation	7,377,537
18	American Express Financial	7,235,831
19	State Farm Mutual Automobile Insurance Co.	7,017,000
20	California Public Employees' Retirement System	6,538,544
21	New York State Common Retirement System	6,279,802
22	Chancellor Capital	6,081,875
23	Teacher Retirement System of Texas	5,835,000
24	First Union Corporation	5,821,609
25	Fiduciary Trust International	5,785,678

are financially poorer for Vagelos's decision. Retirement account holders (including this writer) at the College Retirement Equities Fund—the eighth largest stockholder, with more than $875 million invested in Merck—will have a little less on which to live in their later years. Money managers at Fidelity Investments (FMR, the fifth largest stockholder) may be judged less well by their boss, Edward Johnson III, when he reviews their performance in presiding over their $1.3 billion Merck holding.

One strand of American business culture would certainly question how Vagelos could possibly take it upon himself to make such a decision. Milton Friedman, a Nobel Prize–winning economist, articulated the critique as cogently as any. For him, any diversion of company resources from profitable investment, especially in the name of social responsibility, amounts to executive irresponsibility. To spend stockholders' money on anything but profitable returns is the same as imposing a tax and then deciding unilaterally how the proceeds will be spent. CEOs such as Vagelos are the appointed agents of the company's investors, and such actions violate the fiduciary trust that has been placed in them, or so Friedman argued.[2]

Such actions, Friedman felt, also undermine democratic principles: social allocations should be decided through political process, not economic fiat. Corporate executives, he wrote, "are capable of being extremely far-sighted and clear-headed in matters that are internal to their businesses," yet they "are incredibly short-sighted and muddle-headed in matters that are outside their businesses." For them to make such decisions, then, is to shortchange private stockholders and misallocate public resources. "There is one and only one social responsibility of business," Friedman contended, and it is "to use its resources and engage in activities designed to increase its profits."

The ever-increasing concentration of stockholding in the hands of a small number of professional money managers during the late 1980s and 1990s has reinforced Friedman's message. Institutional investors increasingly demand the highest possible return on their holdings, and they have mastered political clout to match their economic might. The pressure for ever-greater shareholder returns was mounting just as Roy Vagelos did precisely what Friedman counseled against.

Albert J. Dunlap, the chief executive officer who radically downsized Scott Paper Company in 1994–1996 before its sale to Kimberly-Clark and then restructured Sunbeam Corporation in 1996–1998 in much the same way, exemplifies Friedman's principles. For Dunlap, there is only a single constituency worthy of management attention: the owners. The special interests of employees, communities, the public—often lumped together as corporate "stakeholders"—should influence no company decisions. "I don't believe in the stakeholder concept one minute," Dunlap asserts. "I believe in the fact that the shareholders take all the risks, the shareholders own the company." Remember who is boss: "You work for the shareholders. They're the constituency to whom you have to be responsive."[3]

Had he thought like a Milton Friedman or Albert Dunlap, there is little doubt where Vagelos's reasoning would have taken him: Let the United Nations, West African governments, or relief organizations such as CARE underwrite the drug's development and distribution. Their leaders are trained and authorized to make such decisions. It is they who should decide whether river blindness, leprosy, malaria, or AIDS deserves priority. If they have not found Mectizan worthy of their own support—and each in turn had rejected Vagelos's appeal—their collective judgment should be heeded. WHO had even sent an early delegation to suggest to Vagelos that Merck back away from the drug's development. When it comes to a choice between public health and investor value, Friedman's principles point unequivocally in one direction. Fortunately for the many millions of victims of river blindness, Vagelos's thinking was just as clear as Friedman's, but it pointed unequivocally in the opposite direction.

> *By implication:* Clearheaded thinking about why you have been appointed to an office and what those who have placed you there expect of you is prerequisite to clear-minded, if not predictable, decision making.

Doing Well by Doing Good

THE CALL FOR an unyielding focus on shareholder value is a powerful action principle. It is a first axiom of corporate governance, with strategic implications that are unambiguous, and it clearly guides management decisions. What is far more open to question, though, is how to create shareholder value most effectively. Are investors' interests best served by focusing exclusively on the investors themselves, as Friedman and Dunlap argue? Or are they better served in the long run by focusing on customers and letting the customer focus create the value that shareholders have every right to expect? Among the business voices championing the latter course is that of George W. Merck, son of the company's American founder and himself onetime chairman of Merck. "We try never to forget that medicine is for the people. It is not for the profits," Merck says, but he is quick to stress that the objectives are the same: "The profits follow, and if we have remembered that, they have never failed to appear. The better we have remembered it, the larger they have been." What might sound unbusinesslike is little more than advocacy of an alternative avenue for reaching the same ends.

So deeply rooted is this alternative at Merck that it heads up the company's charter: "The mission of Merck & Co., Inc., is to provide society with superior products and services," it declares. The mission is also to render "investors with a superior rate of return," but that will come only on realization of the first. "We are in the business of preserving and improving human life," the statement continues. "All of our actions must be measured by our success in achieving this goal." Financial results should then follow: "We expect profit," the mission statement concludes, but it must come "from work that satisfies customer needs and that benefits humanity." Pension funds and other institutional investors "couldn't care less about any good things that we do," Vagelos observes. They are "interested in the bottom line. But so are we." Mectizan should not really dent the bottom line: "I don't think we are cheating the stockholders."[4]

A skeptical voice may still question whether such formulas are more rhetoric than reality, but at Merck such high-flown thoughts are translated into action, and the actions themselves have ultimately served shareholders' interests handsomely. Tuberculosis, for example, had surged in Japan in the years after World War II, and the war's devastation left few in a position to pay for a powerful Merck product that worked wonders against it: streptomycin. The company finally decided to donate a large supply to the Japanese public. Coming at a moment of great hardship, Merck's generosity has long been remembered. When the company sought access to Japan's domestic market in 1983, Japanese authorities took the rare step of approving Merck's $300 million purchase of 50.02 percent of Banyu Pharmaceutical, Japan's tenth largest drug maker. At the time it was the largest direct investment by a foreign company in a notoriously closed market. "We received help from the Japanese government in making the first acquisition of this kind to be allowed," remembers Vagelos, and it "should come as no surprise that Merck is the largest American pharmaceutical company in Japan today."[5]

"So you see," Vagelos concludes from Merck's experience with streptomycin in Japan, "doing the right thing can bring unexpected rewards later on." Doing well by doing good can also bring immediate windfalls: the Mectizan program has helped Merck attract and retain the best research talent, and it has bolstered employees' pride. Beyond doubt, repeated donations can undermine the earnings of, if not bankrupt, an enterprise. The challenge is to identify areas of mutual gain—ways in which the company and society benefit together rather than at the cost of each other.

Merck tried to strike that balance in the 1980s, when it was approached by the Chinese government for help in combating an outbreak of hepatitis B, a leading source of liver cancer and mortality in the world's most populous nation. China asked Merck to share its technology for the production of a vaccine, and Merck agreed, accepting a token payment of $7 million, a fraction of the actual cost.

A study of a cross section of major firms—the five hundred corporations comprising the Standard & Poor's 500 index—confirms that mutual-gain reasoning can prove superior to mutual-exclusion thinking. Two researchers examined the S&P

500 companies' behavior in eight policy areas where the ests of shareholders and other groups are sometimes viewed as zero sum, including environmental protection, employee practices, and community relations. They found that companies performing better in one year (1989) were more socially generous the following year (1990)—but also that their generosity fostered even higher financial returns the year after that (1991). Just as it had done with Japan, Merck might have to wait years to see its giving repaid with new business opportunities in China or West Africa, but this research suggests that tangible paybacks can also come. Sometimes giving away money is a way of making it.[6]

Among the paybacks realized by Merck is the ownership of a benchmark by which the behavior of other pharmaceuticals is judged. Comparing Britain's largest pharmaceutical—Glaxo Wellcome—with Merck, one business writer concluded in 1992 that the first "is a hollow enterprise, lacking purpose and lacking soul," while the second "builds around it a streak of idealism." The reason: Merck's Vagelos was a "light and airy genius." The message apparently hit home at Glaxo: in 1993, the company announced that it was investing in a molecular biology research program to produce an antibiotic or vaccine for tuberculosis, which has become resurgent with AIDS and is responsible for 3 million deaths a year, mainly among the poor. Glaxo's new chief executive, Richard Sykes, explained his £10-million, five-year investment with an implicit compliment to Merck: "We don't start from the point of saying 'Is there a market here for a drug? If not, it's not important.' That's not right for the future. Today we have a responsibility." In 1996, Glaxo unveiled an even larger program to donate a potent new product for malaria, one of the developing world's great remaining scourges, affecting as many as 500 million people. Other pharmaceuticals have heeded the call, too: DuPont is now bequeathing nylon to filter guinea worms out of drinking water, and American Cyanamid is donating a larvacide to control them.[7]

By *implication:* Identifying ways of bolstering long-term investor and public interest, even if they momentarily reduce shareholder returns, can foster a favorable culture, build a company cadre, and establish a public reputation that can more than compensate for any temporary shortfalls in investor value.

Just Doing

MANAGERS ARE CONTINUALLY taking calculated risks. Indeed, one sign of a manager's executive promise is his or her ability to calculate those risks better than others on the executive waiting list. Moments arise, however, when strict analysis does not serve well. Sometimes what is required is simply instinct.

An example known to many graduates of MBA programs is a decision made by Bowen McCoy, an investment banker at Morgan Stanley. McCoy had taken a six-month sabbatical in 1982 to "collect" his thoughts by trekking through the mountains of Nepal. He was resting at 15,500 feet on his way up the difficult mountain pass of Thorung La, just north of Annapurna, when he encountered an unconscious, nearly naked sadhu, or Hindu holy man. If he carried the sadhu to a lower elevation, McCoy knew, he might end his chance of crossing the pass and completing his month-long trek; he could even endanger himself and others if the unpredictable weather turned stormy. After briefly watching other trekkers help warm the sadhu, McCoy departed for the pass and several hours later celebrated victory on it. Only then did he question whether he had done the right thing in abandoning the sadhu before ensuring his safe descent and physical recovery. McCoy later confessed, "I had literally walked through a classic moral dilemma without thinking through the consequences."[8]

When McCoy evaluated the dangers of delay and the rewards of continuing to climb, a narrowly defined calculus pointed him upward. But a more broadly conceived calculus, one in which his enduring values were entered alongside the momentary risks and rewards, might have led him instead to aid the frozen traveler. Even in the absence of mutual gains, even without indirect advantages to offset tangible costs, some decisions require a transcending of self-interest, whether personal or organizational.

So it was with Merck and Mectizan. As word reached the company's headquarters that the French government would soon approve the drug—and far sooner than expected—Roy Vagelos and his chief financial officer, manufacturing director, and other executives were still debating how to price it. The senior vice president for international marketing was opposed to a giveaway, fearing a backlash against other Merck products in the developing world. Others questioned whether public donation of this drug would discourage private development of future cures and drive down the prices of present products. During monthly meetings they pondered the question time and again, yet despite growing alarm that they were still without a dispensing strategy, no consensus emerged. Tension was rising, Vagelos remembers, over fears of "what would happen if the damn thing was approved and we didn't have a plan." What was clearer was Mectizan's affordability: "We were coming to the realization," he recalls, "that at any price the vast majority of the eighteen million patients that were infected were probably not going to afford" the drug. Finally, on the eve of Mectizan's approval, knowing that a decision would have to be announced, Roy Vagelos brought the debate to a close: Merck would give the drug away forever.

So certain was Vagelos that he had taken the right action—"I thought that the company couldn't have done otherwise"—that he did not inform the governing board before the public announcement. At a directors' meeting shortly thereafter, several questioned why they had to learn from the press that their own company had just committed itself to an everlasting bequest. "You know this happened in a matter of days," he responded. Yes, it should have come before them, he conceded, "but would anybody around the table have made a different decision?" None said yes. "When you really think about it," he later stated, "nothing was going to stand in the way."

By implication: Achieving an organization's imperative is a leader's calling, but sometimes we confront moments when we must do otherwise. Such decisions must be relatively unique, otherwise the inconsistency in our organizational leadership will be evident for all to see; but if they are unthinkingly bypassed, our value as a leader may be doubted by everyone, including ourselves.

Knowing Where You're Going

BOWEN MCCOY MADE a decision over which he remains enduringly ambivalent. "I never found out if the sadhu lived or died," he wrote fifteen years after the encounter, and he still wonders if he chose the right path. Roy Vagelos, on the other hand, made a decision about which he is not the least bit uncertain.

Whether right or wrong in retrospect, the challenge is to anticipate and prepare for such decisions in prospect. "The fact was, we had no plan for dealing with the contingency of the sadhu," recalled McCoy. Such contingencies occur when narrowly defined self-interests compete with more broadly defined objectives. For McCoy, it was a matter of reaching a pass or aiding a victim: "We had to decide how much to sacrifice ourselves to take care of a stranger." For Vagelos, the question was not framed in either-or terms. He knew that in assisting river blindness victims, he was ultimately building shareholder value.

The task, then, is to create a framework for informing such decisions well before they are confronted. Such a framework should explicitly incorporate the diverse considerations that underlie most decisions, providing the manager with an opportunity to reflect on their relative importance before being called to apply them. If such a guiding framework is not available, its absence may deny a manager the balanced set of criteria needed to reach the optimal outcome. In the case of the sadhu, for instance, it might have been useful for McCoy to have reflected more fully on the purpose of his journey: Was it primarily to cross the pass and complete the trek, or was it more to "collect" his thoughts and understand his values? In wondering why he did not carry the sadhu two days downhill to a village where he might recover, McCoy suggested that it should have been more of the latter: "Perhaps because we did not have a leader who could reveal the greater purpose of the trip to us."

Vagelos did not require a leader to reveal such purpose—it was already well inscribed in the company's philosophy and culture. Moreover, a framework for reaching balanced decisions was widely shared in the company, the product of management's explicit steps to build a culture that put patients before profits. Vagelos's decision to distribute Mectizan freely to all who need it forever would surely seem bizarre to the employees of many companies. Merck employees, for the most part, understood his action and realized it meant neither that he had lost his bearings nor that the company had become a charitable foundation. Merck had built a set of values that transcended profitability in its narrowly defined form and in so doing had fostered a framework in which the Mectizan decision seemed not aberrant but consistent. "Some organizations do have values that transcend the personal values of their managers," McCoy wrote. "Such values, which go beyond profitability, are usually revealed when the organization is under stress." And, he warned, companies "that do not have a heritage of mutually accepted, shared values tend to become unhinged during stress."

A parallel moment illustrating the same point confronted one of Merck's competitors, Johnson & Johnson. On September 29, 1982, Mary Kellerman, a twelve-year-old in suburban Chicago, died mysteriously. So did twenty-seven-year-old postal worker Adam Janus and his brother, and Janus's wife fell into a coma.

Medical authorities were considering quarantining the Chicago suburb when they discovered that all of the victims had died of cyanide, and all had also ingested one of Johnson & Johnson's premier products, Extra-Strength Tylenol.

"Tylenol poisoning" became an instant threat to the well-being of millions of Americans and the health of the company. The next day, investors drove Johnson & Johnson's stock price down by 20 percent, a $2 billion decline in total value. Chief executive officer James E. Burke ordered all Tylenol off product shelves and urged the public to return all purchased capsules. The Tylenol poisoning garnered more media attention than any story since the 1963 assassination of President John F. Kennedy.

Investigators soon determined that the cyanide had been introduced through tampering on shelves in isolated Chicago-area stores, not through J&J's manufacturing, but Burke persisted with his costly recall of all Tylenol from all outlets across the country—a $100 million loss and a massive effort that could not have succeeded had thousands of J&J employees not taken parallel steps that pulled the company in the same direction. On the face of it, the company could be seen as overreacting in ways that would cost investors dearly. But Burke's gamble that a short-term loss would be more than restored by long-term gains in company credibility and public trust proved prescient. With a resolve to restore the brand, J&J introduced tamper-proof packaging and within a year had recovered four fifths of its original market.

Just as Merck workers find the company's core values embedded in its mission statement, so do Johnson & Johnson employees draw on a well-known company "credo" that is the basis of annual employee discussions. It, too, focuses on health care providers and users, not on shareholders: "We believe our first responsibility is to the doctors, nurses and patients, to mothers and fathers and all others who use our products and services." A concluding paragraph adds, "Our final responsibility is to our stockholders," who "should realize a fair return." With the credo widely understood, thousands of J&J employees helped remove Tylenol from stores, responded to reporters' questions, and worked to restore confidence in the brand with little explicit guidance from Burke.[9]

McKinsey & Company, a strategy consulting firm, studied steelmaker Nucor, SunTrust Banks, the Body Shop, and Merck to understand why all four have long-standing records of exceptional employee commitment. The conclusion: Their deeply ingrained cultures are the crux. The companies' values, the McKinsey research found, "energize people to go the extra mile" for the firm, a "competitive advantage" for driving performance "that is hard to replicate."[10]

By implication: Knowing where you want go and what your values are can be essential to getting there, to ensuring that all of your interests and concerns are factored into fast-moving decisions, and to avoiding later regrets about being less than clear-minded. Building that understanding into an organization's culture can help all employees be clear-minded and fast-acting as well.

The Gift of Sight

FORMER U.S. PRESIDENT Jimmy Carter wrote in 1993 that the "the campaign against river blindness shows how a major international corporation can change the lives of millions of people" by "stepping beyond the confines of narrow, short-term interest and accepting a broader, global responsibility." Vagelos's leadership, Carter offered a year later, has "helped prove that a corporation can . . . be deeply concerned with the alleviation of suffering throughout the world."[11]

In 1994, WHO orchestrated a consortium with the World Bank, the Inter-American Bank, and private development organizations to support the distribution of Mectizan, finally

Blind mother with son in Southern Chad

giving what had been withheld a decade earlier. In 1995, the Carter Center in Atlanta, Georgia, launched a twelve-year program with the United Nations, the World Bank, and other agencies to control and eventually eradicate river blindness. Private donors stepped forward as well: the International Eye foundation, the Helen Keller Foundation, and Lions International all assisted the distribution. John J. Moores, a software entrepreneur, contributed $11.5 million to the new River Blindness Foundation, established in 1990 at the University of Houston's Department of Optometry and merged into the Carter Center in 1996. The total cost of ending the illness sometime early in the new millennium is estimated at more than $500 million.

By 1992, Mectizan had reached 5 million people; by 1994, 12 million; and by 1996, 19 million. In Nigeria, one of the areas with the greatest concentration of river blindness in the world, the number of people treated rose from fewer than 50,000 in 1989 to more than 6 million in 1996 (see Figures 1.1 and 1.2). In late 1996, the U.S. Food and Drug Administration approved the use of ivermectin for human use in the United States, to be branded as Stomectol. A company "can have an enormous impact," says Vagelos, "if it is willing to do what is required to be socially responsible."[12]

The New York Times wrote in 1989 that Merck's development of Mectizan "will surely rank as one of the century's great medical triumphs." The World Bank commented in 1995 that "the near elimination of river blindness as a public health problem and an obstacle to socio-economic development in West Africa stands as one of the most remarkable achievements in the history of development assistance." That same year, Merck contributed $45 million worth of Mectizan. Jimmy Carter reported that, with the worldwide campaign against river blindness, "villages, once deserted, are now flourishing. And children, once resigned to darkness, are now growing up free for the first time, able to look toward the future." One authority on infectious diseases ranks Mectizan with quinine and penicillin for its vast impact. It remains, however, a partial victory: while river blindness is in retreat in Mali and other West African countries, it is spreading in Uganda, Equatorial Guinea, and elsewhere.[13]

On October 25, 1995, Merck unveiled at its Rahway, New Jersey, headquarters a seven-foot bronze statue, "The Gift of Sight," depicting a boy leading a blind man along a path. Four decades earlier, Roy Vagelos had graduated from Rahway High

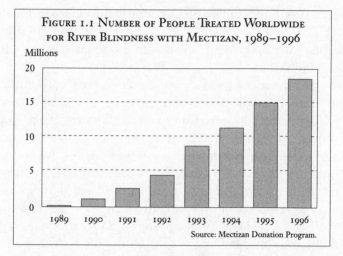

FIGURE 1.1 NUMBER OF PEOPLE TREATED WORLDWIDE
FOR RIVER BLINDNESS WITH MECTIZAN, 1989–1996

Source: Mectizan Donation Program.

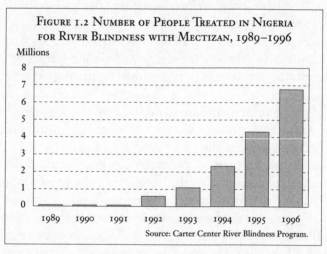

FIGURE 1.2 NUMBER OF PEOPLE TREATED IN NIGERIA
FOR RIVER BLINDNESS WITH MECTIZAN, 1989–1996

Source: Carter Center River Blindness Program.

School and had worked at his parents' diner near Merck head-quarters. The diner was a favorite of Merck researchers, and Vagelos had listened attentively to their words and the spirit behind them. In 1996, Vagelos reported that not a single share-holder had complained about his decision to give away the drug forever. It was, in his view, Merck's "finest moment."[14]

Jimmy Carter and Roy Vagelos visiting a village in Chad

Vagelos had never seen the human consequences of his decision until 1994. That year he and his wife, accompanied by Jimmy and Rosalynn Carter, traveled to a village in Chad on a day when Mectizan was being dispensed. Standing at the front of a long, expectant line, Vagelos deposited one or two white tablets into each raised palm. Nearby a young mother nursed an infant, and he noticed that she was already blind. He took heart from the knowledge that her child would not suffer the same fate.

In a recent interview, Vagelos reflected on the fateful decision he had made a decade earlier. Yes, he said, Merck's generosity had burnished its reputation. Yes, the decision had bolstered its recruitment. But, he was asked, would he have committed his

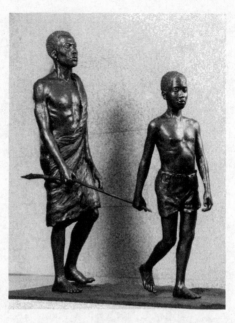

Statue at Merck & Company headquarters

company to such a costly program even without such benefits? Yes, he said, he had "no choice. My whole life has been dedicated" to helping people, and "this was *it* for me." He remained silent for several seconds. His eyes lost focus.

❧

CHAPTER 2

Wagner Dodge Retreats in Mann Gulch

"What the hell is the boss doing, lighting another fire in front of us?"

WAGNER DODGE WAS facing *the* moment, *the* decision of a lifetime. A fast-moving forest-and-grass fire was about to overrun him and the fifteen firefighters under his command. Less than two hours earlier they had sky-jumped into a fiery gulch in Montana. Now an enormous wall of flame was racing at them up the tinder-dry ravine. They knew they were running for their lives, and Dodge knew their time was running out.

Dodge's mind, still remarkably in control, was also concluding that he and his men had almost reached a point of no exit. He estimated that in a mere ninety seconds the conflagration would overtake him and the crew. If he could still discover a way out or invent some way to survive within, it would make the difference between miraculous escape or catastrophic failure, between saving himself and his fifteen men or losing all.

A Fire in Mann Gulch

LOCATED IN A rugged area of central Montana, Mann Gulch runs into the Missouri River in a region named Gates of the Mountains in 1805 by the famed northwest explorer Meri-

R. Wagner Dodge (clutching a handkerchief)

wether Lewis. In such inaccessible areas, fire is always a worry, but on August 5, 1949, the danger was greater than usual. By late summer, central Montana was so bone dry that the U.S. Forest Service put the fire potential at 74 on a scale of 100. Twenty-five miles to the south, Helena was reaching a record temperature for the day of 97 degrees Fahrenheit. A small thundershower moving through the area offered momentary respite. But the storm also meant lightning, and lightning often means fire.

By 2:30 P.M., a crew had loaded onto a C-47 at the smoke-jumper base in Missoula. Thirty-three-year-old R. Wagner Dodge was the crew chief. A man of few words, he had fought many fires during his nine years in the business, and he was deservedly the team boss for the technical expertise he brought to the attack. The fifteen men who checked their parachutes

Mann Gulch and Missouri River, August 20, 1949

and climbed on board with him were young, eager, conditioned. They had been fighting fires all summer and were ready for this one. Some were college students who had volunteered for the summer; others were career firefighters. Several were World War II veterans.

Among those who took their seats for the twenty-minute trip to Mann Gulch were Robert Sallee, underage for the work at seventeen, and Walter Rumsey. The outfit also included David Navon, a former first lieutenant in the 101st Airborne Division who had parachuted into Bastogne, Belgium, during the 1944 German counteroffensive, and William J. Hellman, who only a month earlier had parachuted onto the Ellipse between the

Robert Sallee and Walter Rumsey

White House and the Washington Monument. The men under Dodge's command hailed from Massachusetts and Montana, New York and North Carolina, Pennsylvania and Tennessee.

As the aircraft circled twice around Mann Gulch, Dodge and spotter Earl Cooley scouted a safe landing zone. The men were belted down, but the plane was bouncing about in the turbulence, an early hint of what was to come. Many of them felt half sick, and one, too nauseous to jump, opted to return to Missoula. On Dodge's signal, the others leapt out the open door, targeting a landing zone high on the upper left side of the ravine, marked as point 1 in Figure 2.1.

Dodge and his crew hit the ground at 4:10 P.M. and by 5:00 had gathered their chutes, loaded their packs, and shouldered their shovels. Dodge suggested that his men take some food and drink before moving out. In fire jumpers' parlance, it was a "ten o'clock fire" on the other side of the gulch—one they

The Mann Gulch fire, August 5, 1949

would fight all night and expect to have under control by 10 A.M. the next day. August fires often begin late in the afternoon as lightning rumbles through, and most of them are small enough to be contained by the following morning. The men knew that a brief rest now would probably be their last until the job was done.

This day, though, they were moving without several requisite items, including a map and radio. The map was falsely believed to be in the hands of a firefighter already in the area, and the radio had been destroyed when an equipment parachute failed to deploy. Still, on Dodge's orders they moved down the gulch single file, confidently prepared to confront the blaze.

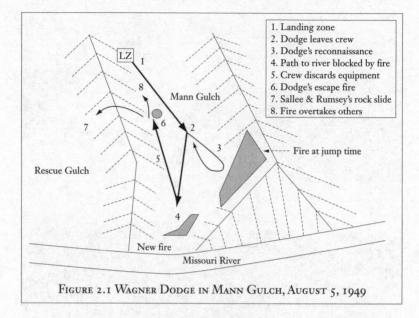

1. Landing zone
2. Dodge leaves crew
3. Dodge's reconnaissance
4. Path to river blocked by fire
5. Crew discards equipment
6. Dodge's escape fire
7. Sallee & Rumsey's rock slide
8. Fire overtakes others

LZ 1

8

Mann Gulch

7

6 2

3

Fire at jump time

5

Rescue Gulch

4

New fire

Missouri River

FIGURE 2.1 WAGNER DODGE IN MANN GULCH, AUGUST 5, 1949

The firefighter already in the area linked up with Dodge and his crew, but the full complement of sixteen men was a team only in the loosest sense. The men had all undergone a three-week training program earlier in the summer, and they had been disciplined to work together, react quickly, and follow their commander's lead. But Dodge had to exercise his command without the authority of military drill. Even more difficult, he was an unknown quantity to many of the men under him. Several had worked with him before; all knew of him. But they had never worked together as a single group, under Dodge or anyone else, and Dodge himself was not even sure of all their names. Under U.S. Forest Service policy, it is the amount of rest, not the amount of camaraderie, that determines how men are assembled for a day's jump group. Those with the longest respite since their last fire are the first to go. A hardened set of individuals this group was; a hardened combat platoon it was not.

Three Terrible Discoveries

AS DODGE APPROACHED the fire line, he told his men to wait in the center of the gulch (point 2) while he moved ahead to scout within a hundred feet of the front. It was during that time, at point 3, that he made the first of three terrible discoveries of the day. Here he found that the blaze was far more dangerous than he had guessed from aerial reconnaissance. A ground wind was coming across the river and over the ridge, at twenty to forty miles an hour, whipping the flames up and blowing them down his path. A vigorous wind is an oxygen supply, nature's giant bellows. Alarmed, he retreated to the rest spot and instructed his men to head for the mouth of the gorge. He himself retreated further back to the landing zone to retrieve some food he had forgotten, leaving his men to move down the gulch without him.

Dodge's instructions were logical. The fire was more threatening than expected, but safety would be assured if he could place his crew between the fire and the river. Should the fire force them into the river, so be it: they would swim out some yards, stay low to avoid smoke, and, once the fire swept by, climb back onshore. The Missouri River was Dodge's insurance.[1]

As the men moved down the gulch without Dodge in the lead, the firefighters became divided in two. As much as five hundred feet separated the two subgroups, neither of which was quite sure where the other was. Twenty minutes later, at about 5:40, Dodge finally regrouped his men and resumed the lead, moving them further toward the mouth of the gulch. Here he made a second, more terrible discovery (point 4): the winds were swirling around the flaming ridge, sweeping burning branches and glowing embers into the air and across the front of the gulch. In the few minutes since their arrival in the gulch, fiery eddies had closed the escape route. Dodge's alarm bells—all of them—were sounding.

At 5:45, Dodge reversed course, saying nothing to his men, but they surely knew why, since they too had seen the wind-whipped smoke across the gulch's mouth in front of them. The crew kicked into a run up the left-hand side of the gulch. Within minutes, Dodge passed word down the line that all equipment—packs, saws, axes, shovels—was to be discarded and that they must move as fast as they possibly could (point 5). He knew, and they must have known, that what had been a routine jump into a ten o'clock fire was now becoming a dash for their lives.

It is hard to imagine what could be worse than what Dodge and his men had already encountered in their short time in Mann Gulch. Less than an hour had passed since they had stashed their parachutes and confidently set out to do their job. But Dodge, at the head of the line, made his third and most terrifying discovery of the day just a few minutes later.

A forest fire rarely moves at more than four or five miles an hour, an advance that smoke jumpers can always outrun. But Mann Gulch was part of a transitional zone—an area where mountains yield to plains and forest timber to prairie grass—and as the men fled from the fire, the forest gave way to shoulder-high grass, dense, dry, and ready to explode.

The Plains Indians feared a prairie grass fire almost as much as anything. They knew that the worst could not be outrun, and now Dodge knew it too. His mind still in steely control, Dodge estimated that as fast as he and his men could move up what was now becoming a grassy slope, the towering wall of fire would move faster. Within a minute or two, Dodge estimated, perhaps sooner, he and his men would be overtaken by flames.

The roar was deafening. Sap in scattered trees was superheating and exploding. Smoke, embers, and ashes swirled in all directions. The apparent options offered Dodge no escape: stand and be fatally burned; turn and be fatally burned; run and be fatally burned.

The Solution

AT 5:55, DODGE abruptly stopped, lit a match from a match-book he carried, and threw it into the prairie grass in front of him (point 6). His fire, almost instantly a widening circle of flame, burned fast. By the normal measures of fire fighting, what Dodge lit appeared to be a "backfire"—one intended to burn off enough fuel in a limited strip to prevent the real fire from advancing. And indeed he would be asked, at a subsequent government investigation into the events of August 5, why he had chosen this moment of extreme urgency to light such a backfire. In response, Dodge would assert that this was not and could not have been a backfire: with less than a minute remaining until he was engulfed by flames, a backfire would not have cleared enough grass to stop anything. Why, then, had he paused to light the fire? The answer seemed both impossible and simple: he had lit the fire in order to take refuge inside it.

As the ring of his new fire spread, it cleared a small area of all flammable substances. It was not much of a safety zone, but it would have to do. He jumped over the blazing ring, moved to its smoldering center, wrapped a wet cloth around his face, pressed himself close to the ground, and waited. As he had anticipated, the surging fire wall rounded both sides of his small circle, leapt over the top, but found nothing to ignite where he lay motionless. Within moments the front passed, racing up the ridge and leaving him unscathed in his tiny asylum. He stood, brushed off the ash, and found he was no worse for wear. He had literally burned a hole in the raging fire.

But he had not forgotten his crew. Just before his lighting of the escape fire, Robert Sallee and Walter Rumsey had been second and third in a line of sprinting men that stretched behind Dodge many dozen yards down the hill. Like the other fire-fighters, Sallee and Rumsey had left the aircraft when Dodge said "Jump," they had moved toward the mouth of the gulch when he said "Go," and they had dashed uphill when he said "Run." Now, as Sallee and Rumsey stumbled on a stopped

Dodge, they saw their boss motioning them to come inside an expanding ring of fire. "This way!" he shouted. Though Sallee and Rumsey could not hear Dodge in the deafening inferno, they could see what he wanted from his frantic waving. They also saw an enormous fire wall at their back, and it was about to overwhelm both them and Dodge's circle.

The Fatal End

SALLEE AND RUMSEY glanced at Dodge but kept going, rounding his fire circle, mounting the ridge to their left, and moving down the other side into what is ironically called "Rescue Gulch." Fires do not stop at the ridge tops; they only slow momentarily. The Mann Gulch fire swept into Rescue Gulch as well, but Sallee and Rumsey chanced upon their own oasis, a strip of stone without vegetation, a rockslide some seventy-five feet wide that had denied purchase to grass and trees alike (point 7). They too squeezed toward the middle, the fire raced down both sides, and a few minutes later, suffering from neither burns nor smoke, they worked their way back toward Mann Gulch.

The remaining thirteen men also rushed by Dodge and his widening circle of flame. Dodge heard one man say, as he glanced at the escape scheme, "To hell with that, I'm getting out of here!" Sallee, who paused higher up after speeding by Dodge, looked back and later estimated that most of the men had passed within twenty to fifty feet of Dodge, just outside the burning ring. After that, however, their stars were not propitious: the thirteen chanced upon no bare spots. As Dodge had anticipated, they were quickly overtaken by the prairie grass fire they could not outrun (point 8).

Unscathed, Dodge, Sallee, and Rumsey gathered and went in search of the others. Several of the men survived a few hours, but all were fatally burned, most not far from where they had started less than an hour before. They had left their landing zone at about 5:00 that afternoon. The hands on the watch of

James O. Harrison were melted into the dial at 5:56. It was the worst fire-fighting disaster in Forest Service history and would remain so for forty-five years, until fourteen men and women were killed on July 6, 1994, on Storm King Mountain near Glenwood Springs, Colorado, combating a vicious wind-driven grass fire that also suddenly engulfed them.

A Credibility Spiral

LEADERSHIP IS A product of both today's actions and yesterday's groundwork. The fatal combination that emerged in Mann Gulch was partly what Dodge did or did not do on August 5, but also partly what he did or did not do well before the smoke jumpers ever climbed aboard the aircraft. We will first review his decisions in the air and on the ground in the gulch and later turn to what he might have done earlier in the summer to prepare for that fateful August afternoon.

First is the question of why Sallee, Rumsey, and the other thirteen smoke jumpers refused to join Dodge inside his circle of fire. It was, after all, an immediate solution, a lifesaving solution, a communicated solution.

Sallee later reported, "I saw him bend over and light a fire with a match. I thought, with the fire almost on our back, what the hell is the boss doing, lighting another fire in front of us?" Sallee was close to Rumsey, and he expressed a conclusion reached by both: "We thought he must have gone nuts." Yet they had, it must be recalled, dutifully followed all of Dodge's earlier instructions. When he had said to plunge out the open door of the airplane, they had done so; when he had moved them toward the mouth of the gulch, they had gone; when he had said to drop their equipment and run for their lives, they had obeyed. Why had his authority suddenly failed him?

One explanation—that the trailing crew members did not see or understand Dodge's frantic waving—may apply to some. But the two survivors said that they could see Dodge and what he intended, and Dodge himself reported that he had seen most of the firefighters come near enough to his circle of fire to see his signals.

A more plausible explanation is that by this point Dodge had simply lost much of his credibility. A leader's credibility can be defined as the authority to make binding decisions based on a record of having made them well before. Dodge was crew chief by virtue of the latter. But in less than an hour, his credibility had been shattered. His decision on where to land had placed the men behind a dangerous fire. They had marched toward it, then moved around it, and finally raced from it. The accumulation of erroneous decisions finally made his latest action—the lifesaving one—too dubious to accept. Dodge's credibility had collapsed; worse, he had not yet realized it.

> *By implication:* If you have made several problematic decisions in a row, be prepared to have your leadership questioned. It may be a moment of personal trial, a point when the cooperation of others is most needed but least forthcoming.

Missteps and Few Words

EXACERBATING DODGE'S DOWNWARD credibility spiral were two small missteps, too minor to draw much notice at the time but arguably big enough to accelerate the downspin. First, when Dodge returned to the drop site at the upper end of Mann Gulch to retrieve his food, he sent his crew on without him for a few minutes, relinquishing his leadership. Thus he momentarily commanded the battle from behind the lines, not the front. In pondering why the generals in World War I so often displayed incompetence in command, Peter Drucker turned to the explanation offered by his own high school history teacher, a wounded veteran of the Great War: "Because not enough generals were killed; they stayed way behind the lines and let others do the fighting and dying."[2]

Second, when Dodge told his men to drop their shovels and

axes, he was asking them to give up a large part of what defined them as a crew under his command; he was, in other words, ordering his soldiers to shed their uniforms.

In both instances, Dodge's actions made sound logistical sense. The first permitted a more rapid movement toward the safety of the Missouri River; the second allowed a more rapid movement away from the accelerating blaze. Yet both chipped away at Dodge's credibility when he most needed it later. A solution lay not necessarily in avoiding such actions, for in this instance it is hard to imagine not ordering the equipment disposal, but in a persuasive communication of why he acted thus.

But probably most damaging to Dodge's credibility was a management style that fostered little two-way communication. Wagner Dodge was a boss of few words, a person who neither expected much information from his people nor gave much in return. As the men flew over Mann Gulch, sixteen pairs of eyes and ears were gathering information on the conditions below, and some might have guessed that the swirling smoke and air turbulence signaled dangerous ground conditions. Yet Dodge relied on only a single pair of eyes, his own. Similarly, in moving toward the fire, then around it, and finally away from it, others reached their own assessment of the best way out. Yet in no case did Dodge ask for their appraisal. He had a diverse human information system at his disposal but chose to avail himself of none of it. Imagine, by way of analogy, a chief executive who never asks his salespeople what they are hearing from their customers or a hospital president who fails to ask his nurses what they are learning from their patients.

At the same time, Dodge also gave little information. He did not share his appraisals, barely explained his actions, scarcely even communicated his growing alarm. "Dodge has a characteristic in him," Rumsey would later tell the Board of Review. "It is hard to tell what he is thinking." When Dodge sent his crew members toward the mouth of the gulch after the brief reconnaissance of the fire, he instructed them to move out of the "thick reproduction" because it was a "death trap," Sallee later reported. But otherwise he dispensed little information, and Rumsey and Sallee observed that he did not even look particularly worried. When he suddenly reversed course near the mouth of the gulch and the crew was moving uphill, Navon, the former paratrooper, was still taking snapshots. Dodge testified at the hearing that he had not communicated directly with his men from the time he retreated for his food until he ordered them to drop all their equipment.

Near the end, as the crew was overtaken by crisis and panic, circumstances permitted little discussion. But up until that time, communication had been feasible. Without revealing his thinking when it could be shared, Dodge denied his crew members, especially those not familiar with him, an opportunity to appreciate the quality of his mind. They had no other way of knowing, except by reputation, whether his decisions were rational or impulsive, calculated or impetuous. Later, when the quality of his mind did display itself in a brilliant invention—the escape fire—his thinking was still too much of a cipher to those whose trust he urgently required.

> *By implication:* If you want trust and compliance when the need for them cannot be fully explained, explain yourself early. If you need information on which you must soon act, ask for it soon. Being a person of few words may be fine in a technical position, but it is a prescription for disaster in a position of leadership.

Other Escape Fires

WAGNER DODGE COULD never have anticipated the specific events in Mann Gulch. Yet it is instructive to ask what he might have done in June and July to prepare for them, not knowing precisely what lay ahead but anticipating the possibility that flawless action and effective leadership were likely to be essential for whatever came along.

Dodge masterminded a winning idea that could have saved

the entire enterprise. The Board of Review concluded that all of his men would have survived if they had "heeded Dodge's efforts to get them to go into the escape fire area." But when the innovation was ready for use, nobody believed it could succeed. And Dodge's escape fire was a genuine innovation. Native Americans on the Great Plains had invented the concept a century earlier, and since the Mann Gulch disaster it has become a standard lifesaving measure in the official survival repertoire. But before 1949, the Forest Service did not train its smoke jumpers in setting escape fires, and on August 5, 1949, nobody in Mann Gulch had ever heard of the tactic.

Why was it that Dodge was the only member of his sixteen-man force to invent the escape fire? All found themselves in the same tightening vise, all saw that their time was almost up, all desperately sought a way out. Yet only Dodge seemingly had the capacity to discover *the* lifesaving solution. When asked how he had come on the idea of the escape fire, he replied, "It just seemed the logical thing to do."

Two explanations for the failure of simultaneous invention come to mind, both pointing to what Dodge might have done earlier in the summer. First, he was an autocrat, an instruction giver, and once in the gulch there might have been no other way to lead. But with earlier opportunities to meld a team and mold a culture, he might have encouraged each member to learn how to reach his own judgments and make his own decisions. This is not to say that fostering individual discretion is the same as allowing discretionary direction. The challenge for Dodge was to instill individual judgment while aligning it around common purpose. Empowering team members to reach their own decisions that will simultaneously pull the team in the same direction is no easy task. It is a learned capacity Dodge would have had to have cultivated well before August 5.

A second explanation again refers to Dodge's style as a man of few words. He had fought fires for nine years and had been a crew foreman since 1945. Some on his crew had combated fires for less than three months. Sallee and Rumsey were making their first smoke jump. Dodge's mind held memories of hundreds of fire, soil, forest, and wind conditions he had seen, dozens of strategies he knew to have worked, and some he had seen fail. It was this repository of practical experience that had led to his promotion to crew chief—and it was this storehouse he had at the ready when he realized that he and his crew had but a moment to rescue themselves. Unfortunately, though, it was his database alone. Dodge might have shared his wisdom earlier, telling and retelling the amazing, sometimes curious, occasionally disastrous stories of his fires of the past. Second-hand accounts can never fully substitute for the personal seasoning of years on the front line, but they can furnish a diverse set of prior conditions against which to test the present. In being tight with words, Dodge denied his men the benefit of his nine years of experience.

The value of downward communication is amply confirmed in any number of studies. Research on flight crew performance during cockpit simulations, for instance, has revealed that leaders of higher-performance cockpit crews share more plans, offer more predictions, describe more options, sound more warnings, and provide more explanations.[3]

> *By implication:* If you expect those who work for you to exercise their own judgment, provide them with the decision-making experience now. If you count on them to understand the conditions as best they can, share your past experience with them now. If your leadership depends on theirs, devolving responsibility and sharing stories is a foundation upon which it will reside. Thinking strategically when confronted with a crisis or challenge is a learned skill that requires sustained seasoning.

The Leader's Ally

AS A THOUGHT experiment, a "what if" analysis, ask yourself what would have happened if Sallee or Rumsey had followed

Dodge's blandishments. Or suppose Dodge had cultivated a loyal ally or second in command whose faith was virtually unshakable. If Sallee, the next in line as the crew raced up the gulch, had been that ally and had entered the circle of fire, others almost certainly would have followed as well. The premise is simple: Everybody is crazy from time to time, but it is rare that two people are at the same moment. This was one of the discoveries of the famous experiment by Solomon Asch: If everybody around you says that line A is longer than line B when the objective fact is obviously the opposite, you will cave in. But if you have just one other doubter, just one naysayer who breaks the mold, you are emboldened to break it too. If Sallee, as the loyal ally, had joined Dodge, others would have been more likely to be lured into the escape circle, and we might well have never heard of a fire in Mann Gulch.

By implication: If you have difficult decisions to make and insufficient time to explain them, a key to implementation may be loyal allies who are sure to execute them through thick or thin. Establishing those allies now is the only way to ensure that their support will be at the ready when needed, and it will sometimes be needed when it is far too late to be created.

Panic and Performance

SOME OF DODGE'S crew members might have rushed by him and his lifesaving fire less from a rational calculus and more out of sheer panic. Sallee and Rumsey thought Dodge must be crazy to be starting a new fire. But others, by the time they neared Dodge's fire, were surely being driven by terror, and in such a state rational judgment is an early casualty. Psychologists tell us that panic sets in when the mind succumbs to stress and fails to take in new information about a threatening event, or fails for similar reasons to take advantage of prior experience germane to the threat. Either way, it is hard to imagine that

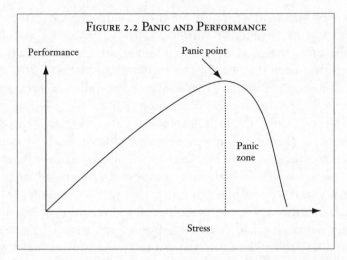

FIGURE 2.2 PANIC AND PERFORMANCE

the thirteen men behind Sallee and Rumsey, those whose backs were even closer to the raging flames, were not overwhelmed with fear.

As panic short-circuits the mind, our mental processors grind to a halt. Then, unable to reach an informed judgment on what to do next, we reach into our memories for what worked well before. A psychologist's label for this is "reversion to last learned behavior." If we manufacture mainframe computers but the market is sinking and our creditors and investors are demanding more, let's do again what has been key to our success in the past: making mainframes. Similarly, if we have a wall of flame behind us, running from it—a successful strategy in the past— would seem to make good sense now. Anybody near a raging bonfire knows to back off; anybody caught in a building fire knows to rush out. Yet in this instance what made perfect sense in the past would prove disastrous in the present.

Panic overwhelms smart decision making, but it is also true that modest levels of stress can improve it. This is the curvilinear relationship between stress and performance, as shown in Figure 2.2. To the left of the panic point, the adrenaline feed

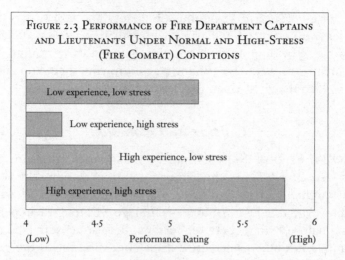

FIGURE 2.3 PERFORMANCE OF FIRE DEPARTMENT CAPTAINS AND LIEUTENANTS UNDER NORMAL AND HIGH-STRESS (FIRE COMBAT) CONDITIONS

concentrates the mind, mobilizes energies, and eliminates distractions. To the right of the panic point, however, we no longer think so clearly, too overwhelmed by stress to reason or calculate.[4]

This can explain the firefighters' flight past Dodge, but how is that Dodge was able to keep such a cool head when others could not? An explanation comes from a study of urban firefighters, those who ride trucks rather than jump aircraft to reach a blaze. Focused on department captains and lieutenants, the study revealed that the performance of experienced officers improves under high uncertainty and stress, while the performance of inexperienced officers declines (see Figure 2.3).[5]

This helps us understand why Dodge's experienced intellect invented the escape fire while others were focused only on flight. It is also a reminder again that experience is a critical foundation of leadership. A warning is contained therein as well: Modestly stressful periods can enhance productivity—we all know of managers who are forever fostering minor crises to get things done. But highly stressful periods worsen the performance of inexperienced people if they are pressed beyond their panic point.

By implication: In periods of anxiety and stress, it is your least experienced associates who will reach the panic zone first. Providing newcomers with as much early training and mentoring as possible is one way of moving their panic point well to the right when the heat is on.

Culture and Cohesion

UNDER FOREST SERVICE policy, Dodge took command of a just-assembled crew as he climbed on board the aircraft. While this might appear odd to those who work in an age of dedicated teamwork, the just-in-time assemblage ensured each person maximal rest time between events. It also ensured administrative flexibility, since crew dispatches varied with the scope of each fire and could range from two men to several planeloads.

Managerial careers are filled with comparable events. Like Dodge, you have probably found yourself more than once assigned to oversee a group of people with whom you are little familiar and within which acquaintanceship is equally scarce. You have just been promoted, rotated, relocated, or otherwise reassigned, and those who now report to you may predate you by no more than days. You are a church minister who has taken over a congregation with an ever-changing membership, a fast-food manager who has taken over a franchise with an ever-churning workforce, or maybe a soccer coach who has taken over a team whose players are as unfamiliar to one another as they are to you.

Seen through today's lens, Dodge would have surely preferred it otherwise. Building a self-contained, mutually reliant team is one of the proven ways of delivering optimal performance under duress. But it requires months, even years to develop the culture and cohesion that are the engines of such work-team performance. Given the seasonal nature of his business, the best Dodge might have done, had policy allowed it, was to form a dedicated team in June within which he could have built some unity by August.[6]

Building a team with its own culture and cohesion brings another key advantage. For well-formed, highly committed groups, the panic point is shifted far to the right. As stress intensifies, their performance curve continues to rise well after others' have plummeted. They can endure extraordinary threats with an equanimity that individuals and poorly developed groups could never bear. French Resistance cells challenging the German occupiers during World War II were a case in point, as were the Allied fighting units that landed on the beaches of German-held Normandy.

Or consider one of the most famous military attacks of all, George E. Pickett's charge at Gettysburg. After the Union army had stalemated the Confederate forces during two days of pitched battle in July 1863, Robert E. Lee readied his rebel forces for one final, decisive blow against the Union center. It was to be a daunting task. Twelve thousand troops under Pickett's command were to march across an open mile of farmland. They would have artillery support, but they would also be assaulting a well-fortified Union line behind a stone wall on an extended ridge. General James Longstreet, ordered by Lee to execute the attack, was convinced of impending failure. The thousands of combat veterans of Virginia and North Carolina who were assembling to mount the attack could see it might well be their last. Yet in full view of Union cannons and infantry, the Confederate troops marched the terrible mile. Pickett's charge ended in bitter defeat, with all but one of his thirty-two regimental and field officers killed or wounded and half his troops down or gone. But the men of the Army of Northern Virginia, loyal to their regimental commanders and comrades, went unflinchingly into the devastating fire. Collectively, they did what neither individuals nor less well-formed teams could ever do.

By implication: If your organization is facing a period of uncertainty, change, or stress, now is the time to build a strong culture with good lines of interior communication, mutual understanding, and shared obligation. A clear sense of common purpose and a well-formed camaraderie are essential ingredients to ensure that your team, your organization, or your company will perform to its utmost when it is most needed.

Our actions today may make the difference between success or failure tomorrow. The challenge is to anticipate what problems lie ahead and what preparatory steps are required now to meet them later. Enabling all to make informed decisions, informing all to understand your decisions, and organizing all to discipline their decisions are among the enduring legacies of Wagner Dodge's fifty-six-minute struggle for survival in Mann Gulch.

❖

CHAPTER 3

Eugene Kranz Returns Apollo 13 to Earth

"What do you think we've got in the spacecraft that's good?"

H EY, WE'VE GOT a problem here."
The day was April 13, 1970. The voice was that of astronaut Jack Swigert, speaking from aboard the spacecraft Odyssey.

Almost immediately, NASA's Mission Control queried back: "This is Houston. Say again, please."

Astronaut and mission commander James Lovell responded this time: "Houston, we've had a problem."

For flight director Eugene Kranz, the message from Apollo 13 presaged the test of a lifetime.

Only nine months earlier, on July 20, 1969, Apollo 11 had landed Neil Armstrong and Buzz Aldrin in the Sea of Tranquillity, fulfilling John F. Kennedy's promise to place a man on the moon before the end of the decade. Five months earlier, Apollo 12 had placed Pete Conrad and Alan Bean in the Ocean of Storms. Just fifty-five hours earlier, at 1:13 P.M. on Saturday, April 11, 1970, Apollo 13 had lifted up from the Kennedy Space Center on what to this moment had seemed a flawless trip to the moon's ridges of Fra Mauro. Now, suddenly, the bottom was falling out.

NASA technician George Bliss was both transfixed and horrified by what he saw on his computer console in a Houston back room. "We got more than a problem," he warned colleague Sy Liebergot. The video screen told why: One of Odyssey's two oxygen tanks had broken down. The pressure in two of its three fuel cells, devices that use oxygen to generate electricity, was plummeting.

As Gene Kranz sifted through damage reports, the picture was distressing. The astronauts and their protective shell were unscathed, but it was evident that some kind of explosion had ripped through vital equipment. Two days into the flight, three quarters of the way to the moon, the astronauts were hurtling away from Earth at 2,000 miles per hour. The only practical way they could return was to round the moon and depend on its gravity to fire them back like a slingshot. But this would require more than three days and demand more oxygen and electricity than Lovell and his crew had left.

As flight director for Apollo 13, Kranz was the responsible official, and he was watching his mission spin out of control: his crew would consume their oxygen and power long before they neared Earth. Even if they survived to reenter the Earth's atmosphere, they would have no way to control their capsule's fiery plunge. Kranz could neither retrieve the astronauts nor replenish their supplies. He knew what options were out, yet he also knew he must somehow engineer a safe return. He understood as well that his actions in the hours ahead might determine whether the U.S. space program experienced or avoided its biggest disaster.

The Explosion's Wake

HUNDREDS OF OFFICIALS and engineers confronted the singular task of bringing the astronauts back alive. Four rotating flight teams—dubbed White, Black, Gold, and Maroon—were scheduled to spell one another during the mission's long days ahead. A backup crew for Apollo 13 was on call to lend its expertise. Dozens of space program contractors were ready to assist.

Yet no one on the ground bore the burden that Eugene

Eugene Kranz during Apollo 13 Mission

Kranz carried that evening and would continue to carry over the next four days. NASA's policy was unflinchingly clear: the flight director had the final call on all decisions. Moreover, "The flight director can do anything he feels is necessary for the safety of the crew and the conduct of the flight regardless of the mission rules."

As Sy Liebergot, the frontline electrical official, gazed at his console in the minutes just after the explosion, he allowed himself to hope that the ominous screen displays might reflect sensor failure rather than a genuine problem. During NASA's countless simulations of the flight, he had often seen disastrous instrument readings that had later proved inaccurate. The astronauts themselves were reporting that their oxygen tanks seemed fine, lending momentary support to Liebergot's hopeful search for instrument error.

But Kranz was already learning from other flight officials that the problems were indeed real. The guidance officer reported that an onboard computer was signaling a major glitch. The

Mission control room during Apollo 13: Flight director Eugene Kranz
observes astronaut Fred Haise on the viewing screen forty-three
minutes before the explosion

communications officer reported that the craft had mysteriously switched antennas. (As would be learned later, one had been hit by the explosion's debris.) And the astronauts themselves soon reported that one oxygen tank had emptied, two of the three fuel cells were generating no electricity, and two panels supplying power to the entire spacecraft were losing voltage. Lovell added even more distressing news: "We are venting something into space." A glowing cloud was hovering outside Odyssey, suggesting rupture of its oxygen tanks.

"OK," called Kranz, sensing signs of panic in Mission Control. "Let's everybody keep cool. Let's make sure we don't do anything that's going to blow our electrical power or cause us to lose fuel cell number two." Then he addressed what would have to be done: "Let's solve the problem." And finally he moved on to self-discipline: "Let's not make it any worse by guessing."

But now, more bad news from Odyssey. Though a moon landing had been eliminated by the loss of the first oxygen tank and fuel cell, the second system should still carry the astronauts safely home. Lovell noticed, however, that the pressure needle for the second tank was falling as well, and Liebergot was discovering the same thing. Normally the tank should register 860 pounds per square inch (psi); now it was approaching 300. The explosion had come at 9:07 P.M., and the clock was now just past 10 P.M. At that rate of loss, the spaceship would exhaust all of its electricity and air sometime between midnight and 3 A.M.

Kranz telephoned the home of Chris Kraft—the former flight director and his onetime mentor, and now deputy director of the Manned Spacecraft Center. Kraft's wife pulled him out of the shower, and he heard Kranz urging, "Chris, you'd better get over here now. We've got a hell of a problem. We've lost oxygen pressure, we've lost a bus [an electrical power distribution system], we're losing fuel cells. It seems there's been an explosion." Kranz, age thirty-six, had worked with NASA for a decade, overseeing all Apollo missions since taking over from Kraft when the prior Gemini series had come to an end. He was an experienced hand who sounded no undue alarm, solicited no unneeded counsel. Kraft raced to the space center, just ten miles away. When he arrived, Kranz brought his former mentor up to speed: "We're in deep shit."

With the oxygen for Odyssey's life support systems in rapid decline, Kranz barked rapid-fire demands for information and support to attack the problem:

> *To the telemetry and electrical officer:* "Will you take a look at the prelaunch data and see if there's anything that may have started the venting?"
> *To the technicians running NASA's fast, on-site computers:* "Bring up another computer . . . will you?"

To the guidance and navigation officer: "Give me a gross amount of the thruster propellants consumed so far."
To Sy Liebergot: "What does the status of your buses tell you now?"

Off line, Liebergot and his backup engineer, George Bliss, were reaching even more forlorn conclusions: The single remaining oxygen tank was below 300 psi of pressure and losing another 1.7 psi each minute. If tank pressure fell below 100 psi, it would have insufficient force to move its precious contents into the fuel cells for power generation, and that point was just 116 minutes away. They made several attempts to stem the flow, but none succeeded.

> *Liebergot:* "George, it looks grim."
> *Bliss:* "Yes, it does."
> *Liebergot:* "We're going down. We're losing it."
> *Bliss:* "Yes, we are."

Now Liebergot was back on line with Kranz, arguing that the astronauts must move immediately into the attached lunar excursion module (LEM). Dubbed Aquarius on this mission, the LEM had been designed to set two astronauts on the moon and sustain life for several days. For three astronauts, Aquarius would be overcrowded, the power system would not work for long, and it would vaporize on reentry. But for the moment it would have to do. The dying command module would support the astronauts for a matter of minutes; the LEM at least offered hours. Kranz again sought instant analysis. "I want you guys figuring our minimum power needed in the LEM to sustain life," he instructed a LEM technical group, which had anticipated no real action until the planned moon landing two days later. "And I want LEM manning around the clock."

The oxygen loss from Odyssey was accelerating to 3 psi per minute, and Bliss now estimated that they had eighteen minutes left before total power shutdown. A few moments later, he revised that down to seven minutes. And then, a moment later, to four.

The Black Team had just taken over from White, and Glynn Lunney, who would spell Kranz at the director's console while the White Team stood down, sent up an urgent command: "Get 'em going in the LEM!" Lovell and Haise moved through the connecting hatch, and while Swigert stayed behind to wind down Odyssey, they powered up Aquarius. They worked frantically to transfer irreplaceable guidance data from the command module into the LEM computer in the seconds before everything was lost. Finally, Lovell radioed Houston, "Aquarius is up, and Odyssey is completely powered down."

There was momentary relief, but with days to go, they had bought only a little time. "OK, everybody," counseled Lunney, "we've get a lot of long-range problems to deal with."

Oxygen and Power

AMONG THE MISSION'S first long-range problems was that the return trajectory would miss the Earth by some forty thousand miles. The astronauts would need to fire the LEM's rocket in just five hours to close the gap. Producing the precision adjustment, however, would require immediate, massive recalibrations of instruments. By now the teams in Houston were humming, and they delivered the requisite data to Jim Lovell and his crew with an hour to spare.

While Glynn Lunney staffed the director's console, Kranz remained only feet away, his mind turning over what to do next. He had already passed word that as soon as Houston had the fuel burn plan set, he would meet with his entire White Team in a nearby room. As it gathered, Kranz laid down his new mandate: "For the rest of this mission, I am pulling you men off console. The people out in that room will be running the flight from moment to moment, but it's the people in this room who will be coming up with the protocols they're going to be executing. From now on, what I want from every one of you is simple: options, and plenty of them." Their new name would be the Tiger Team, and for the remainder of the flight they would work and live in Room 210.

A mere twenty feet by twenty feet and windowless, Room 210 was bare except for several overhead TVs and tables along the walls, but its location was good: adjacent to the operations room and just a floor below the control room. Above all, it permitted the team to assemble all past and current data in one place. Now, Kranz believed, they could determine what had happened and was happening, essential for deciding what should happen next.

Kranz pressed them to focus on solutions. He sought to build, he later reported, "a positive frame of mind that is necessary to work problems in a time-critical and true emergency environment." And he wanted quick answers to specific questions:

"How long can you keep the systems in the LEM running at full power?"

"Where do we stand on water? What about battery power? What about oxygen?"

"In three or four days we're going to have to use the command module again. I want to know how we can get that bird powered up and running from a cold stop . . . and do it all on just the power we've got left in the reentry batteries."

"I also want to know how we plan to align this ship if we can't use a star alignment. Can we use sun checks? Can we use moon checks? What about earth checks?"

"I want options on . . . burns and midcourse corrections from now to entry."

"What ocean does it put us in?"

Once again, Kranz insisted on strategies and solutions without guesswork: "For the next few days we're going to be coming up with techniques and maneuvers we've never tried before," he concluded. "And I want to make sure we know what we're doing."

Kranz left his men to do their work and returned to the control room. Glynn Lunney of the Black Team had focused everybody on the forthcoming course correction, and minutes later Lovell and his colleagues executed a flawless blast of the LEM's engines. In one of the first bits of good news since disaster struck, they had corrected their path perfectly.

Good news, though, was still in terribly short supply. The new course required nearly four days for return, and Aquarius was provisioned for less than two. The LEM's oxygen supply was not a problem since enough had been placed on board for several moon walks, yet its supply of lithium hydroxide was another story. This chemical was carried to remove carbon dioxide accumulating in the cabin, but its LEM capacity was for two men for two days, not for three men for twice that long. The available electricity would last for even less time if Aquarius remained fully powered. Water, too, was in desperately short supply.

Kranz decided he wanted more seasoned talent crunching the numbers. He sent the Tiger Team's electrical specialist back to the consoles on Tuesday morning and in his place recruited Bill Peters from the Gold Team. Other flight directors had sometimes found Peters slow to react and explain. But Kranz had constructed a relationship with him, and he knew that he brought exceptional experience: Peters had worked every space mission since Gemini 3 in 1965. "Peters was utterly brilliant," Kranz recalled, but he could not explain himself well and one had to work with him "to bring out the pieces."

After consulting with Kranz and the lead engineer for Grumman Aerospace, the LEM maker, Peters was heartened by his preliminary calculations: He could find ways to cut Aquarius's electrical flow from 55 amperes to 12, though this would require draconian measures on board: no computer, no guidance system, no heater, no panel display. Communications would stay up, a fan would stir the air, and a little coolant would circulate. Otherwise, all systems would be off.

Kranz also recruited another outsider, John Aaron, the Maroon Team's twenty-seven-year-old electrical specialist. He understood power better than anyone else, he was innovative, and he was unflappable—"Mr. Cool under pressure" in Kranz's phrase. Kranz charged Aaron with a similar task for conserving Odyssey's power, and together they took a first cut at the figures. Their numbers were encouraging, and Aaron designed the plan. He believed he could find the power to rev up the command module for reentry—but only if almost all engineering corners were cut.

Aaron patiently presented his plan to a skeptical Tiger Team, reporting that the powering up, normally a full day's affair, could take no more than two hours. Bill Strahle, a guidance and navigation officer, interjected, "John, you can't do it in that time." Aaron responded, "Well, now, that's what *I* thought, Bill. But I think if we're willing to take a few shortcuts, we just might be able to pull it off."

Late on the evening of Tuesday, April 14, nearly twenty-four hours after the accident, Lovell and crew rounded the moon and were scheduled to fire the LEM's rocket to accelerate their return to Earth. The engine burn, like virtually all other maneuvers of the past day, would be crucial, but this one would be especially so. The smallest error of alignment or duration would send the ship in a wrong direction with virtually no fuel remaining for any correction. Though the Gold Team was still on duty as the time of the scheduled firing approached, Kranz decided to install his own Tiger Team at the controls. His men quietly walked into Mission Control, muttered apologies to their sitting counterparts, and took over the consoles. Under Kranz's direction, the "big burn" worked. Another essential milestone for the journey home had been reached, and the room erupted with cheers.

The moment's glow had barely passed when three men made their way from different directions to Kranz's workstation.

Chris Kraft was one; Deke Slayton, astronaut and director of flight crew operations, the second. Max Faget, engineering director for the entire Manned Spacecraft Center, trailed slightly behind. "So what's our next step here, Gene?" opened Slayton, one of the original seven Mercury astronauts.

> *Kranz:* "Well, Deke, we're gonna work on that."
> *Slayton:* "I'm not sure how much there is to work on. We're going to put the crew to bed, right?"
> *Kranz:* "Eventually, sure."
> *Slayton:* "Eventually may not do it, Gene. Their last scheduled sleep period was twenty-four hours ago. They're going to need some rest."

Now Kraft jumped in.

> *Kraft:* "How do we stand with that power-down problem, Gene?
> *Kranz:* "It's coming along, Chris."
> *Kraft:* "We ready to execute it?"
> *Kranz:* "We're ready, but it's a long procedure and Deke thinks we ought to get the crew ready to sleep first."
> *Kraft:* "Sleep? A sleep period's six hours! Take the crew off stream that long before powering down, and you're wasting six hours of juice you don't need to waste."
> *Slayton:* "But if you keep them up and have them execute a complicated power-down when they're barely awake, someone's bound to screw something up. I'd rather spend a little extra power now than risk another disaster later."

Max Faget appeared, and Kranz drew him into the discussion.

> *Kranz:* "Max, Deke and Chris were just telling me what they think our next step ought to be."
> *Faget:* "Passive thermal control, right?"

Slayton, alarmed: "PTC?"

Faget: "Sure. That ship's had one side pointing to the sun and one pointing out to space for hours. If we don't get some kind of barbecue roll going soon, we're going to freeze half our systems and cook the other half."

Slayton: "Do you have any idea what kind of pressure it's going to put on the crew to ask them to execute a PTC roll now?"

Kraft: "Or what kind of pressure it's going to put on the available power? I'm not sure we can afford to try something like that at the moment."

Faget: "I'm not sure we can afford not to."

The three-way argument escalated for several minutes, with each point and counterpoint more fiercely asserted than the last. Kranz said little throughout, mainly listening to what his three superiors had to say. Finally, he held up his hand, and they stopped speaking.

"Gentlemen," Kranz said, "I thank you for your input." The discussion was over, his decision made: "The next job for this crew will be to execute a thermal roll. After that, they will power down their spacecraft. And finally, they will get some sleep. A tired crew can get over their fatigue, but if we damage this ship any further, we're not going to get over that."

With the decision made, Kranz turned to his console, and Slayton and Faget turned to leave. Kraft lingered, considered objecting, but then quietly moved off as well. His protégé was in control, and he had ruled firmly. The astronauts spent the next two hours performing their assigned tasks and finally began a long-overdue slumber.

The Return

WITH THE TRAJECTORY successfully fixed for the return to Earth, Kranz and his Tiger Team resumed their calculations and planning in Room 210. The biggest challenge still: restarting

Mission control room during the final twenty-four hours before
Apollo 13 returned to Earth

the moribund command module. Aquarius had been life-sustaining, but the LEM would disintegrate on reentry. Odyssey would be life-returning: the command module came with a heat shield to endure the reentry's 5,000 degrees Fahrenheit. For that, though, Odyssey would have to be coaxed back from dormancy—with a defunct regular electric supply and a mere two hours of power remaining in its auxiliary batteries.

It was now late Wednesday evening, and the Tiger Team had been working relentlessly since Monday evening, struggling to surmount problem after problem if reentry were to succeed. Most of the team members had worked nonstop for more than forty-eight hours, and Kranz finally ordered a six-hour respite. Yes, they needed their sleep, but even more compelling was the fact that the most critical troubleshooting might finally be behind them. John Aaron, the electrical officer borrowed from the Maroon Team, had evidently found a way around Odyssey's repowering problem.

It was a collaborative solution. One of the command module's chief engineers, Arnie Aldrich, had worked with Aaron to ensure that the switches for the various systems would be thrown in a workable sequence so that early systems would be ready for later ones as needed. Kranz himself had examined each step, and astronaut Ken Mattingly had tested everything in a nearby command module simulator. Mattingly had been scheduled to serve as the command module pilot for Apollo 13, but after he had been exposed to German measles, NASA had replaced him with Swigert. Severely disappointed at first, Mattingly now applied his insider's knowledge to testing and refining Aaron's scheme. Ultimately, it worked—at least on the simulator.

To add to the tension, the fate of Apollo 13 had become a global drama. The Soviet Union volunteered rescue vessels. Religious groups across America and around the world prayed for the astronauts' safe deliverance. The Chicago Board of Trade added its own supplication, briefly suspending trading at 11 A.M. on Thursday "for a moment of tribute to the courage and gallantry of America's astronauts and a prayer for their safe return to Earth."

By Thursday evening, just eighteen hours before splashdown, the list of procedures to restart Odyssey was finalized and ready for transmission. Kranz, Aaron, and Aldrich pushed their way through the rows of consoles in Mission Control to deliver the list. Mission Control would require nearly two hours to radio the start-up sequence, line by line, to Jack Swigert, who would have to copy each of the hundreds of technical instructions by hand.

Swigert and crew successfully followed the start-up protocol, moved back into Odyssey, and jettisoned Aquarius. By mid-Friday, the command module was approaching Earth's outer atmosphere at 25,000 miles per hour, and Kranz took the director's console for the final time. With four minutes to go before Odyssey hit the atmosphere's upper layers, Kranz stood and asked each of the system officers if they were ready. "Let's go around the horn once more before entry," he said. Each officer declared his readiness. Kranz gave the mission communicator, astronaut Joe Kerwin, the green light: "You can tell the crew they're go for reentry."

Soon all radio contact with the crew was lost as intense heat enveloped the plunging craft. Four minutes of anxious silence passed on the ground until the fiery spray around the capsule subsided; then Kranz instructed Kerwin to resume contact. "Odyssey," Kerwin called. "Houston standing by, over." No response. Kranz: "Try again." Kerwin did, again and again, to no avail, and another minute passed, more blackout time than experienced on any other mission.

Then, faintly, came the scratchy but unmistakable voice of astronaut Jack Swigert: "OK, Joe." Moments later Jim Lovell, Jack Swigert, and Fred Haise were floating down on three parachutes for a soft landing in the Pacific. Eugene Kranz punched the air.

Sy Liebergot faced weeks of recurrent nightmares about undervoltages. Jim Lovell declared the mission a failure, but, he added, "I like to think it was a successful failure." And Grumman Aerospace, maker of the LEM, sent a mock bill for more than $312,421 to North American Rockwell, producer of the command module, for a "battery charge, road call," and "towing fee" for returning Odyssey home.

A Mission that Cannot Be Allowed to Fail

EUGENE KRANZ, JAMES LOVELL, and their crews matched wits with a technology failure, and they won. They orchestrated thousands of actions—many minute, some momentous—to fix what seemed unfixable. In the end, they triumphed over one of NASA's worst nightmares.

At the center of the swirl stood Gene Kranz, a man whose

Eugene Kranz with cigar and Astronaut Jim Lovell on the viewing screen after recovery by carrier Iwo Jima

self-discipline, determination, and "unnerving cool" steadied and then galvanized the energies of all. He orchestrated the victory through the deft combination of the two attributes of leadership at his disposal: personal and organizational. The personal is what we usually mean by leadership: the force of personality, the power of persuasion. The organizational is what we often fail to appreciate at first but almost always find close behind: the ability to meld and exploit a team of associates. Taken singly, neither brand of leadership would have been enough to bring the astronauts home. Joined together in the person of Gene Kranz, they proved lifesaving.

As Apollo 13's system failures became all too evident in the minutes after the explosion, mastering the moment required more than management; it also demanded steely determination among hundreds of engineers, who somehow had to stretch precious resources, barely enough for two men for two days, to support three men for four days.

Chris Kraft later reported that it was "as serious a situation as we have ever had in manned spacecraft." Decisions on how to extend the resources had to be made swiftly, and wrong decisions could have turned a momentary lifeboat into an eternal coffin. "There will be great risks and little margin for error or delay," warned John Noble Wilford in *The New York Times* the morning after the explosion. Two factors more than any others threatened to overwhelm Kranz's engineering team as it faced the emergency: plummeting expectations and premature actions.[1]

Alleviating the Gloom

THE FIRST THREAT to Kranz's associates was the pessimism of circumstance. In the explosion's immediate aftermath, the astronauts' life-support systems were crashing around them, leading to grievous prognoses. The damaged command module had hours, not days, of fuel remaining. "We're going down," Sy Liebergot warned. "We're losing it." He would later say, "Without the electrical power, the command module was dead. Without the electrical power and without oxygen, the crew were dead. . . . We were on the point of losing everybody and everything."

As the astronauts hurriedly settled into the lunar module, the remaining life-support systems still seemed far short of sufficiency. The LEM was unharmed but habitable for just two days. On first reading, it would appear that returning Lovell, Haise, and Swigert was simply beyond NASA's reach.

When managers in any field of endeavor anticipate near-certain failure, they can easily be drawn into a vicious circle of self-fulfilling prophecies, turning probability into certainty. Eugene Kranz instinctively understood the psychic perils inherent at the moment. "Let's everybody keep cool," he insisted just after the explosion. "Let's solve the problem." Rather than focusing on what was not working, he exhorted his team to concentrate on what was. As Sy Liebergot and others reported the failure of one system after another, Kranz urged his associates to see that the glass was half full: "What do you think we've got in the spacecraft that's good?"

Later, when it seemed that his engineers simply could not fashion a lifesaving scenario, Kranz reasserted his expectations: We "don't concede failure," and "we will never surrender. This crew is coming home." Ed Harris, playing Kranz in the Ron Howard film *Apollo 13*, uttered a paraphrase that perfectly summarized Kranz's attitude: "Failure is not an option."

Both on the surface and beneath it, Kranz remained convinced that all the technical problems could and would be solved—he would later affirm that he had never believed he would not get the men back. Even when he harbored doubts, he harbored them privately: "You do not pass uncertainty down to your team members." Others might have hesitated, but he did not, and as flight director he set the tenor for all concerned. The problem would be solved. "At no time did we ever consider that we weren't going to get the spacecraft and crew home," recalled Kranz. He baldly told a press conference, "It's not a question if we're going to get them home; it's a question of how much we're going to have left when we get them home." (Later he overheard one reporter complaining to another, "Arrogant son of a bitch, isn't he?")

Such unwavering optimism is a product not of blind faith but of trained confidence. "Once you think of surrendering, once you think of capitulation, that is the path you go down," warns Kranz. "As soon as you start thinking that way, you really have lost . . . the mental sharpness, the mental edge that is going to take this survival situation and bring it to a successful conclusion."

When the astronauts began repowering Odyssey for the final plunge into Earth's atmosphere, John Aaron asked Jack Swigert to test the current after Swigert switched on the reserve batteries. The meter registered 2 amperes, signaling that a piece of equipment was somehow on when it should have been off. "Sweating blood," Aaron warned Kranz of the unexpected drain on one of the spacecraft's scarcest of all resources. Kranz, though, displayed no alarm. He "knew that his flight controllers were naturally nervous about problems in their own areas," in the words of an account by Henry Cooper, "and he had enough confidence in them to assume that they would find the trouble and fix it."

Aaron did. He asked Swigert to look for several obvious culprits, but none proved responsible. Aaron then requested that the auxiliary batteries simply be disconnected until they were absolutely essential. When the batteries were finally reconnected, the spacecraft's improved telemetry now permitted Aaron to pinpoint two offending switches, and Swigert quickly flipped them off. His team, as Kranz had confidently anticipated, had solved the problem.

By implication: Expecting high performance is prerequisite to its achievement among those who work with you. Your high standards and optimistic anticipations will not guarantee a favorable outcome, but their absence will assuredly create the opposite.

The power of affirmative expectations in driving human behavior is evident in research as well as experience. Consider one illustrative study that measured the impact of two new practices on industrial productivity. In one set of manufacturing plants, employees were rotated among jobs as a way of ensuring continuous challenge. In another set, the jobs themselves were enlarged as an alternative means of instilling challenge. In some plants, senior managers expected the new programs to work; in others, they saw little hope for improvement. And whether the jobs were being rotated or enlarged, the attitudes of senior management proved self-fulfilling. High expectations, not specific job practices, went along with high productivity gains, low expectations with low gains. The bottom line: If you are not sanguine about success, those who work for you will be even less so.[2]

Looking back, Eugene Kranz observes, "The leader has to be unflappable. No matter what is going on around you, you have to be cooler than cool. You have to be smarter than smart."

Making Fast, Accurate Decisions

REVERSING THE GLOOM was only the first of Kranz's challenges. Even after he successfully accomplished that, he still faced an almost continuous stream of decisions, each bound by time and each with the potential to become the single disastrous decision that would undo all that had thus far been accomplished. If the astronauts did not move from the command module into the LEM within minutes of the explosion, they never would. If their course correction when rounding the moon were not executed at the precise moment, they would sail away from Earth forever. If they could not reverse the carbon dioxide buildup, they would be asphyxiated. If they could not restart the command module in the most energy-efficient way, they would lack power for reentry.

"If there's one thing I and each flight director had to be aware of," says Kranz, "it is time, because that is a consumable. Other controllers have navigation jobs, propulsion jobs, life-support jobs." But he had a time job: "If you don't . . . make the maneuver at [the right] time, you're going to be flying by the earth." He knew his team had been "incredibly resourceful" on prior missions, and he knew his contractors had built a "resilient" spacecraft. Now, "If I could buy some time for the people in the early hours," Kranz recalls, "we would find a way to get them back."

Kranz knew that fast decision making would be essential, but he also knew it could mean sacrificing accuracy. Like the classic trade-off between risk and reward or between quality and cost, fast action can easily translate into rash action. When time is of the essence and not all information is at hand, we tend to backslide into what analysts term "satisficing," stopping at "good enough" even when we know our solution is short of optimal. But what may serve us well in everyday life can court disaster when minutiae count: Odyssey's return depended on detail.

As Odyssey neared its plunge into Earth's upper atmosphere, its path mysteriously "shallowed." Indeed, the angle of reentry was so low that the command module threatened to skim the surface of the atmosphere and bounce back into space, much like a thrown stone skipping across water. "Is it something in our computation processors?" wondered Kranz. "Is it something associated with the platform alignments that we did? Is there something associated with maneuver execution? Why, why, why?" He worried about "those 'lurkers' " that can "bite you at the wrong time." Nothing could be left to guesswork: "Here we had zero margin for error. We could not overlook anything. Therefore we had to have an explanation for everything that was happening," including the bewildering drift. (NASA's commission of inquiry later determined that wisps of steam from the LEM's cooling system had nudged the spacecraft off course.)

In requesting fast answers to key questions, Kranz repeatedly warned against the "satisficing" pitfall. Don't guess at anything, he told his engineers; know. As the Tiger Team planned Odyssey's final plunge toward Earth, Kranz moved to the front of Room 210 and reminded his controllers that they would have to be extremely accurate since the spacecraft's crippled state had made it far more intolerant of errors than ever before. "The key thing," he would say, "is to be right."

To be right is first to listen, then to decide. "The principal characteristic of a flight director is to be a good listener," Kranz would later recall. As the fate of Apollo 13 hung in the balance,

Kranz had a wealth of console displays to study, and consult them he did, but far more important were the human displays he had on hand. Twenty specialists—flight planners, craft specialists, trajectory analysts, the astronauts themselves—were reporting to him simultaneously, and if the astronauts were to survive, this human input would spell the difference. "They're providing you with information verbally," he observes, and "the flight director's job is to listen to all of these people . . . and then to form an impression of what is going on and what we are going to do about it." Kranz's flight world was akin to researcher Henry Mintzberg's executive world: In watching what top managers do every day, Mintzberg found that they work primarily through personal dialogue with subordinates. Technical data merely supplement what they hear first from people.[3]

The information acquired through good listening is then filtered through and tested against the frames of experience. "You've got all of the sources of information, and then you have your own knowledge," says Kranz. "You're accepting their input, then you're testing its validity, and then you're adding all the pieces together to get the total picture."

Effective decision making also requires adjudication of conflicting claims. Kranz did not avoid this task even when all the claims were meritorious and all were coming from above. Chris Kraft, Deke Slayton, and Max Faget—each superior to Kranz in the chain of command—insisted on opposite actions in the moments after the key course correction. Kranz heard them out, interrupting little, but once each had said his piece, he decided at once. The fact that two of his three bosses, including his mentor, had vigorously urged against his chosen course slowed him not in the least. "Firmness at the helm" he recalls, "was the only thing that was going to get us through it."

By implication: When both speed and precision count, sharing information and keeping everybody's eye on *both goals simultaneously* are essential for achieving both.

Organizing for Optimal Decisions

WHILE EUGENE KRANZ continually demanded fast *and* accurate decision making from his teams, his exhortations worked only because he had fostered an organizational foundation that allowed them to work. Recall what he did in the hours after the explosion: First, he reassigned his White Team—renamed the Tiger Team—to troubleshoot the entire mission, ensuring that a single group was positioned to integrate the thousands of actions that would be required over the next four days. Second, he restaffed the team with more experienced engineers, ensuring that the best talent was at work on the toughest problems. And third, he mobilized hundreds of others—ranging from Chris Kraft to Ken Mattingly—to support the Tiger Team's decision making.

Just as important, once the emergency apparatus was established, Kranz avoided further meddling. He left the problem solving to those who could do it best, such as Tiger Team electrical specialist John Aaron, whose long leash allowed him to solve Odyssey's power problems. While Kranz avoided micromanaging, he also avoided undermanaging: he insisted on reviewing Aaron's emerging plans at many steps along the way.

Kranz defines his role this way: "My job was basically to orchestrate all the players, recognize the problems, point people in the direction if we had more than one way to do a job, get the players to bring their stuff in, listen to them, and send them back."

Even with the best troubleshooting, optimal outcomes can be blocked if all the options are not on the table. Implicit in the mission's unrelenting effort to husband power, for example, was an abiding effort not to foreclose later alternatives. Saving power would keep open the possibility that the astronauts could be landed near an aircraft carrier during daylight; a power deficit could dictate the opposite. "Being a pilot," recalls Kranz, "you always want to keep as much runway ahead of you as you can. . . . You always want to have as many options out in front of you, because those are the things that give you the ability to change course." It is akin to playing "multidimensional chess: You have to think options."

Until the blowout, the mission, in Jim Lovell's words, had been "the smoothest flight of the program," and Joe Kerwin, the mission communicator, had radioed the astronauts just hours before the explosion that "we're bored to tears down here." But rather than bask in the mission's apparent success, Kranz used the flight's respites to prepare his next steps. "We always try to use every second, every minute when things are going right," he observes, "to individually prepare ourselves for what is coming next." NASA embodied the concept in one of its three foundations for mission operations: each team member must "always be aware that suddenly and unexpectedly we may find ourselves in a role where our performance has ultimate consequences." Kranz deemed it his duty to anticipate the future: "Everything has to go perfectly in this business, and it's up to us to steer it on the path so that happens."

By implication: Construct decision-making teams and procedures for intensive problem solving before they are needed. Bringing to the fore those most qualified to make the decisions, regardless of background or obligation, will aid decision making.

A Team That Would Not Fail

MAINTAINING COLLECTIVE OPTIMISM and avoiding poor decisions rest on yet another, deeper foundation. Optimism is a collective construction, a shared view of the world based on a complex blend of what is and what ought to be. Decision making is a collaborative construct as well, for in this case no individual could hope to solve more than a tiny fraction of the mission's problems. A sense of teamwork was thus essential to the enterprise because only teamwork can sustain optimism in the face of relentless adversity and only teamwork can result in actions that are more than the sum of their parts.

Eugene Kranz had built his teams in two cross-cutting ways. First, he had nurtured camaraderie and understanding within the individual flight teams by repeatedly testing them through simulated crises. Instructors studied the teams under duress, assessing whether they worked efficiently and reached sharp, technically sound decisions. They studied whether some members failed to communicate clearly, seemed distracted by family problems, or were simply not up to the task. Those who didn't measure up were quickly weeded out.

By the end of the training, Kranz observes, "the team has come together," and its members had developed "the ability to compensate for each other when the chips get down" and "an attitude so positive that, given a few seconds, basically we can solve any problem." You "learn to communicate and assess data; you learn to make reasonably crisp and authoritative decisions; you learn to admit when you don't know what's going on and ask for help." His team had acquired what is required: the ability "to make basically one hundred percent correct decisions in extremely short periods of time." So strong was the team that it could transcend individual frailty: "The individual can fail, but the team cannot," Kranz will say. But even isolated deficiencies were to be prevented. "Each person on the team," he adds, is a "potential hero working among heroes," and when their moment for heroism came, they would have to be ready.

Kranz fostered the same mutual understanding and joint readiness across his organization, building a team of teams. At Kranz's insistence, equivalent members of the four flight teams shared offices. This, he reasoned, should ensure that the four electrical engineers, for instance, would know one another well before they would have to communicate and trust one another on such issues as the faltering voltage. It also encouraged a "uniformity of decision" from shift to shift, providing seamless handoffs between the flight teams and a consistent interface between them and the astronauts.

"It's where you start your team building," argues Kranz. "The first thing I did in establishing the team building is to look at 'co-location': I want similar people working together as an element of a team." He grouped people across levels, and he grouped outside contractors with inside employees. Occasionally the arrangements violated civil service rules, but when told to conform, Kranz invented ways around them.

Implicit comprehension was a key objective of the team building: "You learn to use the nonverbal communication," Kranz says. "You develop the feeling whether this guy needs a few more seconds to work out a problem. Sometimes you'll change your polling procedures" in surveying the controllers before taking a decision. "You're going to come to him last, you're going to give him a few more seconds."

As a final reinforcing measure, Kranz arranged his flight teams into their own baseball league. The flight teams then challenged the astronaut teams on the football field. Other seasons produced still more competitive sports, even judo.

The team-building payoffs were evident in Room 210. The forty or so people working there had to solve dozens of interrelated problems on the fly, weaving hundreds of specific steps into broader fabric. They had to restructure technological systems so tightly coupled that tiny changes in one could create havoc in another. When a guidance controller proposed deicing Odyssey's thruster jets by briefly firing the engines, another controller immediately protested that the deicing could ruin the guidance system of the still-attached Aquarius. Those responsible for the flight's dynamics, guidance, and later retrofiring objected that the firing could divert the spacecraft from its required trajectory. Yet they quickly found an effective solution, reaffirming the collective virtues of the endless simulations and sports.

By implication: Developing teams and teams of teams through training and exercise can create the implicit understandings that make for fast and accurate decision making when the teams are under duress but must act.

The Two Faces of Leadership

EUGENE KRANZ ENDURED the crisis with an unshakable faith that it would be resolved the right way. His optimism stemmed from an optimistic appraisal of the decision-making apparatus he had fostered since taking control of the Apollo missions just two years earlier. "I thought that as a group we were smart enough and clever enough," he would later say, "to get out of any problem." Kranz's latticework of teams and specialists served as half the leadership formula. His driving optimism and demand for accuracy among the teams and specialists added the other half.

Managers are vested with certain areas of authority from the day they arrive: they can revise budgets, assign people, and give raises. These are the levers of office shown in the bottom rectangle in Figure 3.1—the ones Kranz was handed the minute he first stepped through the door of his new office. Like all successful managers, though, Kranz realized that the vested powers of office are only a platform to build on. As opposed to merely managing, leadership can be defined as moving above those vested powers in both personal and organizational ways, as shown in the upper rectangles in Figure 3.1.

Personal leadership includes the exercise of individual qualities of leadership, as seen in Eugene Kranz's insistence on fast and accurate decisions and in his abiding optimism about a successful return. Organizational leadership includes the exercise of change and development of other people, as seen in his team building before the mission and team restructuring during it. Leadership, then, can be viewed as leveraging what you are given to achieve far more.

Neither facet of leadership is a birthright. Both can be mastered, but mastery is lifelong, often beginning with early men-

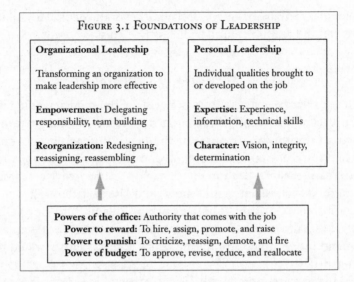

FIGURE 3.1 FOUNDATIONS OF LEADERSHIP

Organizational Leadership

Transforming an organization to make leadership more effective

Empowerment: Delegating responsibility, team building

Reorganization: Redesigning, reassigning, reassembling

Personal Leadership

Individual qualities brought to or developed on the job

Expertise: Experience, information, technical skills

Character: Vision, integrity, determination

Powers of the office: Authority that comes with the job
Power to reward: To hire, assign, promote, and raise
Power to punish: To criticize, reassign, demote, and fire
Power of budget: To approve, revise, reduce, and reallocate

toring by those who understand both. For Eugene Kranz, several "incredibly gifted 'teachers' " served as early models for lasting lessons:

Flight desk manager at McDonnell Aircraft: "His theme was accountability. When you sign that airplane off for flight, you're signing off the lives of the crew on board. You're signing off that airplane that's very valuable. You're signing off responsibility for the future of McDonnell Aircraft."

Flight officer at McDonnell Aircraft: "He really taught me enthusiasm."

Primary flight instructor: "He taught me to watch out for the people around me. . . . If you want to fly safely, you take care of every person in this chain that you fly airplanes on."

Chris Kraft, NASA flight director: "He taught me about risk"—and in the most direct way. Kranz had been serving under Kraft in one of the early missions of the space program when, in the middle of the flight and with no warning, Kraft had turned full control over to him. Kranz recalls being kicked out of the nest so abruptly as a "defining experience."

The day after the successful splashdown of Apollo 13, *The New York Times* editorialized: "For three-and-a-half days all three astronauts had lived at the brink of death in a crippled vehicle whose reserves were so near exhaustion that it had margin neither for human error nor for further malfunctioning of its equipment." The "almost incredible feat" of a safe return "would have been impossible were it not for the steady nerves, courage and great skill of the astronauts themselves" and the "NASA network whose teams of experts performed miracles of emergency improvisation."[4]

Gene Kranz had dreamed of going to the moon himself. As a high school junior, he had authored a term paper on the logistics of moon flight. As a university student, he had majored in aeronautical engineering. As an air force officer, he had served as a jet fighter pilot. And when the Mercury spaceflight program placed a want ad, he was among the first to volunteer. He would never qualify as an astronaut. But in 1970, he received both NASA's Distinguished Service Medal and the Presidential Medal of Freedom. Three years later, as he was turning forty, NASA awarded him its medal for Outstanding Leadership.

❖

CHAPTER 4

Arlene Blum Ascends
Annapurna

"The expedition needed a strong leader but not a dictator."

ARLENE BLUM had braved violent winds and mammoth avalanches to push high up the slopes of Annapurna, one of the world's most awesome mountains. She was determined to place some of her climbing team on the summit—not just for herself or for her expedition but on behalf of women the world around. Blum was leading more than an expedition to one of the planet's most dangerous spots; she was leading a cause.

Annapurna is a part of the most exclusive of all mountain groups, the fourteen Himalayan peaks that all tower above 8,000 meters, more than 26,000 feet. None of the "Eight-Thousanders" had been scaled until 1950, when Maurice Herzog led a French team to the summit of Annapurna. Three years later, New Zealand's Edmund Hillary and Nepal's Tenzing Norgay attained the ultimate Himalayan summit, Mount Everest.

If mountaineering is a sport of adventure and risk, expedition mountaineering is a sport of extreme adventure and risk. By the mid-1970s, Arlene Blum had come to thrive on its special blend of adrenaline and camaraderie, delighting in the grand vistas and mental challenges that come with vertical slopes and thin air. She had already climbed in Alaska and on Everest, and now, in October 1978, she was leading an expedition of women to attempt Annapurna.

Organizing a Himalayan expedition is akin to running a start-up with dozens of full-time employees for several months of outdoor work under extreme conditions. The red tape is an irritant, personnel a headache, logistics a nightmare. Add in the large consequences of even small missteps—a slip off a cliff or into a crevasse—and a Himalayan expedition can seem ludicrous to even the most seasoned outdoor enthusiast, still more so if one is called on to lead it. But Arlene Blum was undaunted. She had recruited a crack group of ten climbers, hired 235 porters and Sherpas, and was now leading them, loaded with six tons of equipment, up the slopes of Annapurna.

Expedition mountaineers have diverse motives; each maintains his or her own "balanced scorecard" on the way up, thriving on the spectacular views, the esprit de corps, or the sheer physical challenge of the act. But traditionally expedition climbers have shared a single ultimate purpose, an unambiguous bottom line: to reach the top. George Mallory, the renowned British climber who made three attempts on Mount Everest in the early 1920s, articulated the main point when he was asked by a journalist, "Why do you try to climb this mountain?" Before disappearing near the summit of Everest in 1924, in what is still one of mountaineering's great unexplained mysteries, Mallory replied with a four-word phrase that has become part of our lexicon: "Because it is there."

To the uninitiated, such a purpose can appear irrational, even absurd. But to the expeditionary climber, to place a foot on the top of the world and see it dropping off in all directions is the driving ambition. Raymond Lambert, a Swiss alpinist who climbed to within 800 feet of Mount Everest's top a year before Hillary and Tenzing succeeded, is remembered best not for getting there but for falling short. He "had to console himself ever after with the knowledge that he had paved the way for Sir Edmund Hillary's conquest," recalled an obituary. He "came within 800 vertical feet of immortality."[1]

Arlene Blum

Arlene Blum and her contemporaries were not yet 800 feet from immortality, but they had trekked and climbed far up Annapurna's daunting heights. Killer avalanches were thundering across their path, and fierce storms were threatening worse. Arlene Bum had to decide whether to sustain the drive or reverse the course; go for the summit or concede defeat.

Creating the Expedition

THE HIMALAYAS ARE filled with sacred peaks. Machhapuchhre, a Matterhorn-like spire over Nepal's second largest town, Pokhara, is an abode of the gods and off limits to all mortals. Its 22,943-foot summit remains one of the few major peaks in the world where climbers have never set foot. Others, such as Mount Everest, are the homes of lesser spirits. Many have been given the names of the deities with which they are associated: Annapurna, for instance, means "harvest goddess," one of Hinduism's benevolent deities, a figure of sustenance and plenty.

For Arlene Blum, just getting the chance to assault Annapurna's heights had been a seemingly endless climb. Despite a long history of women in mountaineering—including an ascent of Europe's highest mountain, Mont Blanc, by Marie Pardis in 1808—expedition climbs were still inhospitable to women in the 1970s. Even Junko Tabei, the Japanese translator and "housewife" who had been the first woman to reach the summit of Mount Everest in 1975, had been criticized by a Japanese newspaper for leaving her husband and children at home to pursue a "selfish hobby."

Blum's experience had been little different. She had applied to join an expedition to Afghanistan in 1969, only to learn that her otherwise exemplary high-altitude experience left her disqualified: "One woman and nine men," the organizer wrote, "would seem to me to be unpleasant high on the open ice," undercutting the "masculine companionship which is so vital a part of the joy of an expedition." A year later she saw an advertisement for a commercial climb of Alaska's Mount McKinley—now better known as Denali—with a stricture that women could come and cook at the base camp but not move above it. When asked why, the leader explained that women were too frail to carry the necessary loads and too weak to bear the stress. Even a male climbing friend warned her off, saying, "You should not sacrifice life on the same altar of egotism that causes men to join the Marines, shoot buffalo," and "drive fast cars."

Like so many avocations we embrace, Blum's encounter with the world of mountaineering had been by accident. She had been an out-of-shape student during her junior year, 1965, at Oregon's Reed College, far from her urban roots in Chicago, when a chemistry lab partner asked if she would come with him to climb nearby Mount Hood, an ice-covered volcanic peak of 11,245 feet. They studied late and started climbing only at 2 A.M. The pitch-dark start, however, meant that they reached the summit in a brilliant sunrise. Blum was hooked.

Told that women could only assist climbers of Denali, not

climb it themselves, Blum helped organize a team of six women in 1970 that successfully scaled the mountain, North America's highest point at 20,300 feet—and did so on their own. By 1972, she had set her sights on even higher points in Nepal, and after a chance encounter with British climber Alison Chadwick during an attempt on an Afghan peak, the two resolved to form a women's team to tackle Annapurna—26,545 feet—in 1975. Nepal tightly restricted access to its renowned summits, allowing but two parties a year, and it denied Blum and Chadwick a permit. But when Blum returned to Nepal in 1976 with an American expedition to Mount Everest, she learned that a permit was available for Annapurna for 1978. Now, a decade after her dawn on Mount Hood, she was determined to reach one of the great summits of the world, towering nearly three miles higher.

Though it was the first 8,000-meter peak to be conquered, Annapurna remains a formidable challenge. The human body deteriorates with prolonged exposure above 20,000 feet, and the summit is another mile above that. Its slopes are swept by thunderous avalanches; temperatures plunge below zero. The first successful expedition had encountered appalling conditions on its retreat. Maurice Herzog had lost a mitten on the summit and later lost his fingers from frostbite. Lionel Terray and Gaston Rébuffat, two of the great figures in French mountaineering, had been blown into a crevasse and emerged temporarily snow-blind.[2] Of thirteen previous attempts, only four had placed climbers on top, and nine mountaineers had perished in the process. Of those who had begun the ascent, one in ten had not returned.

For the American Women's Himalayan Expedition, Blum wanted seasoned climbers with substantial experience above 20,000 feet, but since so few women have found space on previous expeditions, the field was thin. Still, she was able to recruit nine others with strong records. Among them were two long-time friends: Vera Watson, a 46-year-old computer scientist, and Irene Miller, a 42-year-old physicist at IBM with daughters aged 12 and 16. The others were Joan Firey, age 49, an artist and physical therapist; Piro Kramar, age 40, a surgeon; Alison Chadwick-Onyszkiewicz, age 36, an artist; Vera Komarkova, age 35, a plant ecologist; Elizabeth Klobusicky-Mailänder, age 34, an English teacher; and Annie Whitehouse, age 21, and Margi Rusmore, age 20, both university students. Chadwick was British, Klobusicky lived in Germany, but the rest resided in the U.S. Most serious climbers dream of a Himalayan climb, a visit to mountaineering's Mecca, and Himalayan climbers are believed to be at their best in their thirties. For some of the women, this expedition might be their last shot. To raise the $80,000 required to finance the expedition, Arlene Blum and her compatriots had sold 15,000 T-shirts emblazoned with the expedition's slogan, "A Woman's Place Is on Top."

After flying into Kathmandu, the capital of Nepal and gateway to the mountains, the party motored along eighty miles of twisting mountain roads to the town of Pokhara in the shadow of Annapurna. Then it traveled on foot for another eighty miles. For ten days team members wended their way through one of the deepest gorges in the world to the more accessible back side of the mountain. "The summit, floating more than four vertical miles above us in the clouds," wrote Blum, was "so remote that our desire to stand there seemed arrogant." They were now looking at six weeks of endless shuttling of supplies—tents, food, sleeping bags, climbing gear, and oxygen tanks—among the five camps they would establish between base camp and the top.

A key objective was to place a camp on the Dutch Rib, a slice of rock and ice connecting the mountain's lower glacial highways to its upper snowfields. Doing so would require arduous technical climbing up a nearly vertical face hung with mammoth icicles. There, on top of a sinuous ridge, they would perch a tent as a vital way station for bringing essential supplies up and spent climbers down. With a thousand feet of free space on either side, the narrow platform would have to do, but its location was precarious. (A year later, when three American climbers were

American Women's Himalayan Expedition

camped in much the same spot, hurricane winds thrown up by a nearby avalanche ripped them from the ridge to their deaths.) Still, they decided, the site would work. They designated it Camp 3, and they would require just two more tent sites for a final push to the summit.

Avoiding the Avalanche

DAILY SNOWFALLS ACCUMULATE high on a mountain. On slopes of 30 degrees or more, the smallest trigger can suddenly transform a serene landscape into a boiling cauldron. When hit by an avalanche, a climber is told to "swim" toward the surface of the fluid flow of snow, ice, and air as it bounds down the mountainside. As treacherous as "swimming" a flowing avalanche can be, though, the ultimate terror begins when the avalanche stops. A climber caught near the top can often break free; those caught deeper down are trapped. As the tons of snow compress downward, air is forced upward. Tiny pockets of oxygen might remain in the bowels of the avalanche, but even the largest pockets are exhausted within twenty minutes. And the snow and ice are only part of an avalanche's arsenal of horrors. Avalanches are known to create wind blasts of 200 miles per hour, and as nature's battering ram and giant scythe, they can dislodge a steel bridge or shear off a stand of trees.[3]

Not surprisingly, then, avalanches are one of the most feared hazards of the Himalayas, and Annapurna is especially notorious. In 1970, Henry Day led a British-Nepalese ascent over the "Sickle" route used by Herzog two decades earlier, and he warned Blum about the exceptional avalanche dangers on the route she was planning: "I do not believe the Sickle is a justifiable route," Day observed, "now that I am the father of two."

The worst danger zone for Blum and her companions was a swath of crumpled glacier between Camp 2 and the bottom of the Dutch Rib. The glacier was a chute for avalanches coming off the vast upper slopes, and it funneled one after another across the route the climbers had to traverse continually as they moved their supplies ever upward. In some mountain areas, avalanches are rarer in the early hours of the day, when temperatures are low, and working around their rhythm can mitigate the risk. Here, avalanches seemed to descend at random. The chute might require thirty minutes or more for the uphill crossing of its half-mile width—half that time in going down—and when one is ferrying a forty-pound supply pack at 18,500 feet, sprinting free of harm's way would be feasible only at the very edge. Given the route she had chosen, Blum had little choice but to pass this way, and she carried responsibility for all those who would cross.

The passage was usually uneventful but almost always terrifying. One day, six of the climbers moved across without incident. Shortly thereafter, a snowslide swept through and obliterated all evidence of their passage. Later, three climbers were nearing the far side of the avalanche run when Annie Whitehouse witnessed a horrifying sight. "I was just beginning to cross the mounds of avalanche debris," she wrote in her diary, "when I saw, but didn't

The Dutch Rib on Annapurna

hear, a great cloud of snow and ice coming down from the right side of the Sickle. It looked as though the three members ahead of me were directly in the path. . . . All I saw was a great cloud of snow engulfing the area where they'd been." Miraculously, though, they are not there when it hit, having scurried a few feet beyond the chute before the blast arrived. Not long afterward, an avalanche stripped away spare climbing gear stored at the bottom of the Dutch Rib in a seemingly bombproof cache.

So capricious were the avalanches that Blum once wondered whether stopping the few minutes to attach her crampons

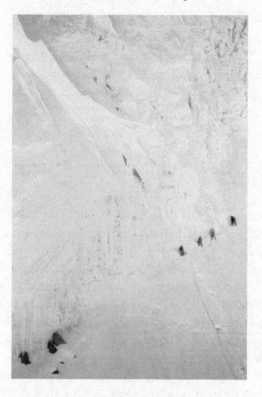

Close-up of the Dutch Rib

before crossing the chute might prevent her from being hit—or, because of the delay, cause her to be hit. Later, no more than five minutes after she finally passed through the chute, another avalanche roared down it. One afternoon the whole mountain seemed to give way, with avalanches cascading every few minutes and one nearly overwhelming Camp 1 and its six inhabitants. So grave was the threat that Blum raised the unthinkable: packing it in. She polled her teammates in several tents:

> *Blum:* "These avalanches are getting to be too much. Do you think it's safe for us to stay here?"

Long silence.

Blum: "Things that aren't supposed to happen are happening twice a day right now. I feel as if something is telling us we should give up before one of us dies."

Another long silence.

Whitehouse: "I don't feel like talking about it. I just want to climb this mountain."

Miller: "I've been climbing for twenty years, and I've never been on a mountain that's so unstable. The avalanches are completely random. Sometimes it seems almost immoral to keep going."

Blum: "I feel like we did everything right except selecting our peak. I know we've got the ability to climb the mountain. We've already done the hardest part, but I don't know if we can stay here for three more weeks and keep walking under these avalanche slopes day after day without someone getting killed."

Miller: "I've never felt good about Annapurna because of the avalanche danger. I wish we'd picked another peak, too, but we're here now. I guess we'll have to go on."

The avalanches never diminished, the qualms never subsided, yet a decision to reverse course was never seriously considered either. One team member, Liz Klobusicky, had to return to her teaching job in Germany. As she was bidding adieu, she confessed, "I'm terrified for all of you." But the momentum of the enterprise remained upward, and nobody quit or balked at crossing the avalanche fans. "I'm not sure it was particularly intelligent or laudable of us to stay," Blum later wrote. "But it definitely was heroic."

Selecting a Summit Team

EXPEDITION MOUNTAINEERING IS an enterprise in which everyone must stand on the shoulders of others, a "pyramid of people." Nobody can reach the top without the unrelenting efforts of all. But it is also an enterprise in which everyone wants to reach the top. That, after all, is the sport's allure, the reason mountaineers are willing to risk the avalanche superhighway. The problem—and the leadership challenge for Arlene Blum— was that there is room for few on top. Not literally, of course, but so extreme are the conditions at 26,000 feet that often only a single pair of climbers is likely to have a realistic shot at the summit. When Herzog and colleague Louis Lachenal reached the Annapurna pinnacle, and when Hillary and Tenzing attained the Everest crown, a dozen team members were supporting them below and none would get close to the top.

The sport's obsession with the summit was a formidable drawback in Blum's eyes. If the rewards of making it vastly outweigh those for all other contributions—a winner-take-all mentality—she worried that as individuals vied for the summit team, they would lobby her to favor their own chances even at the cost of the team's objectives. And once it became clear which few would have a shot at the summit, it could demoralize the others, whose continuing energies would still be critical for a successful ascent and safe descent. When planning the expedition, Blum even considered refusing to announce later who had reached the summit so that all of her climbers could glory in the full credit for attaining it.

Serendipity plays a role in determining what history records. Who is healthy and who is high on the mountain when the weather clears are important contributing factors. Still, the final order of ascent remains in part a leader's prerogative, and Arlene Blum had to make two critical decisions. Later, in years to come, she would repeatedly relive both, mentally undoing and redoing each and wondering again and again if they had been right or wrong.

The first decision was the composition of the initial summit party. Blum knew this decision could not be made cavalierly, nor could it be imposed without the others' concurrence, for this was an enterprise of consent. She told her team that the first summit party would comprise three women and they would go for the top between October 14 and 16. A second attempt, by two women and two Sherpas, would follow two days later, and a third team of those who still wanted a stab at the summit might come later.

Alison Chadwick objected that the numbers did not add up. Realistically, a third assault was unlikely to materialize, and even a second attack was a long shot. After a Himalayan expedition places a first group on the summit, Chadwick knew, the momentum tends to reverse completely. The summit climbers are spent, risks no longer seem acceptable, and descent becomes the mental imperative. Four previous expeditions had reached the summit of Annapurna, and in each case it was only the first pair who had made it.

Chadwick persisted. "I think all the members of the team—all nine of us now that Liz has left—should have a reasonable chance for the summit," she argued. The first two teams totaled only five climbers. "What about the rest of us?" worried Chadwick. "Everyone should have some guarantee of being on a summit team after they've risked their lives doing carries to Camp 3." She proposed that the second party consist of three women and only one Sherpa, and that a third try should be elevated from possible to definite. Blum responded that she could not guarantee a second attempt, let alone a third. If anybody felt that a shot at the summit trip was the price for continuing to traverse the avalanche chute in support of others, said Blum, that person should stop carrying supplies to Camp 3.

The Sherpas weighed in with their own objections. A tribal group of Tibetan origin, they had become a standard component of most Himalayan expeditions, experienced and conditioned mountaineers whose strength and tenacity had been indispensable to many ascents. Blum had considered dispensing with them to make hers a truly female force. When reality had intervened in that plan, she had sought to employ two women, or Sherpanis, along with three Sherpas for the high-altitude climbing, but no Sherpanis had been available. Now the Sherpas she had employed announced that they, too, wanted to reach the summit. It was a matter of pride, but they also wanted to enhance their reputations for future expeditions.

Lopsang Tsering was the *sirdar*, the head Sherpa, and he urged that the first summit group be made up of one woman and one Sherpa, arguing that the smallest, best-suited party was most likely to succeed. He also contended that a single team would be enough: "Too many people going to the summit. Annapurna is very dangerous. When one member and one Sherpa reach summit, then we are all very happy and go home." Blum resisted, explaining that all on her team have been dreaming of the summit, but he insisted: "You are leader. . . . You must tell your members that everyone cannot climb mountain."

The weather was holding, and Blum announced the first team: Irene Miller, Vera Komarkova, and Piro Kramar. Combining the earlier concept of distinct second and third teams with two women each, Blum announced that the final team would consist of the other four women who still want to try for the summit, plus Sherpas Chewang Rinjing and Mingma Tsering. Privately, Blum was prepared to allow one of the Sherpas onto the first team if circumstances dictated, and she so instructed the team.

The summit-bound women reached the high camp at 24,200 feet, just half a mile below the summit. They had asked Rinjing and M. Tsering to accompany them there, and, knowing that, if they asked one Sherpa to try the summit with them, he would insist the other come as well, they now invited both to make the final ascent.

The three women rose at 3 A.M. on October 15 and spent four hours preparing for the final ascent. In stepping outside to

Irene Miller

fasten her crampons and load her pack, Kramar discovered to her horror that her right index finger had been extended through a hole in the glove and was now frozen white. An eye surgeon, Kramar could not risk amputation and resigned herself to remaining behind.

Late that same afternoon and more than a mile lower on the mountain, Arlene Blum was crossing the avalanche zone one final time, terrified as ever, when she spotted another climber on the far side who had radio contact with the top. "Did they make it?" Blum called out. The nod was affirmative. Miller, Komarkova, and the Sherpas had stepped onto the summit at 3:30 P.M. "We've done what we set out to do," Miller wrote in her diary. "There's no point higher." Emotion overwhelmed Blum, "a mixture of triumph for the summit, relief at having made it across the avalanche slope for the last time, exhaustion

Vera Komarkova

from the tension of the descent, and, most of all, joy in knowing that a woman's place was indeed on top." Irene Miller would say that getting to the summit was "the hardest thing I've ever done in my life."

A Second Decision

ARLENE BLUM'S second critical decision was made the same day, not long before the first party reached the summit, but its consequences would be felt tragically two days later. The second summit party was to consist of three Americans: Alison Chadwick, Vera Watson, and Annie Whitehouse. A fourth member, Margi Rusmore, had also been named, but a frozen foot would force her to sit it out. The team was already at Camp

3 on the Dutch Rib, just two days' climb below the summit now that the higher camps were well established.

"I'm so excited about going to Camp 4 today!" exclaimed Watson, hoping that the others felt the same. Chadwick was ready too, and the weather was holding nicely. But Whitehouse was strangely ambivalent, worrying about whether they had sufficient support to ensure they would get up and back safely. "I've been thinking about it all night," she worried. "I just don't feel our team is strong enough for a second summit attempt. It doesn't really seem safe to me."

Watson was crestfallen. Chadwick was shocked: "Don't be silly, Annie. Come with us. We can do it—I know we can." Whitehouse feared that the Sherpas, who might be essential for evacuation if anything went wrong, would not even wait at Camp 5, let alone accompany them to the top. Two Sherpas would soon reach the summit with the first party, and the Americans recalled the earlier warning that one Sherpa on top would be enough to make them "all very happy and go home." M. Tsering of the summit party would drive the point home the next day, when he reached Camp 2. "Let's go to Kathmandu," he said, "and have a party." Still, Chadwick believed that some Sherpas would stay, and she insisted that "we can do it ourselves if not," but Whitehouse was not swayed: "The weather could change in a few hours, and then where would be?" Without "oxygen or support from Sherpas, I don't feel safe."

Even though Blum had named Whitehouse to the summit team, she did not press the point. "Annie has to make her own decision," Blum warned, and "you can't talk someone into taking that kind of risk" against her better judgment. Whitehouse soon announced a firm decision not to proceed.

Undaunted by losing a third of their team and knowing that support was thin, Chadwick and Watson prepared to move up on their own. They might try for a subsidiary summit—itself an unclimbed 26,000-foot point—or they might simply turn back. The important thing was to make an attempt. Indeed, in some ways, the less support they had, the better. Chadwick had earlier told Blum, "For this Annapurna trip to really mean some-thing, we've got to get to the summit alone, with no Sherpas along." She had come close to doing it alone three years earlier when climbing without oxygen at nearly 26,000 feet on another Himalayan giant, Gasherbrum III. Watson herself had been the first woman ever to make a solo ascent of Aconcagua in Argen-tina, South America's highest mountain at 22,835 feet.

"Be careful. Don't take any risks," Blum cautioned Chadwick and Watson as they left Camp 3 at 11:30 that morning. Watson's enthusiasm had waned during the course of the discussion, and now she talked of achieving just a personal best, ascending above 23,000 feet. Chadwick remained eager to go as high as possible, and she left for the heights with an air of confident optimism: "We'll be fine."

On October 16, a day after the first summit success, Chad-wick and Watson were pushing above Camp 4 when they met the exhausted summit group on its way down. The Sherpas were not the least bit interested in going back up with them. Still, Chadwick and Watson were now determined to go for the unclimbed subsidiary peak, and by radio they asked Blum to describe a guidebook photo of its ramparts. Blum warned that the steep rock near the apex "seems risky for a party of two."

By the next morning, all the rest of the expedition had descended to Camp 3 or lower, leaving nobody at the two high-est camps to render assistance if required. Blum made one last appeal by radio: "I'd rather you wouldn't go up there without Sherpa support. You've done a great job already, and you can come down now." Chadwick and Watson remained resolute, and late in the afternoon the expedition's film crew spotted the two of them well on their way to Camp 5, the last camp before the summit.

At dinner that evening, Arlene Blum tried to make radio con-tact with the climbers, but she could not raise them. Radio fail-ures in extreme temperatures are not uncommon, but the next day, the film crew could detect no movement through its giant telephoto lens anywhere below or above Camp 5. Another night passed with no radio response from above, and still another day with no sign of human movement.

M. Tsering and another Sherpa went up to search, and a few hours later an agitated voice crackled on the radio with an alarming discovery: not far from the Camp 4 they could see a red jacket, much like Chadwick's. A crevasse blocked them from approaching, but from fifty yards they confirmed the worst: The two climbers had evidently lost their footing somewhere on their way to Camp 5, perhaps where the icy route steepened just below the tent platform. The path was steep enough for descending climbers to have to belay one another down it, but ascending climbers tended to move up it without such protection, knowing that facing into the mountain going up was more secure than facing outward going down. Even then, if a boot crampon were to come lose or a snow step give way, a secure footing could vanish in an instant. Whatever the cause, the two women had fallen more than a thousand feet.

The slightest misstep on an icy slope can mean disaster. Had the Sherpas accompanied Chadwick and Watson, they could probably not have helped. In all likelihood, the Sherpas would have been on a separate rope, tied to each other but not to the others, as had been their practice throughout much of the expedition. "I kept wanting to play the record backward—to change the summit teams, the lead climbers, the mountain; to change ever having wanted to climb an eight-thousand-meter peak," remembers Blum. "But the record would not reverse."

Becoming a Leader

LEADERSHIP IS A learned skill, and Arlene Blum was enrolled in the school of direct experience. She had not begun with a blank slate, for she had already helped lead a group of six women up Denali. At the Denali summit, her group's leader had collapsed from altitude sickness, and it had been Blum who had organized a grueling and dangerous evacuation of the stricken climber. Still, the scale of an Eight-Thousander is another magnitude, as are the human challenges and natural risks. Without formal tutoring in the skills of expeditionary leadership, she would have to acquire them as her team moved up the mountainside.

Launching the expedition itself had been an act of creating something out of nothing, of transforming a transcendent vision into the mundane matters of permits, tents, and teams that would make it happen. Many dream of building an enterprise, of walking on clouds, but few carry their concepts to fulfillment. As Blum and her companions passed through customs at the Kathmandu airport on August 9, 1978, it was opening day.

Moving a band of mountaineers from civilization to wilderness requires a deft but firm hand, and such did not come naturally for Blum. Her penchant was for companionship and collaboration, not command and control. But chaos would have been the consequence, and as the team was assembling its gear, porters, and Sherpas in Kathmandu, Blum was already appreciating the need to revise her instincts. "I was learning the hard way," she remembers. "Although I didn't yet sound like an authentic army general, I was moving in that direction." But since she was presiding over a consensual enterprise, "the trick" was "to move just far enough."

An early test for Blum came in the person of Joan Firey, a team member with years of climbing experience and a paragon of certainty. Ever optimistic about the team's prospects and confident of her own judgment, Firey was responsible for organizing the food supplies, which should have included prodigious quantities of local rice, fruit, and meat. Her frugal nature, however, had led her to minimalist buying, enough for lean cuisine but little more on the mountainside.

Viewing the larder, Blum anticipated a motivational debacle. In her experience, at high altitude the correlation between food sufficiency and human energy was close to exact. Luxury foods would add verve when it was most needed, but Firey asserted, "We will have to make do with what we have." Blum would not have it: "Buy that food today, Joan. I'm not going to see this expedition fail because we don't have the food we need."

Several months earlier, in a Stateside meeting with a clinical psychologist, Firey had confessed that she did not trust Blum's leadership and would even prefer to be the leader herself, but other team members now rallied to Blum's defense, and in doing so they presented her with a dilemma that would plague her in the months to come: "They wanted me to be a strong, decisive leader, but they also expected to contribute to major decisions." The principles resonate with modern sensibilities, but the challenge is in the application. "What does it mean," Blum asks rhetorically, "to be the 'strong leader' of ten tough-minded women who all want to contribute to each decision?" She knew that she would have to resolve the dilemma.

Joan Firey, charismatic and decisive, already represented one side of the divide. The other side was more familiar to Blum. She recognized that her motives for going on prior expeditions had been a blend of personal sharing and self-understanding, "to know my companions and myself better." But those would not suffice when larger responsibilities demanded more: "My primary goal would have to be the overall success of the expedition, not friendship."

As soon as the expedition had established Camp 2 at 18,500 feet, Blum's solution was put to a test. She announced her plan of attack on the Dutch Rib: the four most experienced ice climbers—Komarkova, Klobusicky, Kramar, and Chadwick—would lead, two Sherpas would support them, and others would transport supplies. Her marching order seemed squarely in the interests of the collective, even if it was disquieting for some individuals, but it was greeted with stony silence by all. Later that evening, Blum overheard a comment from another tent: "All Arlene cares about is public relations with the Sherpas, not about giving women a chance to climb."

At breakfast the next morning, there were more gripes. "I think we should have a discussion about how decisions are made in this group," Kramar complained. Watson struck home: "I think the climbing plan was made undemocratically and should be changed so that everybody gets an equal chance to lead. . . . If I get to the summit on someone else's fixed rope all the way, I'm not going to feel like I climbed the mountain." Added Firey, "A lot of us are unhappy about the way that decision was made." Remaining silent in her growing distress, Blum finally heard soothing words. "I think most of us have forgotten how hard Arlene's job is," said Miller, "and I don't think we're giving her adequate support. She's getting pressure not just from us, but from many other directions, too, every day, every hour."

Hours of acrimonious exchange followed. Near lunchtime the problem of the privileged position of the Sherpas became moot. They had just washed their clothing and announced that they had nothing dry for that day's climbing in any case. By then, Blum had become convinced that her plan was right but the process all wrong. "I had learned another lesson about leadership," she wrote. "If there had been an open meeting, my plan would probably have prevailed, and at a much lower cost." She knew where she wanted to go but was less sure of how to get there: "I'd had the confidence in my plan to get it accepted but had lacked the confidence in myself necessary to do it openly."

Blum promised more consultation during the days ahead, saying she would discuss decisions personally with those at her own camp and by radio with others. Yet one of the comments during the morning's discussion suggested the limits of communal decision making. Margi Rusmore, though the youngest on the team, was not without experience. She had "majored" in mountain climbing in high school and at age seventeen had reached the summit of Denali, the youngest woman at the time to have climbed to North America's highest point. Youth is no inhibitor of insight. "We can't all be a bunch of prima donna climbers and lead the whole mountain," she cautioned. "If the plan is best for the expedition as a whole, then we should try it." Later, reflecting on the fateful determinations that Blum was reaching, many with implications for summiting or surviving, Irene Miller would say, "I was grateful that I didn't have to make the decisions."

In constituting the final summit teams, Blum conferred more but still decided which plan was best. She heard members' concerns, tested their moods, gauged their stamina. When Chadwick and the Sherpas protested that some would miss having a chance at the top, the dispute was amicable and short-lived by comparison. When Whitehouse dropped out of the second summit team, and when Chadwick and Watson decided to move up, it was a decision made within a consultative framework that Blum had finally created. If at 14,000 feet she had not appreciated all the pitfalls of team leadership, she had mastered many of them by 21,000 feet.

By implication: A new position of leadership will engender the experience you lack on arrival, and seeking feedback on your performance in the position will ensure that you take advantage of the experience.

Managing Motives

ALL ORGANIZATIONS ARE challenged by the need to link personal goals to collective welfare. Common objectives can be reached only if individual aims become aligned with the goals, if private purpose and public aims are matched. Though researchers have mastered the science of creating light coherence to produce laser power, leaders still struggle with the art of human coherence to generate organizational muscle. Two motivational issues account for much of the struggle.

The first is the diverse set of motives that lead participants to join an organization. While all seek to set foot on a summit, their reasons for doing so are as varied as people are. For Blum, it was not to prove that women could reach great summits, which she already knew, but to send that message "to people all over the world." Watson wanted to summit in the Himalayas; Chadwick hoped to prove she could do so without men or oxygen.

Even in far more narrowly defined activities, the diversity of human motivation is impressive. Consider one of the most clearly defined sporting events of all, the men's one-mile race. Since Roger Bannister first broke the four-minute mile, a dozen runners have successively held the world record. In broad terms, what they had to endure to achieve such excellence—the endless hours of training, the pain, the self-denial—was much the same, but each was driven by distinct personal motives:

> *Roger Bannister* (1954, 3:59): "Running presents a perfect test of judgment, speed, and stamina."
> *John Landy* (1954, 3:58): "One's effort could be pinned down and quantified precisely."
> *Derek Ibbotson* (1957, 3:57): "I ran to prove to my father that I was better than my brother."
> *Herb Elliott* (1958, 3:54.5): "I ran at first to remorselessly beat everyone I possibly could."
> *Peter Snell* (1962, 3:54.4): "I ran for recognition."
> *Michel Jazy* (1965, 3:53): "I ran so I would not have to fight the war in Algeria."
> *Jim Ryun* (1965, 3:51): "I ran to get a letter jacket, a girlfriend."
> *Sebastian Coe* (1981, 3:47): "I ran because I was meant to run."
> *Noureddine Morceli* (1993, 3:44): "I run to be known as the greatest runner . . . of all time."[4]

The issue for Arlene Blum—or any organizational leader—is to recognize, understand, and work with such varied motives. "I focus on the fact that everyone wants to win," offers Robert L. Crandall, chief executive officer of American Airlines, but he adds, "You must recognize that everyone has a different reason for wanting to win." Only late in the expedition did Blum appreciate all that was behind Chadwick's early resistance to Blum's plans for the summit and Chadwick's later determination to reach the summit herself.

The second motivational issue derives from the scarce space at the top. While all are drawn to climb to the summit, few in fact will get there. Nor is much value added to an expedition if a second group reaches the top. Had others followed Herzog and Lachenal on Annapurna, or Hillary and Tenzing on Everest, they would have contributed little to their enterprises' essential success, the first ascent. Worse, second- or third-party efforts can detract from a mission if they end in disaster, tainting an otherwise unambiguous success. And given the mood and momentum of a climbing team after one party has reached the summit, the probability of accidents worsen, as time passes and support wanes.

The leadership imperative for Blum was to keep the contest open as long as possible, not only for the summit but also for the critical challenges on the way up. As long as the prospect of pioneering the route and reaching the summit remain alive for all, everyone's energies remain alive as well. This may have been one of Blum's miscalculations in announcing that the four most experienced ice climbers would lead the way up the Dutch Rib: her associates were not yet ready to recognize the collective limitations to their own aspirations. Each would have to struggle up the slope and face repeated risks if the expedition were to be successful, but the willingness of each to do so depended on the perception that she might lead on the Dutch Rib and have a chance at the summit.

After Chadwick and Watson departed for their ill-fated attempt at the top, Blum found satisfaction in the fact that everyone who was still able and aspiring has had a chance. The Sherpas had placed two of their own on the summit; Miller and Komarkova had reached it; Whitehouse had declined the opportunity; Kramar and Rusmore had frozen limbs; and the others, including Blum herself, had by now opted not to try.

Thus, finally, after an initial misstep she managed to offer upward opportunity for all who would avail themselves of it.

By *implication:* Recognizing people's diverse motives for participating is an essential first step in mobilizing their contributions. Creating an opportunity for all to succeed—whatever their motives—is an essential second step in harnessing their contributions even when the room at the top is not big enough for all.

Managing Uncertainty

UNCERTAINTY IN ACHIEVING a summit is a given. Were it not, there would be little mystique in reaching the top. The degree of uncertainty, however, can vary widely from moment to moment. On some days, victory looks clinched; on others, much the opposite. Bright sun, calm air, and working limbs inspire the former attitude. Heavy snowfall, cruel winds, and frostbite make for the latter. Prospects can even change by the hour. Early on the afternoon of May 10, 1996, Jon Krakauer, a writer for *Outside* magazine, and more than a dozen other climbers were nearing the summit of Mount Everest with clear weather all around. Late in the afternoon a sudden storm hit the summit pyramid, plunging the wind chill to −100 degrees Fahrenheit, and half of the climbers would not survive the night.[5]

Such cycles of hope and despair present a countercyclical enigma. When optimism and confidence run high, they can be self-defeating: one's adrenaline level drops, one's attention drifts, and what should not be taken for granted becomes a given. It is said that one of the most dangerous moments during a climb is just after the summit has been reached. It is then, in the elation of victory, that distraction can be greatest. Conversely, when pessimism and discouragement run deep, they can also be self-limiting. A victory that seems beyond reach can undercut the will to achieve it even when it is not out of the question.

The challenge is to compensate, to mitigate both the optimism and the pessimism. Too much of either can be counterproductive. This helps explain why Blum's teammates were so reluctant to acknowledge overtly that the avalanche dangers between Camps 2 and 3 were far greater than had been anticipated. Talking about them would have brought subjective perceptions too closely into line with the objective reality. Avoiding such a discussion allowed the luxury of downplaying the reality, a hedged assessment essential for continued commitment to the climb. Chadwick helped Blum understand the collective conscience: "The problem with talking about it at all is that if we admit we are really worried and try to have a rational discussion, we would inevitably come to the conclusion that we should give up."

Later, Blum accompanied the first summit team for part of its final climb from Camp 3 to Camp 4. The wind was savage, stinging their faces and obscuring the treacherous route. Blum announced that she was turning back, and Irene Miller understood Blum's implicit assessment: "Yeah, this wind really takes it out of you." Miller herself looked wan from the high-altitude slogging through thick snow, and she acknowledged a fatalistic state of mind. "I've left some letters at Camp 2 for my friends in case I don't come back," she told Blum. "Will you make sure they get them?" Blum accepted the task but none of the mood: "Oh, Irene, you'll be all right." She offered Miller chocolate and counsel: "You've done really well so far—it's going to be beautiful up there—it looks like you'll have a full moon if you have to come down in the dark." And a final bolstering for a faltering perception: "I think the weather's going to be good for the next couple of days."

To the second summit team, Blum delivered a different message. She reminded Alison Chadwick of the risks she was facing in going for the summit, dampening her optimism to ensure she did not misread the dangers. Conversely, when Whitehouse voiced her ambivalence about a summit bid with Chadwick and Watson, Chadwick played down the hazards. "When you came along on this expedition, you made a decision to take risks," she argued. "Every time you crossed that avalanche slope, your life was in danger. This risk isn't any larger, and the rewards could be so much greater." But Blum responded with a counterpoint. "I'm uncomfortable with the sparse support left for your attempt," she warned, and "I think you should give it up if the Sherpas all go down."

As Chadwick and Watson were about to leave Camp 3 for their ill-fated attempt, Chadwick was ever the optimist, telling Blum not to "worry so much." Chadwick had earlier enthused over the prospect of reaching an unclimbed summit: "What a coup that would be—the two of us doing a first ascent of a twenty-six-thousand-foot peak. That would make the climbing world sit up and take notice, wouldn't it?" Once again, Blum counseled caution: "Remember, if you don't feel strong or the weather looks like it is changing, don't go any higher."

At first glance, such efforts to dampen high spirits might seem the antithesis of leadership: Why not go for it all while you're on an emotional high? But counterinterpreting objective conditions can be more than caution; it can be a survival skill. In 1963, an American expedition set out to place the first U.S. climbers on the summit of Mount Everest, the roof of the world. Two of the climbers achieved the summit by the route pioneered by Hillary and Tenzing; two others made it by an entirely new way up the more difficult west ridge. In all, the climbers spent more than two months above their base camp, often in harrowing conditions. But a research study of the expedition showed that one of the team's most potent weapons had been a collective psychology that was consistently countercyclical: when objective conditions offered reason for optimism, the climbers' collective mood turned cautious; when conditions were dismal, their mood turned upbeat. Thus their spirits rarely got too high to encourage recklessness or so low as to cause despair.[6]

If the subjective interpretation of an uncertain objective verges toward one end of the spectrum or the other, a team's realization of the objective can be undermined. Blum and her fellow climbers cautioned one another against both overoptimism and excessive pessimism.

By implication: When a summit, product, or project seems well within reach, dampening overconfidence can ensure that energy remains focused on achieving it; when it appears almost out of reach, encouraging greater confidence can ensure that the motivation remains focused on achieving it.

Managing Meaning

THE EXPEDITION'S SLOGAN, "A Woman's Place Is on Top," and its title, the Women's Himalayan Expedition to Annapurna, established an expectation. If the expedition were not only for climbers to conquer the summit but also for women to climb an Eight-Thousander on their own, it would augment the rewards of success. If successful, it should help pave the way for women's admission into mountaineering's inner circles.

Several months before the ascent, *The Washington Post* provided its readers with its answer to the inevitable question of why. "America's first all-female Himalayan expedition sets out this August for Annapurna, the world's 10th highest peak," wrote reporters Ron Brodmann and Bill Curry. Organized by Arlene Blum, the "10-woman team plans to storm Annapurna's summit by a . . . difficult route. If they succeed, they'll be the first American group to make it to the top of the 26,545-foot mountain." Women across the country, they noted, were volunteering their professional services as lawyers, accountants, and publicists to support and raise money for the expedition. An all-female film crew had been recruited, and the climbers wanted Sherpanis, not Sherpas, to guide them.[7]

Inevitably, such high expectations entail high risks. If the expedition were to fail, the pain would be all the greater because so much had been laid on it. "We felt all the eyes of the world were on us," Blum would later say. Americans would have fallen short, but, even more important, women would also have fallen short. While nothing is gained if nothing is ventured—and the climb promised to strike another blow for women's equality—the operational downside may be an excessive willingness to tolerate risk. Ascending any serious peak is a risky business, but ascending with one gender's reputation contingent on the outcome may require the climbers to tempt fate once too often.

In laying the mantle of "cause" on the expedition, its leader anticipated the downside. "I am concerned about this expedition," Blum cautioned four months before departure. "If a man doesn't make it to the top, nobody says, well, men can't climb mountains." She sought to dampen public expectations to avoid untoward pressure on her team to succeed: "There's so much focus on our attempt, I worry. For us the expedition will be a success if no one gets killed."[8] Later, as the climbers deliberated continuing in the face of the violent avalanching, Blum told her team, "It's not worth it if anybody dies." As the first summit team was ascending the final mile, she reminded herself, "All that mattered was that some of us get up this mountain and all of us get off it alive."

Knowing that she and her associates might be tempted to compromise their judgment, Blum pressed for clear thinking, shorn of context. In deciding to go for the second summit bid, Chadwick argued, "You've got to remember that this attempt is what our expedition is all about—a real all-women team. No Sherpas, little oxygen." But Blum remained skeptical, fearing that Chadwick's determination to "make the climbing world sit up and take notice" could lead to an underestimation of the mountain's hazards.

The larger-than-life context and the successful surmounting of the summit would later strike, as hoped, a symbolic blow for equality. Arlene Blum would become, in the words of Nina McCain of *The Boston Globe*, a "world-famous climber who in 1978 led an all-women's team on the first American ascent of

Annapurna." Maurice Herzog, the first on Annapurna, would write, "I am convinced that this success will lead to further triumphs of women in the fields of adventure, exploration, and discovery."[9]

For those still trapped in gender bias, the expedition would establish that women could equal what men had achieved. But in guiding the expedition to its triumph on the summit, Blum's actions remind us of one's responsibility for managing both one's actions and their attendant risks when the end results have symbolic power.

> *By implication:* Infusing collective action with transcendent meaning can add greater reward to successful completion of a task, but it can also add greater risk to those involved. When a broader purpose is aimed for, crafting an appropriate balance between expectations on the outside and risk taking on the inside is the challenge.

An Enduring Legacy

ARLENE BLUM went on to climb other mountains. She walked the length of the Himalayas on a 2,500-mile trek in 1981–1982, and she carried Annalise, her four-month-old daughter, on a two-month, 600-mile hiking trip across the Alps in 1987. She also joined Amelia Earhart, Mary Leakey, and Margaret Mead as one of only eleven recipients of a Gold Medal from the Society of Woman Geographers. Along the way, Blum's work as a professional biochemist played an important role in the U.S. government's decision to ban makers of children's sleepwear from using the fire-retardant chemical Tris, which she helped identify as a possible carcinogen.[10]

But her Annapurna expedition, at age thirty-three, was a turning point. "The experience of leading that historic expedition," Blum says, "changed my life." Before the expedition she had been a scientist and mountaineer; now she is a writer and

Arlene Blum and Annapurna

leadership developer. With aging and becoming a mother, she has become more leery of taking personal risk: "When you're young, you think you can beat the odds. You think you're immortal. I don't think that anymore."[11]

Blum brought a unique blend of qualities to the slopes of Annapurna: She dreamt of a team on a summit, and she transmuted a private idea into public ambition. She persisted in her pursuit, aligning thousands of small steps, one at a time, to achieve a far larger step. Despite being a natural worrier and friendship seeker, she mastered the unnatural skills of making decisions with confidence and directing others. "I learned that a group of ordinary people, when they share a vision, can take on an incredible challenge and do things they never dreamed possible," she recalls. "If you can get a clear picture of your goal—really see it, feel it, taste it—then I'm convinced you can make it happen."[12]

A midcareer manager in one of my teaching programs offered a parallel portrait of his boss: "He is a calculating adventurer, deriving a thrill from taking a risk and watching it pay off. He dreams and creates visions that enable others to do their best. He motivates team members by emphasizing that the team is doing something that has never been done before." Behind it all is "his strong confidence in himself and in those he trusts." Like Arlene Blum, this boss makes his vision his team's vision. Through trust and confidence, he creates the conditions that allow both individuals within the team and the team itself to reach whatever summits they have set for themselves. Thus, on both the frequently hazardous slopes of the Himalayas and the often slippery terrain of the workplace, is "calculated adventure" turned into tangible reward.

❖

CHAPTER 5

Joshua Lawrence Chamberlain Defends Little Round Top

"We know not the future, and cannot plan for it much. But we can . . . determine and know what manner of men we will be whenever and wherever the hour strikes."

I T WAS MAY 24, 1863, and Colonel Joshua Lawrence Chamberlain had been in command of the 20th Regiment of Infantry, Maine Volunteers, for all of four days. His troops, aged eighteen to forty-five, were marching through Virginia, part of a Union army that was on a collision course with a menacing Confederate army. The Civil War was entering its third summer, but that morning neither secession nor slavery was much on his mind.

An aide was delivering to Chamberlain what should be good news: his undermanned unit was about to acquire a new batch of 120 badly needed troops. The 20th Maine had mustered a thousand men at commissioning time; now, less than a year later, it stood at 358 men—the cumulative attrition of straggling, desertion, injuries, and death after five major engagements in less than a year, including the disastrous Federal forays at Fredericksburg and Chancellorsville.

But the good news came with a price: the new soldiers were mutineers. Chamberlain learned that their unit, the 2nd Regiment of Maine, had just been decommissioned. The 120 men were refusing reassignment to any other regiment, and Union commanders had taken them under armed guard. The soldiers, still in uniform, were worn, ragged, and famished; in a blunt attempt to break their will, Federal officers had withheld their rations for three days.

In his formal order transferring the insurgents to the authority of the 20th Maine, General George G. Meade of the Fifth Corps of the Army of the Potomac instructed Chamberlain to "make them do duty or shoot them down the moment they refused." It was wartime, the mutineers were facing court-martial, and mutiny was a capital offense.

Chamberlain had no choice but to accept the mutineers, yet he did have options: He could force the men forward under armed guard. He could try to recruit them, persuading them to take up arms with the 20th Maine. Or he could wait until the men were derelict in their duties and shoot them.

The last choice was the least likely, and not just because it was the most absolute. A firing squad would make Chamberlain's own return home impossible since the malcontents were from Maine, some even from Bangor, near his hometown. The remaining two options—one imposing armed control, the other requiring self-control—appeared nearly as untenable as a firing squad. Standing sentry over the mutineers would impose a crippling burden on the fighting unit. Yet their fierce defiance made recruiting them seem equally improbable.

Although Chamberlain had no way of knowing it, in forty days he would lead his men into one of the Civil War's momentous battles as two armies collided near the town of Gettysburg, Pennsylvania. Whatever his approach to that day's challenge—whether he chose to cajole or coerce the mutineers—his solution would be fateful for the events soon to unfold on the battlefield.

Joshua Lawrence Chamberlain

The Gettysburg Collision

IN A THRUST at the Union on its own territory, Robert E. Lee had moved the 70,000 men of his Army of Northern Virginia across the Potomac River, up through Maryland, and onto Pennsylvania soil. On June 28, 1863, one of his three army corps—under the command of Richard Ewell—was threatening the state capital at Harrisburg; the other two, under A. P. Hill and James Longstreet, were not far west of Gettysburg.

Under relentless prodding by President Abraham Lincoln and his general in chief, Henry W. Halleck, General Joseph Hooker had also been shifting the seven corps of his 90,000-man Army of the Potomac northward. Hooker's orders were to keep a wary eye on his adversary, buffer Washington, D.C., from threat, and attack if he could flush Lee into the open,

Robert E. Lee

but Lincoln and Halleck had given up on "Fighting Joe's" resolve to fight. On Sunday, June 28, they relieved him of his command and installed George Meade, a forty-seven-year-old Pennsylvanian who knew the countryside—a cautious but determined "snapping turtle."

One small fighting unit of George Meade's vast army as it converged on Gettysburg was the 20th Regiment of Maine. An even smaller part of Meade's plans was the 20th's leader, Joshua Lawrence Chamberlain.

Chamberlain had been with his unit from its formation at summer's end in 1862. "Come out for your country—answer the call," he had appealed in a Bangor speech when the North had first mobilized. "Be ready to stand at your post." Answering his own call, he had asked Bowdoin College for a leave from the faculty to enlist. Conservative Bowdoin, however, was not taken with the thirty-three-year-old religion professor's ardor for

George G. Meade

national service, and the faculty rejected his request. Faculty opponents even sent a representative to warn the governor that Chamberlain "is no fighter, but only a mild-mannered common student."

Chamberlain was nevertheless commissioned by the governor as a lieutenant colonel in Maine's newest regiment. His faculty colleagues were angered when they read about it in a Portland newspaper but recognized they had little choice but to grant him his leave.

In September 1862, Chamberlain left his wife, Fannie, three-year-old Wyllys, and five-year-old Daisy and set off for Washington with Maine's 20th Regiment of Infantry. Within days, the unit was marched to Antietam, Maryland, where the bloodiest single day's battle of the war was fought. Chamberlain and his men remained on the periphery of the battle, but Union forces successfully repulsed Robert E. Lee's invasion of

Maryland. With a victory finally in hand, President Lincoln issued the preliminary Emancipation Proclamation to abolish slavery.

Chamberlain was without West Point pedigree, formal military training, or management experience of any sort. Yet here he was on May 24, nine months after enlisting, a colonel in command of not only the men of the 20th Maine but also the malcontents of the 2nd Maine—and a fresh commander at that. The 20th Maine's original officer had been promoted just four days earlier and Chamberlain elevated to take his place.

The Mutineers

THE NATION'S UNITY would face one of its gravest tests in July, but Chamberlain's challenge that day in late May was far more immediate: he would somehow have to soften the resistance of the renegades. Their service would be invaluable, their continued insubordination too dear. It was an unusual trial in a regimental commander's list of tribulations.

The 2nd Maine had nominated one man to explain its resistance. We do not know precisely what the spokesman said to Chamberlain, but Michael Shaara, author of the Pulitzer Prize–winning account of the Gettysburg battle, *The Killer Angels*, has speculated on that conversation for us. We will draw on his account, as did the makers of the 1993 film *Gettysburg*. Keep in mind, though, that Shaara's book, while praised for its historical accuracy, won the 1975 Pulitzer Prize for *fiction*.[1]

"They been tryin' to break us by not feedin' us," grumbled the mutineers' spokesman. Then came a litany of complaints, all understandable if not persuasive: "I been in eleven different engagements. . . . I've had all of this army and of these officers . . . this idiot Meade . . . this whole bloody lousy rotten mess of sick-brained pot-bellied scabheads that ain't fit to lead a johnny detail." The mutineers had come to fight with the 2nd Maine, he said, and only the 2nd: "We are good men and we had our own good flag." The insurgents, it seemed, had signed papers for three years of service, but the other men of the 2nd Maine had signed for shorter terms and had already been sent home. The reason for remaining, in any case, had been fading as the Union suffered loss after loss: "We ain't gonna win this war. We can't win no how because of these lame-brained bastards from West Point, these goddamned gentlemen, these *officers.*"[2]

The mutineers' grievances were bitter, their rebellion full blown. Yet in defiance of what would seem obvious military logic, Chamberlain quietly divided the malcontents among his companies to "break up the 'esprit de corps' of banded mutineers," he later explained. Chamberlain placed their names on his official roster and gathered them to explain why. He voiced his appreciation for their grievances, beginning with the demand that they be returned home with the 2nd Maine, and then turned to what the future required (see the box on the following page).

Whether persuaded by Chamberlain's words, the provision of food, or the display of muskets, all but a handful of the insurgents acquiesced in the days that followed, melding into the companies, taking up arms, and augmenting the ranks. Their decision ended the burdensome guard duty and expanded the regiment's fighting strength by a third.

Little Round Top

As an unanticipated product of a thousand small decisions, Union and Confederate armies were converging around a single point on the map. On the afternoon of Tuesday, June 30, Union general John Buford led cavalry through the Pennsylvania town of Gettysburg in search of Lee's troops; on the far side of town, not more than a mile to the west, he found what he was looking for: Confederate infantry was marching toward Gettysburg in strength. The next day, the bloodiest encounter of the Civil War began in earnest as southern troops poured in from the west and north and northern troops rushed up from the south.

Joshua Lawrence Chamberlain's Re-created Comments to 120 Mutineers of the 2nd Maine Regiment, May 24, 1863

I don't know what I can do about it. I'll do what I can. I'll look into it as soon as possible. But there's nothing I can do today. We're moving out in a few minutes and we'll be marching all day and we may be in a big fight. . . .

I've been told that if you don't come I can shoot you. Well, you know I won't do that. Not Maine men. . . .

Here's the situation. I've been ordered to take you along, and that's what I'm going to do. Under guard if necessary. But you can have your rifles if you want them. The whole Reb army is up the road a ways waiting for us and this is no time for an argument like this. I tell you this: We sure can use you. We're down below half strength and we need you, no doubt of that. . . .

This Regiment was formed last fall, back in Maine. . . . Some of us volunteered to fight for the Union. Some came in mainly because we were bored at home and this looked like it might be fun. Some came because we were ashamed not to. Many of us came . . . because it was the right thing to do. . . .

This is a different kind of army. If you look at history you'll see men fight for pay, or women, or some other kind of loot. They fight for land, or because a king makes them, or just because they like killing. But we're here for something new. . . . This hasn't happened much in the history of the world. We're an army going out to set other men free. . . .

Here you can be *something*. Here's a place to build a home. It isn't the land—there's always more land. It's the idea that we all have value, you and me, we're worth something more than the dirt. . . . What we're fighting for, in the end, is each other. . . .

I think if we lose this fight the war will be over. So if you choose to come with us I'll be personally grateful.[3]

Chamberlain's regiment, which had been speeding northward with the Army of the Potomac, crossed into Pennsylvania early on the afternoon of July 1. His men's apprehension grew as they heard cannons ahead and passed cavalry horses dead by the roadside. By early evening, still sixteen miles south of Gettysburg, Chamberlain and the Fifth Corps halted their march to prepare supper and make camp for the night. Little of either was ready, however, before a hard-riding Union messenger arrived with urgent instructions: two Federal corps had battled the rebels all day near Gettysburg, and the Fifth Corps was to advance immediately.

The men of the 20th resumed their northward tread through the countryside, wearied by the unrelenting pace of the past days but carried by anticipation of the coming battle. Colonel Strong Vincent, a Pennsylvania native and Chamberlain's immediate superior, confided a premonition to another officer with whom he rode across the moonlit farmlands: "What death more glorious could any man desire than to die on the soil of old Pennsylvania, fighting for the flag?"

Chamberlain's marching unit was halted after midnight, and his men were afforded a brief rest along the roadside. A bugle broke their slumber just three hours later, and the 20th Maine advanced the last several miles to Gettysburg with neither breakfast nor coffee, arriving by 7 A.M. behind the front lines just south of town. The Federals had formed a defensive position that came to be known as the "fishhook," as shown in Figure 5.1. Troops and cannon were arrayed along Culp's and Cemetery Hills, on the northern end of the hook, and on Cemetery Ridge, extending south. At the southern extremity stood a modest, partially bare hill, Little Round Top, that would become the eye of the fishhook later in the day. At the moment, though, it was undefended.

On July 2, George Meade opted to remain entrenched behind his defensive perimeter, but Robert E. Lee was ready for offense. He instructed Longstreet to assault the Union left, the southernmost extension of the fishhook, and by 4 P.M. Longstreet's divisions were in motion against the Federals. Meade had been making continuous adjustments all day in the positions of the seven corps he had brought to the field. Now,

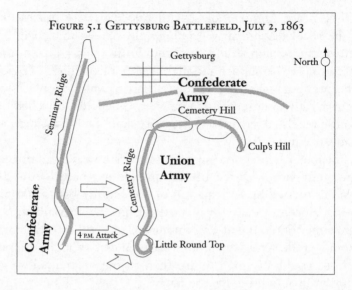

FIGURE 5.1 GETTYSBURG BATTLEFIELD, JULY 2, 1863

with Longstreet's massive late-afternoon attack finally becoming all too evident, Meade rushed his Fifth Corps forward in support of a Union front that was crumbling. As part of the advance, Colonel Strong Vincent took his brigade—the 20th Maine and one regiment each from Michigan, New York, and Pennsylvania—to a wheat field just west of Little Round Top.

About the same time Chamberlain arrived in the wheat field, a thirty-three-year-old brigadier general, Gouverneur K. Warren, mounted Little Round Top to inspect its potential. The army's chief topographical engineer with an excellent feel for strategic ground, Warren was startled to discover not only that Little Round Top was undefended but also that southern troops were massing in the trees just below. "The discovery was intensely thrilling to my feelings," he later wrote, "and almost appalling." A Confederate commander among those assigned to take Little Round Top and its larger sister hill, Big Round Top, just to the south, was equally thunderstruck by the military significance of the high terrain: if he could place just a few artillery pieces on Big Round Top and fell the trees that covered it, he would have a "Gibraltar that I could hold against ten times the number of men that I had."

Warren dispatched an urgent request for a Union brigade to occupy Little Round Top, the most important of the two hills and the most imminently threatened. His staff officer, Lieutenant Ranald Mackenzie, managed to find General George Sykes on the battlefield. Sykes, elevated to Fifth Corps commander on June 28 in the wake of Meade's promotion to the top, in turn dispatched Mackenzie to locate the commander of the Fifth Corps' First Division, James Barnes; but Mackenzie, searching vainly for Barnes, chanced instead on Strong Vincent, whose brigade happened to report to Barnes.

"What are your orders?" demanded Vincent. "Give me your orders!" Reluctant at first, the aide finally confided that he was to instruct Barnes to rush a brigade "to occupy that hill yonder." Without direct orders but emboldened by the exigencies, Vincent declared, "I will take my brigade there." He rushed his brigade onto Little Round Top and assumed personal responsibility for the decision.

The 20th Maine and 15th Alabama

VINCENT POSITIONED THE 20th Maine and his brigade's three other regiments in a quarter circle just below the westward crest of Little Round Top. Chamberlain's troops, on the far left, anchored a Union line that stretched several miles northward along Cemetery Ridge and around Cemetery and Culp's Hills. If the rebels amassing in the valley below could overrun the prominence or sweep around it, the Federal position would be threatened from both above and behind (see Figure 5.2).

In positioning the 20th Maine, Vincent instructed Chamberlain that a "desperate attack" was minutes away and that he must prevail over "all hazards." The order was unambiguous: "I place you here! This is the left of the Union line. You understand. You are to hold this ground at all costs." Indeed, losing the ground

Little Round Top, July, 1863

would in all likelihood be catastrophic: Confederate artillery on top of the heights could decimate the Union line on Cemetery Ridge, already under blistering attack by another Longstreet division, while Confederate infantry beyond the heights could slice into the undefended inside of the Federal fishhook.

But more hung in the balance than a single engagement or even the battlefield. The Army of Northern Virginia had forced back the Army of the Potomac the day before. Further retreat today might well give Lee the victory punch he had come north to deliver. In case of a victory by Lee in Pennsylvania, Jefferson Davis, president of the Confederacy, had readied a proposal for peace talks for delivery to Abraham Lincoln.

Coming at Chamberlain's troops on Little Round Top was a hardened Confederate regiment of 700 men under the com-

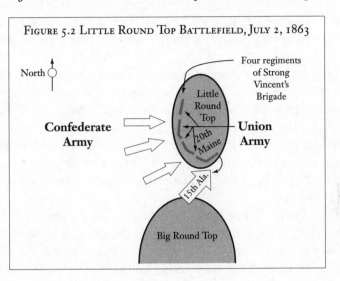

FIGURE 5.2 LITTLE ROUND TOP BATTLEFIELD, JULY 2, 1863

mand of William C. Oates. The infantry of Oates's 15th Regiment of Alabama was working its way around Chamberlain's left flank, anchored as it was "in the air." Chamberlain ordered his line extended to offer a wider defense, a difficult maneuver though one that Chamberlain was confident his regiment's training and discipline would prove up to. Oates directed the attack around what he thought was the Union left, only to learn from the withering fire that the flank was still farther left. "They poured into us the most destructive fire I ever saw," reported Oates.

Although on its feet since 3 A.M., the 15th Alabama attacked and reattacked in a series of assaults on the 20th Maine's defensive perimeter, both sides gaining and giving and gaining and giving. "The edge of the conflict swayed to and fro," in Chamberlain's description, "with wild whirlpools and eddies," but after two hours and five attacks, the Union line remained unbroken, albeit badly damaged. "How men held on, each one knows," Chamberlain later said, but "not I." As Oates pulled back his regiment to regroup, the surviving soldiers of the 20th

Maine reported that they had exhausted their allotted sixty rounds of ammunition and that a third of their comrades were down or dead.

Despite his own grievous losses, Oates mustered his survivors for still another assault. "They knew our weakness now," Chamberlain recalled, and they were "gathering force" for an attack he knew was imminent. "I saw the faces of my men, one after another, when they had fired their last cartridge, turn anxiously toward mine for a moment." He knew he must hold his ground "at all hazards." He could not retreat, but he was about to be overrun.

Chamberlain's spontaneous solution was to use what little lethal force he still had left: bayonets. He passed the word that offense was to replace defense, that his remaining 200 men were to charge forward lest they be forced backward. "Bayonet!" was relayed up and down the line. Chamberlain added another unusual feature: he ordered the right end of his line to remain fixed while the rest rotated around it like a giant hinge.

On signal, around 6:30 P.M., the line of blue charged with fixed bayonets, the men swinging downward in a great human arc. The attacking infantry in gray slowed, paused, and then retreated as the Union troops came swarming over them. Chamberlain had earlier sent his Company B deep into the woods on the left, and they added to the panic by suddenly rising from behind a stone wall with rifles ablaze. The rebels' astonishment turned into rout: the men of the 15th Alabama, Colonel Oates confessed, "ran like a herd of wild cattle."

Taking twice their numbers in rebel prisoners before the bayonet charge was over, the 20th Maine stymied the Confederate push around Little Round Top. Oates, who saw his own brother die in the battle, would later write, "If I had one more regiment, we would have completely turned the flank and have won Little Round Top, which would have forced Meade's whole left wing to retire." But, he added, "There never were harder fighters than the Twentieth Maine men and their gallant colonel."

Still another day of battle followed, and by the end of July 3, some 50,000 men were dead or seriously wounded. On November 19, 1863, Abraham Lincoln dedicated a new cemetery in Gettysburg, saying, "The world will little note, nor long remember what we say here, but it can never forget what they did here."

Enlisting the Troops

FACED WITH THE mutinous men from Maine and with only a few minutes to anticipate your first encounter, what would you say to them and how would you say it? Would you mention your capital authority? Should you appeal to your common roots? Is this a time for a reminder of the common cause? On your choice of words will depend whether the mutineers remain in open defiance of Federal authority or choose to follow you into battle.

Years after the war, Chamberlain would recall that he had "called" the mutineers "together and pointed out to them the situation: that they could not be entertained as civilian guests by me; that they were by authority of the United States on my rolls as soldiers, and I should treat them as soldiers should be treated; that they should lose no rights by obeying orders, and I would see what could be done for their claim." Yes, he would press their grievances over the closing of the 2nd Maine—he twice wrote the governor of Maine, to no avail—but in the meantime, he insisted that they accept his authority and command. To the stick he added a carrot, hinting that a later court-martial might be averted if the mutineers were to take up arms now. Michael Shaara's reconstruction of the encounter allows a parsing of the contents.

Stripped of the exigencies of war, the moment was not unlike those many managers face. Perhaps you have just taken over a new office in the wake of a merger that has led to the departure of your predecessor and rampant anxiety among those remaining. With little warning, you are about to meet the assembled

THE SPEECH	THE MESSAGE
I've been told that if you don't come I can shoot you.	I hold the ultimate stick.
Well, you know I won't do that. Not Maine men.	I will not resort to force because of our common heritage.
We're down below half strength and we need you, no doubt about that.	I need you.
Many of us came . . . because it was the right thing to do.	Our personal calling is noble.
We're an army going out to set other men free.	Our cause is just.
What we're fighting for, in the end, is each other.	We are joined together for one another.
I think if we lose this fight the war will be over.	The challenge is critical.
If you choose to come with us, I'll be personally grateful.	I will value your support.

staff for the first time. You know many of those present, but others are new faces from the acquired firm. Some despise the merger; others fear being laid off; many are skeptical of management. For your part, you need not only their passive support but also their wholehearted energy if you are to succeed in the weeks ahead. Anything short of that may be a prescription for disaster, both for the organization and for your career. Much rides on your words and subsequent deeds.

IBM chief executive Louis Gerstner faced such a moment on June 12, 1995. The day before, IBM had announced that it was acquiring Lotus Development Corporation for $3.5 billion, a purchase first resisted and finally embraced by Lotus Chairman Jim P. Manzi. Preeminent manufacturer IBM, famous for its white-shirt mind-set, would be incorporating a software start-up famous for its freewheeling culture. Lotus, meanwhile, intended to proceed with its program of cost cutting and downsizing, announced just a month earlier. Following mounting losses, Lotus outside director Richard Braddock had been working part-time to supervise a 15 percent reduction in the managerial ranks and a $50 million reduction in the budget lines.

Now, on June 12, Gerstner, with Jim Manzi at his side, was to address 2,200 employees who had been bussed from the company's headquarters in nearby Cambridge to Boston's downtown Wang Center. As he walked onstage, he would need to quell any rebellion in the newly acquired ranks and harness Lotus's energy to IBM's. His speech was brief, offering a vision of where he wanted IBM and Lotus to march together. He issued a call to arms for battle with their competitors, above all Bill Gates and Microsoft, and he bid for the commitment of all to surge forward (see the box on the following page).

Gerstner's message was much the same as Chamberlain's: *I need you:* "You represent the leading edge of fundamental change in this industry." *Our cause is just:* Our standards are "what the customer deserves." *We are joined together for one another:* IBM and Lotus must "find ways to work as a team." *The challenge is critical:* "Over the next couple years, a huge battle will be waged for where this industry is going to go." Gerstner added more. *Cutbacks are not the future:* "We want all parts of Lotus to grow fast." *We will ensure your autonomy:* IBM will work "without in any way destroying what's important to you as a group of people and as a culture."

Both Joshua Lawrence Chamberlain and Louis Gerstner had to transform a strategic vision into human reality by mobilizing those who could make it happen and without whose commitment it would not. Much the same challenge faced President John F. Kennedy in 1961. His early vision: "I believe this nation should commit itself to achieving the goal, before this decade is out, of landing a man on the moon and returning him safely to earth. No single space project in this period will be more

IBM Chief Executive Louis Gerstner's Comments to 2,200 Employees of Lotus Development Corporation, Boston, June 12, 1995

I want to take a few minutes and describe to you why we think this joining of Lotus and IBM makes so much sense. . . .

As we move into [a] new model of [computing], there's two choices emerging in the world. There's the model led by Lotus, and now I hope IBM-Lotus. . . . And there's another guy out there. . . .

And over the next couple years, a huge battle will be waged for where this industry is going to go. Now, I was a customer of this industry for 20 years, and I want to tell you what the customer wants and what the customer needs is an open . . . platform. And I think we have a chance between Lotus and IBM to set that standard, not because we want to own standards. Because that's what the customer deserves. . . .

It is going to be our responsibility and our opportunity to provide that leadership. And I think that the marriage of Lotus and IBM will do that in ways that no other individual company, be it ourselves or any other combination, can do. So, I am very excited to be here today, because you represent the leading edge of fundamental change in this industry, and we think, combined with our resources, we can make sure that your success happens. . . .

My expectations for Lotus are very simple. I want you to win in the marketplace. I want you to beat our competitors. I want you to grow fast. I want you to execute a set of strategies brilliantly to deliver what we all want, which is leadership for our customers. . . .

We did not purchase Lotus because we feel like we're good at downsizing. We're hopefully done downsizing at IBM. There is no way we can get our 3.5 billion dollars back by downsizing Lotus. . . . We want all parts of Lotus to grow fast, to take advantage of a competitor who is looking in 10 different directions at once and who is on the wrong side of the issue in terms of what customers should have. We want to make the term Windows an opportunity in the next 18 months that will be huge for both of us. Those are my expectations. That you succeed, that you execute well and that we find ways to work as a team without in any way destroying what's important to you as a group of people and as a culture.[4]

impressive to mankind, or more important for the long-range exploration of space, and none will be so difficult or expensive to accomplish." The later reality: in the last year of the decade, as Michael Collins circled the moon in the Apollo 11 spacecraft, astronauts Neil Armstrong and Buzz Aldrin took those first giant steps for mankind.

By implication: If you are appealing for the support of a critical group, make your ultimate, shared objectives the platform. Convince its members that the cause is just, the calling noble, the course collective, the challenge critical; remind them that the goal cannot be reached without their energetic engagement.

Small Actions, Great Value

JOSHUA CHAMBERLAIN had no way of knowing on May 28, 1863, how his handling of the mutineers would play out in the days and weeks ahead. Perhaps it would be crucial, perhaps inconsequential in the larger sweep of the war. The best he could hope for was that his reasoned treatment of the 2nd Maine on May 28 would pay dividends if and when history afforded the opportunity. As things turned out, history would more than give Chamberlain and his men their chance.

Just forty days after Chamberlain shed himself of the burden of guarding 120 men in a war zone, the men of the 2nd Maine were standing shoulder to shoulder with the men of his own 20th Maine on Little Round Top. Converted by Chamberlain's actions from costly cargo into strategic asset, they had become, in Chamberlain's own appraisal, "some of the best soldiers in the regiment." They were vital links in the last human chain between the Army of Northern Virginia and the soft inside of the Union fishhook—part of the whirlpools and eddies through which the 15th Alabama was finally unable to pass. Among the Federals swooping down the slopes with their fixed bayonets, the men of the 2nd Maine helped buttress a force that had been nearly—but not quite—overrun. Their armed rather than guarded presence might have been just enough to make the difference.

By implication: Winning the confidence of your people now may well be invaluable in a yet-unforeseen time when you face your ultimate test. No one can know when that day will come or even if it will. But if it does, early investments in winning support among even your most stalwart opponents may make the difference between success and defeat when it counts most.

The forty-day hiatus between the mutineers' recruitment and their indispensable presence on Little Round Top also reminds us that the responsibilities of leadership often magnify the aftereffects of even small decisions. A move that may seem inconsequential now may come to enduringly benefit—or forever haunt—later actions. In a crisis, everything is magnified, for better or for worse. A hot meal, a short speech, a personnel dispersion—all modest deeds at the time—gave Chamberlain the services of 120 soldiers when he needed them most. Chamberlain's fight on Little Round Top was but one of many that day, but it proved critical to holding the Union line, which in turn proved critical to holding at Gettysburg. Colonel Oates of the 15th Alabama later described the strategic outcome of his repulse at the hands of the 20th and 2nd Maine Regiments on that fateful day: "Great events sometimes turn on comparatively small affairs."

By implication: Some of today's modest actions in mobilizing others may prove of little value, but others may have great results. Since you often cannot know which will later become critical, you cannot afford to avoid or ignore any now.

Taking Responsibility

STRONG VINCENT PLACED the 20th Maine on Little Round Top with scant time to spare. Stepping on a boulder for a view over the heads of his soldiers, Joshua Chamberlain surveyed the wooded landscape as his men frantically improvised a crude breastworks. Within ten to fifteen minutes of arrival, perhaps less, he saw the gray-clad enemy coming toward his left: he had barely beaten Oates to the top of the hill. "I was three minutes late in occupying Little Round Top," Longstreet would later tell a group of Union veterans. "If I had got there first, you would have had as much trouble in getting rid of me as I did in trying to get rid of you."

Vincent's decision to take the hill had been his own. The aide he had intercepted had had no authority to sanction any action. Nor had Vincent. But he had taken the action, telling the aide that he would move his brigade onto Little Round Top under his own responsibility. He was fully cognizant of command structure and military discipline. But had he not acted, had he waited for direct orders, had he been reluctant to exercise his own discretion when the situation called for it, Longstreet might have found the three minutes he needed.

By implication: Authority systems help ensure that our decisions contribute to an organization's mission, but they can also get in the way. Recognizing when autonomous action is the right course—and learning to act on that recognition—can be essential, both for yourself and for those upon whom you depend.

Learning to Lead

HENRY HETH'S CONFEDERATE infantry division opened the Gettysburg conflict on the morning of the first day by over-whelming John Buford's cavalry division. George Pickett's infantry division closed the conflict on the afternoon of the third day with its failed charge. In between, George A. Custer's cavalry brigade turned back a Confederate attack on the Union rear. All three were generals, having already proven themselves in the ranks. All three performed well at Gettysburg, given the hands they were dealt. And all three had graduated from West Point dead last in their class.

Chamberlain could claim even less. Not only had he not attended a military academy, he had never had any officer training. Yet when a decisive military moment presented itself for which there was seemingly no solution, he devised one that stirred those far more steeped in battlefield theory. General George Sykes, commander of the Fifth Corps, informed Chamberlain that holding Little Round Top was one of the crowning achievements of the day. James Rice, who would become brigade commander in the wake of Vincent's fatal injuries during the battle on Little Round Top, told Chamberlain on the morning of Friday, July 3, "Your gallantry was magnificent, and your coolness and skill saved us."

The official account of the Fifth Corps later wrapped the hill's defense in larger cloth. Had Vincent and Chamberlain "faltered for one instant—had they not exceeded their duty," wrote historian William H. Powell, "there would have been no grand charge of Pickett, and 'Gettysburg' would have been the mausoleum of departed hopes for the national cause; for Longstreet would have enveloped Little Round Top, captured all on its crest from the rear, and held the key of the whole position." A congressional commendation cited Chamberlain for his "daring heroism and great tenacity in holding his position on the Little Round Top against repeated assaults." William Oates, the opposing regimental commander, rendered the same verdict: Chamberlain's "skill and persistency and the great bravery of his men saved Little Round Top and the Army of the Potomac from defeat."[5]

While the decisiveness of the Little Round Top defense for

the Gettysburg battle is sometimes debated, there can be little doubt that Chamberlain's exceptional "skill" helped carry the fight that day, as did his "coolness," "persistency," and "tenacity." The latter traits are likely to appear on almost any shortlist of leadership qualities. But where or how did Chamberlain acquire the skill to solve a military dilemma that few others might have? How, indeed, can any of us expect to exercise informed leadership of a company or community when we have arrived there without any formal training or experience in its essentials?

The answer, for Chamberlain, was disciplined self-study. His commissioning as an officer was the product of patriotic fervor and professional favor, not of any demonstrated abilities or background in the martial skills of warfare; but once in uniform, he devoured all he could on military strategy and battlefield tactics. He read, he asked, he observed, he listened. He learned his job on the job. Chamberlain had told Maine's governor when he requested service, "I have always been interested in military matters, and what I do not know in that line, I *know how to learn.*" And learn he did.

The first colonel of the 20th Maine, Adelbert Ames, served as Chamberlain's personal mentor in the early months. Ames brought an experienced eye: fifth in his 1861 class at West Point, he had been wounded in the first battle of Bull Run, where his service had garnered a Medal of Honor from Congress. As second in command, Chamberlain shared a tent with Ames, and he continuously sought his instruction. He asked for Baron de Jomini's *The Art of War*; he devoured Silas Casey's *Infantry Tactics*. "I study," Chamberlain wrote his wife, "I tell you—every military work I can find."

By implication: When you are thrust into a responsible position with scant warning and even less preparation, ask what actions are called for in the position, what strategies have worked in the past, and how others have previously responded to the challenges you now face.

Standing Where They Stood

JOSHUA LAWRENCE CHAMBERLAIN was one of more than three hundred commanders of Union regiments engaged at Gettysburg, and lessons abound in the actions of all of them. A personal visit to the Gettysburg battlefield provides one of the best ways of bringing those lessons to life.

Every spring I arrange for students in Wharton's executive MBA program and their families and friends to walk the battlefield. With two guides who specialize in its leadership questions, we seek to understand how the Federal and Confederate commanders, both high and low, faced their hour of decision. We see the ground where Chamberlain led his charge and Pickett ended his.

Robert E. Lee is often praised for the confidence he showed in his commanders and the wide latitude he gave them in the field, but that same confidence may also have cost him the effective use of his cavalry at Gettysburg because its commander, Jeb Stuart, had wandered far afield. We ask: Did Lee's leadership style blind him at a moment of ultimate need? And this: George Meade had been appointed Union commander just days before the battle. Did his newness result in overly cautious leadership on the battlefield? Or was it an asset, causing him to consult with his top commanders before deciding how to respond during the battle's third, climactic day? And of course we roam across Little Round Top, where Chamberlain and Oates were under orders to occupy the same ground. With little guidance from above, each was able to lead his troops into extraordinary actions, and we ask how they did so.

Standing where Meade arrayed his army, walking where Pickett led his charge, ascending where Chamberlain held his ground—all help to put you inside their minds as each faced their fateful decisions. Reading *The Killer Angels*, viewing *Gettysburg*, and reviewing the Civil War are all valuable before arriving on the battlefield, but there are few better ways to appreciate the decisions of Chamberlain and others than by standing where they stood during their defining moments.

Appomattox and Beyond

AS THE FORWARD troops of Pickett's charge surged into the Union defenders on Cemetery Ridge, they breached the Federal line near a turn in a stone wall that came to be known as "the angle." For a few fleeting moments they reached their objective, but they could not hold it. Determined reinforcements drove them back across the wall, the survivors retreated across the field, and the army withdrew across the Potomac. Twenty-one months later, Lee signed surrender papers at Appomattox Court House, Virginia.

Confederate General Lewis Armistead was at the front of those storming the angle, hat on raised sword, but in the tumult he advanced very few yards beyond. As he placed a hand on the muzzle of a captured Yankee cannon, he was mortally wounded, and the spot where he falls became memorialized as the "high water mark" of the Confederacy.

In the months after Gettysburg, Chamberlain continued his service with Fifth Corps. He recovered from a near-fatal injury during a Federal siege of Lee's army at Petersburg, Virginia, in June 1864, and by April 1865, he had risen to brigadier general. Union commander Ulysses S. Grant, who accepted Lee's surrender at Appomattox, bestowed on Chamberlain the singular honor of commanding the April 12 ceremonies in which the infantry of the Army of Northern Virginia was to relinquish its colors.

With three Union brigades at hand and a bugle calling the event to order, Confederate troops marched forward to present their flags. Chamberlain brought his troops to attention and then to the respectful posture of "carry arms." The surrendering general, John B. Gordon, startled by the gesture, ordered his own ranks to return the respect, and the southern troops marched by, in Chamberlain's later words, "honor answering honor." As the final southern banner was being presented to Chamberlain at the end of the long day's ceremonies, he told the bearer, "I admire your noble spirit and only regret that I have not the authority to bid you keep your flag."

Chamberlain's respectful presentation and consoling words became known throughout the South, and he retired from service with widespread respect on both sides. His final rank was major general. His final citation: a Congressional Medal of Honor for his moment on Little Round Top.

❧

CHAPTER 6

Clifton Wharton Restructures TIAA-CREF

"Here's a great institution that is in more trouble than it realizes."

"THE UNSEEN REVOLUTION" was how Peter Drucker described it in 1976. Pension funds—the repositories of our assets and executors of our future—had been transforming themselves from financial backwaters into economic dynamos, but they had been doing so quietly that the "revolution" had slipped by virtually unnoticed.

A decade later, however, the biggest pension fund of all— Teachers Insurance and Annuities Association–College Retirement Equities Fund, or TIAA-CREF—was still on the sidelines. TIAA-CREF was the nationwide retirement system for college and university professors, and its participating institutions had reached a record 3,950, account holders numbered 890,000, and assets amounted to $52 billion. But "Teachers," as the slumbering giant was popularly known, remained an operational backwater, with employees laboring in dingy quarters and account holders complaining about inflexible rules. One retiree wrote a trustee, "I always think of TIAA as the American version of Intourist, the Soviet travel agency. During a long life I have seen adjustments to customer needs made by many big outfits, including airlines and telephone companies, but never by TIAA or Intourist."

In 1986, Stanford University circulated a harsh critique of TIAA-CREF's hidebound approach, which gave individuals virtually no control over their own retirement funds. Fidelity, Vanguard, T. Rowe Price, and other prospective competitors were ready to pounce on unhappy account holders, who wanted a choice not only in how their assets were invested but in who was doing the investing. Teachers was ripe for revolution, and it was ready for an executive to make it happen.

Clifton R. Wharton Jr. was running one of America's great public university systems: the State University of New York (SUNY). Larger even than California's public system with its flagship UCLA and Berkeley campuses, SUNY enrolled 380,000 students at sixty-four colleges and universities from Buffalo to Binghamton, from New Paltz to Stony Brook. Wharton's interest in new challenges was piqued, however, when Andrew F. Brimmer—a consultant, friend, and former fellow director of Equitable Life Assurance—informed him in the summer of 1986 that his name had been submitted to the executive search firm charged with finding a new chief executive officer for Teachers.

Trained as a development economist, Wharton had worked for almost a decade and a half with the private, nonprofit Agricultural Development Council in Cambodia, Laos, Malaysia, the Philippines, Thailand, and Vietnam. Later, he had presided over Michigan State University during the tumultuous era of antiwar protests. He had now served as chancellor of the State University of New York for nearly a decade. He was used to managing vast organizations, yet he was a stranger to the rarefied world of money managers, where billions of dollars of other people's money are gambled on stocks and bonds, and experience and judgment are all that stand between riches and ruin. He had run neither a financial services firm nor an insurance firm, though he had had thirteen years of experience on the Equitable Life board. But he knew how to make a large enterprise work, and he was certainly familiar with Teachers' customer base, college and university faculty. In December 1986,

Clifton R. Wharton Jr. at TIAA-CREF

he was offered the top post of the largest nongovernment pension system in the world.

Capping an already extraordinary career as the first African American to head a predominantly white major university and then to run a state system, Wharton was now asked, at age sixty, to take responsibility for more than $50 billion of other people's wealth and to reform a pension system that was direly out of touch with its markets and its customers. The challenge would be to "transform a major institution from top to bottom" and "to bring this great company into the twentieth century." But the terrain was unknown, the players were contentious, the problems profound. Robert Wilson, the senior personnel administrator at Johns Hopkins University, expressed the view held by many of its customers: "The institution had frozen in place." Teachers "didn't listen to what people were saying," he complained, and it was "completely out of step with the times," run by "a self-perpetuating hierarchy that was totally unresponsive." Teachers was so entrenched, Wharton learned, that he wondered whether it was beyond redemption. "I knew the place had problems," he remembers, "but could it be changed?"

He accepted the offer. Still, he wondered how he would be able to make the necessary changes. "I decided to give it a shot, but I didn't know if it would work," he recalls. "I was not sure how I would do it."

Ready for Restructuring

AT THE TIME Clifton Wharton became chairman and chief executive of TIAA-CREF, it was offering a range of products from retirement planning to life insurance, and it was servicing a broad array of nonprofit organizations. In 1918, the Carnegie Foundation had created TIAA with a $1 million gift around the concept of portability: professors could change jobs among any number of institutions and still keep their retirement fund intact. But portability was gained at the cost of transferability: neither the institutions nor their employees could withdraw their funds once they were deposited. The Carnegie Foundation had also built Teachers around institutional flexibility: each participating college and university could establish its own premiums and define its own retirement age. Unlike many public and private pension funds that preset retirement benefits regardless of the amount contributed by the individual—commonly known as defined-*benefit* plans—Teachers predetermined no benefit level and paid back whatever the individual and employer had contributed, plus whatever gains it had made with the invested funds—known as a defined-*contribution* plan.

During TIAA's first year of operation, $700,000 of its $1 million in assets from the faculty of thirty participating institutions had been invested in railroad bonds, including some of the New

York Central with a maturity date of 1997. More than thirty years later—and reinforced by the lessons of the Great Crash of 1929—the fund was still gun-shy of stocks. But in 1952, William C. Greenough, then a young vice president and later chief executive of Teachers, argued that stocks were a sound investment in the long run. At Greenough's urging, TIAA created the College Retirement Equities Fund (CREF), and by 1986 the pension assets were divided roughly equally between the two sides: TIAA held $27 billion in fixed-income investments—government bonds, home mortgages, real estate—while CREF had $25 billion invested in stocks.

By 1986, too, Teachers had long dominated its market. So well established was its presence that on numerous campuses almost no competition could be found. Some institutions also participated in state pension plans and others included private providers, but if you taught at many, TIAA-CREF *was* your retirement income manager. It had also simplified your investment options to a single decision: how much of your retirement you wanted invested in fixed-income investments by TIAA or stocks by CREF. Even that choice contained an anomaly: you could move your money from the stock side to the fixed-income side but not the other way, and then only on the last day of a month. And even if you concluded that you would rather bet your future on old masters or rare coins than on what appeared to be an overheated stock market, you would remain frustrated until retirement. Even then, you could draw down your TIAA-CREF assets only in the form of annual pension payments. Had you wanted to reinvest your assets elsewhere before after retirement, you could just forget it; you were vested with Teachers forever.

Despite its eccentricities, the Teachers monopoly had worked well for participants for more than sixty years. Akin to AT&T's earlier monopoly, Teachers had served its customers responsibly even when they had had no service alternatives. But just as the rise of MCI and other upstarts had forced an end to AT&T's

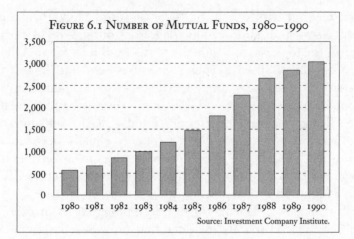

FIGURE 6.1 NUMBER OF MUTUAL FUNDS, 1980–1990

Source: Investment Company Institute.

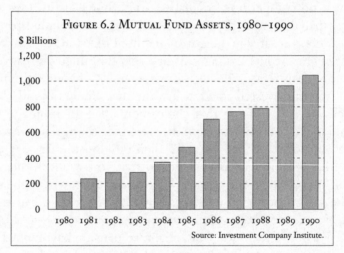

FIGURE 6.2 MUTUAL FUND ASSETS, 1980–1990

Source: Investment Company Institute.

exclusive franchise in 1984, so the spectacular growth of investment companies and their mutual funds in the 1980s presented
TIAA-CREF with much the same competitive threat. The
number of mutual funds, which are a pooling of individual
assets in professional hands, soared during the decade from 564
to 3,105. At the start of the 1980s, the funds collectively man-

aged $135 billion in assets; by the end, that total reached $1,067 billion, nearly an eightfold increase (see Figures 6.1 and 6.2). Mutual funds had become a huge industry, and its thousands of profit-hungry money managers had begun to eye the vast, lucrative terrain that the nonprofit TIAA-CREF still managed to dominate completely.

At the same time, more than a few faculty members were wondering why their pension system permitted no choice despite the rise of thousands of alternatives. CREF managed a single stock fund that invested largely in blue-chip American companies, but restive professors wanted to bet their retirements on other kinds of investment strategies. Some would go for high-growth, high-risk start-ups; others, for emerging markets such as Mexico or Malaysia; still others, for "social" funds that excluded tobacco firms and arms makers. They also noticed that certain mutual fund professionals were far outpacing CREF's performance. Under Peter Lynch's deft hand, for example, Fidelity Investment's Magellan fund achieved an average annual return of 29 percent during the 1980s; during the five years ended in 1987, his CREF counterpart had produced less than 18 percent. An 18 percent rate of return is *very* respectable, but it was not just accounting professors who realized that the gap between 18 and 29 percent was itself very respectable: $100,000 invested with an 18 percent annual return would reach $523,000 after ten years, but at 29 percent it would soar to more than twice that: $1,276,000.

The agitation in the customer ranks reached Teachers' New York headquarters, but there was little reason for alarm, or at least so it seemed. For almost three quarters of a century, TIAA-CREF had held *the* franchise for higher education, and during the past decade, its stock fund had regularly outperformed the standard industry benchmark, the Standard & Poor's 500 stock index. Like most professional money managers, CREF compared its performance not against a few investing superstars but against what would have happened had it spread its retirement

TABLE 6.1 RETURN ON INVESTMENTS BY CREF

PERIOD OF COMPARISON	CREF'S ANNUAL NET TOTAL RETURN	STANDARD & POOR'S 500 STOCK INDEX	CREF'S POINT ADVANTAGE
1987	5.1%	5.1%	0%
1985–1987	19.3	17.9	1.4
1983–1987	17.3	16.3	1.0
1978–1987	15.6	15.2	0.4

assets among Standard & Poor's roster of 500 well-established U.S. firms. Though 1987 proved disastrous for all because of the infamous market meltdown in October, CREF fund managers outpaced the industry benchmark over the previous three, five, and even ten years (see Table 6.1).

Teachers' obvious success reinforced its conviction that wise investing began and ended with its professionals. Left to their own devices, it felt, poorly informed professors would be drawn to potentially more rewarding but unacceptably risky alternatives; some might even opt to move their entire nest egg out of fixed-income holdings, such as U.S. Treasury bonds, into high-yield devices, such as junk bonds, exotic stocks, or initial public offerings.

Fears of the potential for self-inflicted damage if naive faculty were allowed to gamble with their one real asset were not limited to TIAA-CREF officials. Financial officers and presidents of many colleges and universities were privately warning Teachers to resist the call for choice. They worried that too many faculty would make poor investment decisions if allowed to do so, and they feared that their institutions would then face litigation from those who would later discover they had too little upon which to retire. A former TIAA-CREF board member, George Kaufman, described the anxiety: "University administrators are haunted by the image of a starving faculty member crawling up the steps of the administration building and saying, 'But I was faithful to you for thirty years.'" Later research revealed that such fears were unfounded: in 1996, a study of TIAA-CREF participants revealed that when they faced choice, their investment decisions were in fact little different from those recommended by the experts. But a decade earlier, institutional faith in the financial savvy of the professoriate remained low.[1]

The stock market crash in the fall of 1987 fueled the desire for choice. "I knew in August 1987 that the market was unsustainably high," lamented law professor and Teachers policyholder Robert W. Hamilton at the University of Texas, and "I had no choice but to move every penny into TIAA." His timing proved exquisite: On October 19, 1987, the Dow Jones Industrial Average dropped more than 500 points in one day, wiping out $500 billion in market value. During five trading days, the market value of CREF's own stock fund plummeted by $7.4 billion. But Teachers' one-way switching rule prevented a return to the stock market as it later recovered and became one of the great bull markets of all time. Now "I'm stuck forever in TIAA," Hamilton griped. "It seems to me the restriction is outrageous."

In November, just days after the October crash, Stanford University filed a brief with the U.S. Securities and Exchange Commission, asserting that the fund had become "anachronistic, paternalistic, and self-serving," and charging that it was breaking federal securities law. Stanford's general counsel, John J. Schwartz, argued that history had left Teachers behind: "In this country we've long passed the point where private entities like TIAA-CREF can assert total control over the assets of individuals." The mutual fund industry association, the Investment Company Institute, complained in its own filing with the SEC, "We do not believe continuation of CREF's insulation from normal competitive forces meets the statutory standards." Its general counsel compared Teachers' participating campuses to "captive nations."

Teachers' would-be competitors were promoting round-the-clock investment and redemption services, just a toll-free phone call away. Because TIAA-CREF offered no choices, not only was twenty-four-hour servicing little needed, even standard work hours seemed unnecessary. During the summer, for example, the entire staff was allowed to take Fridays off—good for employee morale but not so good for customer service.

TIAA-CREF staff itself was dispersed through drab, cramped quarters, and even the employee cafeteria, on the fifth floor of an office building plagued by slow elevators, was hard to reach. A quarter of the lower-level employees quit every year, low for a fast-food restaurant but high for a financial services organization. The computer systems were so outmoded that Teachers could not offer daily valuations of its investments, already an industry standard elsewhere. Although Teachers was collecting, processing, and distributing vast sums of money for nearly a million people, it had not introduced a new product since 1952.

How Wharton Restructured the Fund

THE LATE 1980s would provide many harsh lessons for corporate dinosaurs and their leaders. At General Motors and IBM, two paragons of past success, customers were complaining and competitors circling, but neither GM's chief executive, Robert Stempel, nor IBM's CEO, John Akers, could see any reason to fix what at first seemed not to be broken, even after market share plummeted and record profits turned into historic losses. At both industrial giants, the bureaucracy was too entrenched and the corporate culture too slow of foot to stanch the hemorrhaging. It was only when their boards acted to force change— replacing Stempel with the hard-charging Jack Smith at GM and Akers with the equally aggressive Louis Gerstner at IBM— that the bottom line began to show a profit.

So it was with Teachers as 1987 dawned. The pension giant was under intense outside demand to right its wrongs; yet its inside culture was so impervious to change that when an internal trustee committee looked into the possibility, it urged against it. Longtime management consultant Eugene E.

Jennings told a reporter, "I have encountered no bureaucracy as entrenched as . . . what you have at TIAA-CREF."

The TIAA-CREF board turned to Clifton Wharton to upend the dominion. His was the only name the nominating committee had proposed to the board, and he took office on February 1, 1987, the first chief executive to come from outside. "He had a very strong and very authoritative personality," recalls John H. Biggs, cochair of the trustee nominating committee. "We thought he could do the job." David Alexander, the other cochair, recollects much the same: "He was clearly a very skillful manager, with a lot of experience in dealing with complex institutions," and he would bring "an overall record in administration that was so powerfully compelling in tangible results."

Wharton listened, he walked the halls, he met the critics. Then, taking a page from the playbook of his years as a university administrator and those of the corporate executives on whose boards he had long served, he constituted a working group to tackle the problems. Known as the Special Trustee Joint Committee, its charge was to review a set of "white papers" that several internal task forces had prepared on what needed to be done. Task force members had reviewed both outside proposals and internal suggestions for how TIAA-CREF should change in light of the changing investment market. Wharton acknowledged that the "revolution in financial services" and the "rapid growth of the mutual fund industry during this decade" forced a strategic reassessment, and he set forth a stiff timetable: formed in June 1987, the committee was to report in September, and the full board was to take action in November. Wharton made himself chairman of the committee, and he brought on three university administrators, a business school professor, a consultant, and executives from a company, a brokerage firm, a money management firm, and two banks.

Clifton Wharton pressed the committee to take action. One participant recalled that the new CEO's favorite expression at its meetings was "Let's get closure on this thing." Soon, with a

Special Trustee Joint Committee meeting on The Future Agenda, *1987*

full draft in hand of the Joint Committee's report, *The Future Agenda*, Wharton took an unprecedented step: he called for public distribution of the strategic plan for comment before implementation, a shrewd move for management advantage but foolhardy for competitive advantage. "Normally you would not share your strategic plans with the competition," he explains, "but the key thing was that we were opening ourselves up to our customer base." Several board members objected that such disclosure was unheard of, but Wharton retorted, "Show it to them. Either we mean what we say—that we want their input— or we don't." Customer response, he argued, was sure to be valuable: "At least we'll find out what they're going to say, and maybe some of the suggestions they will make will very well alter what we're getting ready to recommend."

Wharton also restructured the organization. In April, he created two new revolving positions for young highfliers to work closely with him. The appointments were intended to provide the occupants with "a broadening and development experience," but the eight-month rotation schedule also seeded people throughout the firm who knew what really happened inside the executive office and even the boardroom. On discovering that top management convened to review strategy and solve problems only erratically, Wharton constituted three new groups to guide the enterprise: an Executive Cabinet of the top dozen officers, which would meet weekly; an Executive Council of the most senior seventy officers, which would gather monthly; and an Officer Group of the topmost three hundred managers, which would convene quarterly. All would serve as two-way conduits for troubleshooting, intelligence gathering, and strategic thinking.

Just as important, Wharton also realigned the organization to pinpoint responsibility for customer service. "This was not a modern organization," he recalls. "It was like something from the sixties or the seventies." Drawing on an analysis by the management consulting firm of Booz, Allen & Hamilton, he broke up the classic functional divisions, such as data processing and financial accounting, and regrouped them into four "accountability centers": fixed-income investing, equity investing, pension services, and insurance services. Each was given far greater autonomy, as well as its own personnel and computer systems, but each also had far more "bottom-line" responsibility.

As a tangible reminder of who was now king, Wharton built a compensation system that focused on the customer and rewarded results. Under a plan he installed in 1990, lower-level managers for the first time found their compensation depending on how well they did, with 9 percent of their total pay package placed at risk. For higher-level managers, a third or more of their compensation was now contingent on results. The driver for all was "increased value to participants through improved long-term financial performance and service," as measured by investment returns, business growth, service quality, and cost controls. For the thirty-two top executives, income depended not only on annual results but also on multiyear trends, including whether operating costs were held low compared with the bottom quartile of the large mutual funds and whether customer perceptions were held high as measured by independent audits. Nearly half of Wharton's own income depended on how the firm performed, on a par for the first time with the usual arrangement for CEOs of major corporations.

Contingent compensation is only as effective as the evaluation on which it is based, and Wharton introduced systematic annual appraisals of the top officers—and evaluation of himself by them. He also instituted lateral assessment: each officer was to give Wharton an evaluation of the others, and he in turn would inform each of what his or her peers were saying. (Receiving such feedback for the first time, several officers were shocked to learn that aspects of their behavior had long been viewed by others as dysfunctional.) Wharton also established succession planning, annually reviewing with the trustees the performance and promise of the top officers, middle-rank "comers," and young "high potentials."

The firm's nearly three thousand employees now answered their telephone with a fresh "TIAA-CREF, at your service." To keep customers in focus, Wharton created an advisory committee of twelve higher education association officials and personnel officers to meet quarterly with his management team and annually with a new trustee Committee on Products and Services. He also created the post of ombudsman to serve as an inside customer advocate. Branch manager Thomas Williams reported that the changes had moved employees' attitude from a "defensive posture" to an "aggressive one," and former trustee Peter Bernstein observed that Wharton had "turned an institution into a company."

But above all, Wharton unbundled and modernized what had long been sacrosanct: Teachers' rigidly constrained options.

Over the next several years, he created a diverse menu of invest-ment choices from which an individual could choose: a bond fund, an actively managed equities fund, a passive equities fund, an international equities fund, a social choice fund, and a money market fund. He also introduced the long-sought transferabil-ity, permitting the movement of new funds among the several investment options, including from TIAA to CREF. He arranged for funds switched to TIAA to be credited immedi-ately instead of on the last day of the month. He introduced quarterly reports for policyholders and increased counseling services for both campus administrators and retirement cus-tomers. He added a research-and-development unit to fashion new products.

In collaboration with colleges and universities, Wharton worked to dismantle the de facto monopoly they had estab-lished on campus. Just two years after his arrival, 252 of TIAA-CREF's institutional clients offered faculty the option of picking its competitors to manage their funds, and TIAA-CREF allowed faculty to transfer their old accounts to any of the new alternatives. By 1989, T. Rowe Price Associates drew $350 million away from Teachers, Vanguard Group $750 mil-lion, and Fidelity Investments $1 billion. Dave H. Williams, chairman of Alliance Capital Management Group and a mem-ber of the Trustee Joint Committee, summed up the scope of Wharton's transformation: "The changes he has wrought at CREF are simply astounding in light of what had *not* transpired before."

Readying for Restructuring

SON OF A CAREER diplomat and fluent in Spanish from childhood years spent abroad, Clifton Wharton graduated in 1943 from Boston Latin School, the city's elite public high school, and earned a B.A. in history from Harvard University in 1947 and a Ph.D. in economics from the University of Chicago in 1958. He devoted the first twenty-two years of his professional life to promoting agricultural development in emerging economies, and he published widely.

The first of several critical turning points occurred in 1970. As the newly appointed president of Michigan State University, Wharton was responsible for an enormous campus on which he had never worked before. It was a baptism by fire. Three of the eight elected trustees had fought hard against his selection, favoring the still-popular ex-governor G. Mennen Williams. The dissident trustees bluntly told Wharton that they were determined to oust him as soon as possible, and they acted to block much of what he proposed at the monthly meetings of the governing board, which was widely considered one of the most backward of its kind. With the faculty, the new president played far better. When his name appeared in press articles as a possible candidate for the presidency of Harvard University, the spokesperson for a faculty delegation told him, "You can't leave us! You're the only thing that's protecting us from those idiots!" Eventually, Wharton prevailed, defeating his archenemies on most issues and serving for eight years. By then he had learned to administer a big, contentious system.

Wharton's invitation to head the State University of New York in 1978 was equally daunting, and not just because the system was nearly ten times larger than Michigan State. SUNY was a study in centralized control, akin to the way so many U.S. companies were then run by all-powerful and all-knowing headquarters. The simple repair of a leaking gymnasium on one of SUNY's campuses required approval at a seeming infinity of levels. The state budget office, audit office, comptroller, attorney general, legislature, and even governor got into the act, and by time a repair was authorized, the entire gymnasium floor was ruined. The bureaucratic obstacles, Wharton recalls, were "absolutely unbelievable."

Yet any decentralization would diminish the power of many people from the governor on down. Wharton bided his time and built his base, visiting all sixty-four campuses and meeting newspaper editors throughout the state. He contacted city mayors, county executives, and campus councils and charged a commission with formulating an end to the maze of needless controls. When a legislative committee held hearings around the state on the commission's recommendations, it learned that Wharton had already made its case. Campus presidents, community leaders, and faculty representatives clamored for decentralization, and the legislature got the message. Thus Wharton learned how to restructure a vast, entrenched system.

A third experience rounded out what Wharton would need for the formidable tasks at TIAA-CREF. Several years after taking the Michigan State University presidency, Wharton was invited onto the board of Ford Motor Company. He was already serving as a director of Equitable Life, and in the years that followed he joined other boards as well. By the mid-1980s, as corporate restructuring was acquiring a full head of steam, he was seeing firsthand how executives were transforming somnolent machines into powerful engines. Watching as customer-focused units replaced functional divisions, as incentive compensation overtook flat pay, and as cultures of change ousted ideologies of inertia, Wharton learned by observation how to restructure large, resistant enterprises.

When he took the call from Andrew Brimmer about the TIAA-CREF job, he was confident in his own abilities: "Here's a situation where you can try to do something. It's not just business as usual, and you've got some major challenges. This was interesting!"

By implication: Moving yourself through varied and increasingly responsible management experiences develops the personal confidence and diverse skills required to master different, more ambitious arrays of tasks; moving yourself across varied organizations fosters the capacities essential to leading still different institutions.

Selling Buy-in

CLIFTON WHARTON was not from the George Patton school of action. Just as Arlene Blum had to learn on the icy slopes of Annapurna, so Wharton had learned in the halls of Michigan State University that authority by decree and action by order would not accomplish what needed doing.

Wharton knew he could achieve most when dictating least. He believed that listening could be as important as deciding, that a decision without consultation could be worse than no decision at all. Robert Atwell, president of one of higher education's preeminent associations, the American Council on Education, recalled Wharton's exceptional accessibility: "This guy would come down to Washington at the drop of a hat to listen to us." Caspa Harris Jr., executive vice president of another education powerhouse, the National Association of College and University Business Officers, bluntly told Wharton that "we were not going to have the Big Brother attitude anymore." In response, Harris reported, Wharton was surprisingly attentive: "He listened."

"In situations of change, it is almost as important to have the key actors at all levels buy into the goals and process as it is the substance," explains Wharton. "People have to know that they have contributed to the process. It's not the CEO who just decides something and then says, 'Do it!' " The biggest mistake you can make, he warns, "is to assume that all wisdom is concentrated at the apex." In meeting with college presidents across the country, he would say, "I've been a president; I know what the situation is. What is it that you're concerned about?"

The pressure on Wharton to divulge his command plan as soon as he took office was unrelenting; in fact, Wharton believed it was a mistake even to settle on a plan before hearing everyone out. "When you get into the company, you may have one foot in quicksand and one on a land mine," he warns, "and not even know it." To demonstrate their take-charge attitude, incoming chief executives often proclaim their grand designs in advance. "Some people can do that," Wharton observes. "I can't."

After listening for three months, Wharton presented his conclusions to the trustees. To ensure that they would ask the questions they should, he arranged for his predecessor, who still served on the board, to absent himself from the meeting. (Later, Wharton would brief him privately on everything he had reported to the board.) Many of the institutions and policyholders that TIAA-CREF served, Wharton reported, saw Teachers "as arrogant, paternalistic, defensive, isolated, out of step, resistant to change, bureaucratic, without vision, [that it] lost sight of its original purpose, lacked innovativeness, has poor communications on what it does, and poor service." Teachers had "allowed change to pass it by"; as a result, its products were out of date and its market was slipping. He warned that Fidelity and others were gearing up for a major assault. On the inside, he faulted an antiquated computer system, a weak planning process, and an ineffective reporting structure. He also criticized a "bunker mentality" that rejected criticism and discouraged creativity. When he asked managers why they were doing something a given way, he notes, the most common answer was "That's the way we've always done it."

Criticism of the past is essential to foresee a better future. But honoring the past can be equally important for moving into the future. Those who made the past are now expected to create the future, and without their talents and energies, any blueprint will remain just that. Thus, in his report to the trustees, Wharton also extolled Teachers' virtues: TIAA-CREF's staff was personally loyal and professionally competent, and the investment managers were first rate. As the organization's first outside chairman, he started with no inside loyalty but would require it quickly. He calmed his managers, hearing out their anxieties about reform and their ideas for achieving it. He invited staff from all levels for freewheeling discussions over lunch, and he printed transcripts of the discussions in internal newsletters. Ultimately, he knew, his employees were the ones who would have to carry the change.

When Wharton launched his reform initiative at TIAA-CREF, the Trustee Joint Committee was the primary vehicle, and he used its recommendations to stir the pot. By extensively involving the trustees from the start, he ensured that the board knew where he was going, even though some would grumble that they had not anticipated such a drain on their time. By circulating a draft soon after the start, he also alerted customers and critics alike to his objectives. Wharton writes, "Since our very inception we have never been 'just another insurance company,' but an organization intimately linked to the groups it serves," and for this reason he was widely distributing the strategic plan for comment. He also dispatched his staff members to campuses across the country to tug at the grass roots and to hear out the policyholders and benefits administrators before the plan was finalized. They returned from six hundred visits to institutions with more than eight hundred recommendations for change.

If the skeptics were to accept and the doubters to believe, consultation would be only half the sale; the other half would be Wharton himself. Unless he were visibly, actively, and aggressively behind the restructuring, the endemic cynicism on the outside and entrenched resistance on the inside were sure to persist. Critics had doubted whether he would be able to turn around, in his own words, an "antediluvian, ancient, inflexible monster." He knew that he could bring them along only if he heard their grievances and demonstrated his commitment to resolving them.

From his battles with the dissident trustees at Michigan State University, Wharton had learned the importance of personal persistence against fierce resistance. From his campaign for decentralization of the state system in New York, he had mastered the concept that the executive must lead from the front. From his board experience, he had learned that "the CEO makes a huge difference—but only if he or she walks the talk." After several months of listening, Wharton sallied forth to sell his vision. Speaking before college associations and campus audiences, he seized every opportunity to argue the case for TIAA-CREF's new commitment to choice and transferability, and he visited college presidents across the country, convinced that he had to make personal calls to promote the new way of doing things. Simply put, he says, "I had to show that I was committed to this."

> *By implication:* Buy-in by all those affected by an organization's change hastens its achievement. Consultation with them, engagement of them, and appeals to them are the critical steps for building acceptance of the change.

Delighting in Doing Well

CHANGING BUSINESS can be dreadful business. When employees fear reassignment or even layoff, the stress is palpable, and when those clamoring for change are harshly demanding, the tension can overwhelm. But despite the inside anxieties and outside strains, restructuring Teachers proved a gratifying business for Clifton Wharton.

"I was having an absolute ball," he remembers. It helped to be surefooted: after several months, "I had a very clear sense of where I wanted to go, what I wanted to accomplish, how to go about trying to get there, and what I thought needed to be done." It helped, also, to have a committed, engaged board of trustees: they "were totally supportive, and they were involved with me." And it helped to have a competitive fray that made change appear imperative.

Wharton delighted in the contrast with the past. After seventeen years in higher education, he savored the fact that now when he said, "Jump!" the response was "How high?" Without turning his authoritative powers into authoritarian rule, he applauded fast action. "In higher education," he laments, "you're really ruled by committee." Faculty members "talk and talk and talk and analyze and go on at great length with all their wonderful insights and wonderful contributions—but it goes on for months."

Even without objective conditions from which to take subjective satisfaction, Wharton looked for the affirmative and eschewed the negative. "I've always tried to maintain a sense of humor," he reports, "because if you don't, you can become too torn and depressed" by the stress. His parting words: "If you're not enjoying it, then get out."

By implication: Leading change is like riding a bucking bronco: if you are not finding satisfaction, you may want to switch the horse or even change the event.

Firsts and Lasts

As a young Harvard student, Clifton Wharton became the first black announcer for the college's student-run radio station. It was the first of many firsts: first black director of a major life insurance company, first black chairman of a major foundation (the Rockefeller Foundation), first black president of a major university, first black chancellor of a state higher education system, and first black CEO to command a Fortune 500 service company. All along, Wharton was following an example close by: his father had been the first black diplomat to rise through the ranks of the U.S. Foreign Service to its highest career rank, serving before his retirement in 1964 as ambassador to Norway.

Even when race set Wharton back, he often got the final, sometimes ironic word. He vividly remembers arranging in 1946 to meet several friends in the lobby of one of the great institutions of Washington, D.C., the Willard Hotel. Near the White House, it had been the residence of choice for visiting dignitaries and had provided temporary quarters for several presidents and presidents-to-be, including Abraham Lincoln, who lived there while awaiting his inauguration in 1861. In 1946, though, the Willard was still a segregated facility, and as Wharton innocently waited in its lobby for his friends to arrive, he was unceremoniously told to leave. Years later, a victim of its own insulation from the changing hospitality industry, the Willard was forced to close. When the hotel subsequently sought big capital for radical renovation, Teachers invested $90 million in its restoration and ultimate reopening, an investment that Wharton came to oversee.

By implication: The qualities that make a difference are the special province of no racial, gender, or national group; the opportunity to apply them is the prerequisite for developing them, whatever the group.

Two of You

CLIFTON WHARTON LEFT office in 1993 to join the new Clinton administration as U.S. deputy secretary of state, the first black person to hold this second highest post for American foreign policy. It was not a natural sequel, however, for the capital's violent political winds led to his resignation just ten months later. Wharton had been offered senior positions in government before and had always said no. This time he mistakenly said yes—"I didn't come down to make a name for myself, I came down to be helpful"—but in the words of *New York Times* columnist A. M. Rosenthal, he got a "knife in the dark." He regretted none of his prior moves, but "that one," he reflects, "I would have done differently."

Just after Wharton's elevation to the presidency of Michigan State University, his high school had named him its "Man of the Year," joining writer Theodore H. White and composer Leonard Bernstein among Boston Latin's honored few. Within five years of his initiation of TIAA-CREF's restructuring, Wharton was venerated by his second alma mater, Harvard

University. In bestowing an honorary degree on him, Harvard would say of his service, "Our security in retirement depends on his intelligent leadership. We are in good hands." So impressive was his record that, the university added, "his entry in *Who's Who* might make us wonder if he were three men with the same name."

One person Wharton encountered remained convinced that there were least two. During a robing for an honorary degree at another campus, a faculty member approached him:

> *Professor:* "Dr. Wharton, you don't know me, but I want you to know how much I appreciate all of the wonderful changes you made at TIAA-CREF. I just think it's great; what you've done is wonderful. I also use your father's book in my course."
>
> *Wharton:* "My father didn't write a book."
>
> *Professor:* "*Subsistence Agriculture and Economic Development.*"
>
> *Wharton:* "That's not my father; that's me!"
>
> *Professor:* "You mean there are two of you?"

By the time Wharton left TIAA-CREF in 1993, it had been modernized, its monopoly ended, its choices opened. Wharton had never doubted that choice spelled not the beginning of the end but rather a new start; now the numbers bore out his faith. Customer surveys revealed abiding loyalty, and the few customers exiting after he introduced choice—less than 1 percent—were far outnumbered by those drawn by the fresh choice and improved service. During Wharton's six years at the fund, the number of participating institutions rose from 3,950 to 5,000, the number of policyholders from 890,000 to 1.5 million, and assets from $55 billion to $114 billion.

Like AT&T, GM, and IBM, Teachers learned to compete in a market it had once thought it owned. Wharton established the platform and momentum to compete, and both would outlive his departure and carry his legacy forward. By 1997, TIAA-CREF's participant base reached 2 million and its asset base $200 billion. In moving America's biggest pension fund from the backwaters of an unseen revolution to its forefront, Clifton Wharton fostered a restructuring built to last.

CHAPTER 7

❧

John Gutfreund Loses Salomon Inc.

"It's a harsh world, where mistakes are not charitably dealt with."

JOHN H. GUTFREUND, chairman and chief executive officer of Salomon Inc., presided over one of Wall Street's richest companies. A brilliant bond trader and power broker, he had been featured on the cover of *Business Week* as the "King of Wall Street." Wall Street wannabes and critics also knew him from the pages of Michael Lewis's *Liar's Poker*, where they learned that his formula for success was to wake up in the morning "ready to bite the ass off a bear."

By mid-1991, though, John Gutfreund's dominion was being threatened from below. Earlier he had learned from John W. Meriwether, one of the investment bank's nine vice chairmen, that back in February bond trader Paul Mozer had improperly bid for U.S. Treasury bonds on behalf of a customer but without the customer's knowledge. Three months later, in May, Mozer had been at it again, secretly winning more government securities than allowed by federal rules.

Bond trading had long been the lifeblood of Salomon and its main subsidiary, Salomon Brothers, where Mozer was head of the Government Trading Desk. Throughout the late 1980s, Salomon had been among the top three or four underwriters of U.S. debt, acquiring and reselling as much as $40 billion a year.

In 1990, its trading of securities had accounted for a fifth of Salomon's $5.9 billion in revenue. Seven of its nine vice chairmen had risen to the top through their successful trading. John Meriwether himself was a near legend, considered one of the best bond traders on Wall Street. John Gutfreund and Salomon were riding high, in large part because Meriwether and his traders were riding high: in 1990, they had been responsible for $400 million in company earnings.

Treasury auction rules are not to be trifled with, however, especially by a firm whose chief Treasuries trader, Paul Mozer, was already on notice. When Salomon had submitted a bid in 1990 for an amount larger than the Treasury's entire auction issue, the government had announced that any one dealer could no longer seek more than 35 percent of an auction total. Mozer, who had been responsible for Salomon's aggressive bids, had denounced the rule, angering Treasury officials.

It had been against such a background that Meriwether, alarmed on learning from Mozer what he had done in February, had taken the news to John Gutfreund in late April. They had agreed that the violation should be brought to the attention of federal regulators. Nothing, however, has been done. In May, Mozer had "squeezed" the Treasury securities market with his second improper bid. Weeks had passed, and Salomon had still not informed the regulators of its transgressions. Now the clock began adding its own penalty: each additional day the incendiary news was confined to the chairman's office, the higher the price that would inevitably have to be paid. This inaction would later be described by the chairman of the U.S. Securities and Exchange Commission, Richard Breeden, as a "long and thunderous silence." John Gutfreund was sitting on a time bomb.

An Unauthorized Bid

THE U.S. TREASURY sells $30 billion in new securities every week, some maturing in ninety days, others not for thirty years. Once sold to investors, the $2.4 trillion of government securi-

John Gutfreund, Chairman and CEO, Salomon Inc.

ties in circulation is traded and retraded in a vigorous secondary market. Government bonds do not earn their holders much, but they prevent sleepless nights. U.S. securities are virtually risk-free, the gold standard of investing.

For thousands of would-be U.S. bondholders, access to ownership is through thirty-nine "primary dealers." The government has designated them—and only them—as eligible to submit bids for both themselves and others. In exchange for their privileged access to the federal auctions, they are obliged to bid at all auctions and to resell to others. The aftermarket is vast: $110 billion in government bonds changes hands every day, more than ten times the daily value traded on the New York Stock Exchange. Among those who make a living in buying and reselling these billions of dollars in government bonds, Salomon is one of Wall Street's most formidable.

The Federal Reserve Bank—the "Fed"—conducts the auctions on behalf of the Treasury, and it calls for bids that specify the type of securities (distinguished by the year of maturity), the dollar amount sought, and the interest rate to be paid, termed the "yield." In his bid at the February 21, 1991, auction, for example, Paul Mozer offered for Salomon to buy 35 percent of the $9 billion in five-year government notes at a yield of 7.51 percent, and he quickly learned that he had played his cards well. Salomon accepted customers' orders until just minutes before the standard 1 P.M. auction time. Its runners, on call in the lobby of the New York Federal Reserve Bank, jotted the final bids on a piece of paper for deposit in a box just seconds before a clerk put a hand over the slot at 1 P.M. The Fed announced the winners two hours later, and that day Mozer learned that he had won 19 percent of the bonds, a strong showing.

A key to a primary dealer's success or failure at the auction is its proposed interest rate. Because of the competitiveness and transparency of the market, the difference between the highest and lowest bidders rarely exceeds .02 to .03 percent, or just 2 to 3 "basis points." Primary dealers want to acquire bonds for themselves and on behalf of their customers, with the highest possible yield, but if the yield specified in a firm's bid is too high, the dealer risks getting none of the bonds. On the other hand, if the yield specified is too low, the firm runs the risk of acquiring in great quantity notes that it cannot profitably sell to others. The line between the two is very, very fine.

The Federal Reserve, of course, has the opposite interest: it wants to sell bonds, on behalf of the Treasury, with the lowest possible interest rate and these are the bids it accepts first from primary dealers. From there, the Fed moves up to the next lowest yield and the next one, until all of its securities for that particular auction have been sold. In the argot of the business, the highest interest rate for which bids are accepted by the Fed at any given auction is known as the "stop-out yield." When more bids are submitted at the stop-out yield than can be fulfilled—and that is often the case since dealers obviously want the highest return and the spread among interest rates is so small—the Fed prorates its notes for distribution to the bidders at that level. If sufficient bonds remain for only half of those sought at the stop-out rate, bidders at this yield receive only half of what they want.

The importance of the stop-out yield can be seen in the government auction of February 21, 1991, illustrated in Table 7.1. The lowest bidders offered to buy at 7.50 percent, and they received all they wanted, $3.9 billion of the total. This left $5.1 billion in notes for the next highest interest rate, 7.51 percent. But dealers at this level wanted a total of $9.4 billion, and, as a result, the Fed prorated the remaining $5.1 billion among the competing bidders at 7.51 percent, giving each, including Mozer, only a little over half—54 percent—of what it sought. Bidders that had the misfortune of offering a yield of 7.52 percent—just one basis point higher—were completely shut out, not good for business when customers had expected more.

TABLE 7.1. BIDS AT U.S. TREASURY AUCTION ON FEBRUARY 21, 1991

INTEREST RATE OFFERED	AMOUNT OFFERED ($ BILLIONS)	BONDS SOLD ($ BILLIONS)	BONDS SOLD AS % OF OFFER
7.50%	$3.9	$3.9	100%
7.51	9.4	5.1	54
7.52+	15.8	0	0
	$29.1	$9.0	

For a decade, the Treasury had limited dealers to no more than 35 percent of the total to guarantee that no single dealer would corner a market. To ensure that they receive as much of the 35 percent as possible, however, Salomon and its fellow dealers often submitted very large orders at what they guessed would be the stop-out yield. While awards were limited to 35 percent, bids were not. The strategy, thus, was simple: overbid sharply to garner the lion's share of the prorated bonds at the stop-out—or most favorable—rate.

For Salomon, which bids for both itself and its clients, this strategy had been a proven winner. In 30 of the 230 Treasury auctions held between 1986 and 1990, Salomon and its customers had acquired more than half of the offered securities. On June 27, 1990, Salomon submitted a bid for itself and its customers so large that the aggregate exceeded the entire offer. Two weeks later it carried the logic to its extreme, bidding $30 billion for only $10 billion in offered notes.

To those outside the high-octane world of bond trading, this vast oversubscription might appear bizarre if not pernicious. In response to Mozer's outsized bidding, Deputy Assistant Treasury Secretary for domestic finance Michael Basham called him and instructed him to stop. Mozer did not, and Basham announced that "to maintain the competitive nature of the auction process," the government would no longer accept bids whose aggregate value—for the dealer and its customers taken together—exceeded 35 percent of an auction total. Mozer condemned the Treasury's "rash decision," claiming that it "ties the hands of the larger dealers," and he threatened to protest to the Treasury Secretary. Mozer's harsh words rankled Basham, and by the fall of 1990 the two were no longer on speaking terms, even though Salomon and Treasury had to be in constant contact. The 35 percent limit came to be known as the "Mozer/Basham rule."

Despite the new federal regulation with his own name on it, Mozer submitted the February 21, 1991, bid on Salomon's behalf for 35 percent of the $9 billion auction. He also entered a second bid for another 35 percent in the name of—but unbeknown to—one of Salomon's customers, S. G. Warburg. The two bids came in at what turned out to be the stop-out yield, and the Fed granted both Salomon and Warburg a prorated $1.7 billion of the notes, 19 percent of the total for each. After the auction, Mozer instructed his staff not to inform Warburg that its name had been used and to transfer the "Warburg" notes to Salomon's own account. Thus combined, the two bids amounted to 38 percent of the bonds sold at the February 21

Paul Mozer

auction, a violation of Treasury's decade-old rule limiting a winner to 35 percent of the market. The excess was not great, however, and in any event, Mozer believed that his shrewd but unauthorized bid would not be detected.

Treasury officials, however, noticed an anomaly. Itself a primary dealer, Warburg had, unknown to Mozer, bid $100 million at the same auction. When Treasury called Salomon to ask why Warburg had bid through Salomon when at the same time it had submitted its own bid, Mozer instructed another managing director, Thomas Murphy, to say that Salomon's bid should have been submitted in the name of Mercury Asset Management. Mercury, however, was a subsidiary of Warburg, and thus Treasury wrote to Warburg on April 17, asking it to explain why its two bids—the $1.7 billion bid through Salomon and the $100 million bid on its own—together had surpassed the 35 percent Mozer/Basham limit. Treasury officials sent a copy of the letter to Mozer, who implored Warburg executive Charles Jackson, a personal acquaintance, to ignore the request. His bid in Warburg's name had been inadvertent, Mozer pleaded, and its revelation would prove embarrassing.

When Mozer soon learned that Warburg would tell what it knew to the Treasury, however, he concluded that his options had narrowed to one, and on April 27 he walked into the office of his boss, John Meriwether, to explain his misdeed. Mozer confessed that he had misused Warburg's name, but he also asserted that this had been his only such transgression. Over Mozer's objections, Meriwether took the news to Salomon president Thomas W. Strauss, and the next day they discussed Mozer's action with general counsel Donald Feuerstein. Their boss, John Gutfreund, was traveling, but they informed him of the illicit bid that day. The following day, Gutfreund reviewed the matter with Meriwether, Strauss, and Feuerstein. They recalled Mozer's row with Basham, and they remembered a recent incident when Mozer had exploded at Salomon's chief auditor when he had requested a routine review.

Salomon's top management team was a seasoned group. John Meriwether was a seventeen-year veteran of the firm. Donald Feuerstein had served as its chief legal officer for twenty years and, before that, as staff attorney and assistant general counsel for the U.S. Securities and Exchange Commission. Thomas Strauss had been with the company for twenty-eight years, John Gutfreund for thirty-eight. Their collective Salomon experience thus totaled more than a hundred years. Gutfreund, who had joined the firm in 1953 after army service in Korea, had devoted his entire career to Salomon, watching it grow from 300 employees to 9,000. Even Paul Mozer, who joined in 1979, had given the company more than a decade.

A Market Squeeze and More

ONLY THIRTY-FOUR YEARS old, Paul Mozer earned $4 million in 1989 and another $4.75 million in 1990. Still, he was abashed to learn that bond arbitrage trader Lawrence Hilibrand had received a $23 million bonus. His own 1991 bonus should be closer to that, Mozer reasoned, but it was likely to be so only if he were able to continue his growing dominance of the government securities market.

Undaunted by the disclosure of his illegal bid of February 21 and undisciplined by the firm, Mozer submitted another illegal bid on May 22. The Fed was offering $12 billion in two-year notes, and Mozer went for almost all: he bid for 34 percent in Salomon's name, 17 percent in the name of Tiger Investments, a customer of Salomon, and 35 percent in the name of Quantum Fund, another customer. Many primary dealers had predicted a stop-out yield near 6.83 percent, but Mozer bid a very aggressive 6.81 percent. So low was the level that Salomon and its two customers won the full amount bid. Together they now held 86 percent of the securities sold. Other dealers had virtually been shut out, and as they scrambled to meet their customer obligations, the prices of the bonds soared.

In the wake of the squeeze, some firms were forced to borrow the May 22 securities from Salomon. Boatman's Bank, for example, was committed to delivering $120 million of the notes to customers. Losing its own bid and finding virtually no affordable notes, Boatman's borrowed them from Salomon at a daily rate of $8,000. Other traders absorbed similar costs, and several complained to Washington. The SEC and Treasury began a secret investigation of Salomon's role in the May 22 auction.

Because Mozer was one of Salomon's 158 "managing directors," only John Gutfreund could suspend or dismiss him. Yet by midsummer the Salomon chief executive had still not disciplined his rogue trader. Nor had Gutfreund notified the U.S. Treasury of Mozer's illegal bids of February 21 and May 22, though he now knew of both. In June, Gutfreund paid a visit to Treasury Undersecretary Robert Glauber to mend Salomon's relations with Treasury in light of the May squeeze but disclosed nothing.

Instead, Salomon conducted an internal investigation that revealed even more damaging news: Mozer's initial claim of a single lapse had been patently untrue. In a December 1990 Treasury auction, Salomon had bid 35 percent for its own account and another 11 percent using a customer's name without authorization. On February 11, Salomon had made an unauthorized offer for $1 billion of government securities for a customer—the result of a practical joke gone awry. And in April, Salomon had bid its maximum 35 percent and another $2.5 billion for a customer. Salomon had then immediately bought $600 million of the notes from the customer at the auction price.

On August 8, more than three months after first learning of Mozer's illicit February bid, Gutfreund finally telephoned Gerald Corrigan, chairman of the Federal Reserve of New York, Treasury's Robert Glauber, and SEC Chairman Richard Breeden. The next day Salomon issued a press release stating that "irregularities and rule violations with its submissions of bids in certain auctions of Treasury securities" had been reported to the government. On August 14, Salomon went further and admitted publicly that its chairman had known of the improper February bid since April but had not revealed it until now. As first drafted, the release explained that top management had failed to notify the government because of the "press of other business," but Salomon directors modified this transparently ludicrous excuse to "a lack of sufficient attention."

The next day, a *Wall Street Journal* headline read, "Top Salomon Officials Knew About Illegal Bid." Sniffing more than insufficient attention to an illegal bid, some holders of Salomon's own debt securities asked the firm to purchase them back, a request that Salomon had always honored. But the normal trickle soon turned to a flood, and after spending $700 million to repurchase its notes, Salomon closed the floodgates by midday, suspending trading in its own securities.

Earlier in the year, Gutfreund had said that "all my life is here" at Salomon, but as he gazed at the *Journal* headline, he knew it soon would not be: "I knew I was reading my own obituary," he later recalled. Federal regulators were angered by what appeared to be a cover-up on their watch, and Gutfreund learned during a telephone conversation that evening with Corrigan that the Fed was contemplating ending Salomon's "primary dealer" status. The next morning, Gutfreund decided to resign.

Under New Management

THE LARGEST SALOMON stockholder was the legendary Warren Buffett, one of America's shrewdest investors and richest men. His Omaha-based company, Berkshire Hathaway, had amassed more than $10 billion in equity investments. Unlike most mutual funds, he placed the capital not in hundreds of separate holdings but in only a select few, including some of the marquee names of American business: Capital Cities/ABC, Wells Fargo Bank, Gillette, *The Washington Post*, Coca-Cola— and Salomon. His stock picks had led to spectacular returns, giving Berkshire Hathaway an annual growth rate of 15 percent from 1956 to the early 1990s, outperforming all other institutional investors. *Forbes'* 1991 listing of the nation's richest people included the dynastic names of American capitalism— Rockefeller, Mellon, du Pont—but among the top ten was Warren Buffett, with an estimated personal net worth of $8 billion.

Buffett had known John Gutfreund for more than a decade and had been impressed with his frequent willingness to put clients' welfare ahead of the firm's interest. In 1987, Gutfreund had pleaded with Buffett to make a friendly investment in

Salomon as a defense against corporate raider Ronald Perelman, and the two had arranged for Buffett to purchase $700 million of a special Salomon stock, giving him a 12 percent voting stake. Buffett and longtime associate Charlie Munger had also taken seats on the board of directors. In defending the decision to his board, Gutfreund had argued that Buffett could be a help to him in running the company. Though surprisingly reluctant to proffer unsolicited advice to the managements in which he has entrusted so much, Buffett had been pleased to be asked, and Gutfreund had telephoned him often, sometimes twice a week. "I go to him if I've got something that I can't ask anybody inside the firm about and get a reliable answer," Gutfreund related. "Warren is a terrific call."

At 7:45 A.M. on Friday, August 16, 1991, Gutfreund telephoned Buffett, but this time not for advice. He reported that he and Strauss were resigning and he wanted Buffett to take the reins at the crippled firm. Buffett called back an hour later to say he would accept the position—temporarily. During the day, trading in Salomon stock was stopped. At the company, activity ground to a halt. Gutfreund announced at noon, "Warren is the CEO," but that evening, when Gutfreund and Buffett met with Gerald Corrigan of the New York Federal Reserve Bank, Corrigan coldly warned Buffett to be ready for "any eventuality."

Twelve hours after Gutfreund's exit, Soviet president Mikhail Gorbachev was temporarily ousted in an abortive coup attempt, and the tumultuous events inside Salomon's New York office became a sidebar to Moscow's historic upheaval. "There are a lot of ways of getting off the front page," observed a Salomon salesman, "but sending in the Red Army has got to be the most creative." The respite, however, proved momentary.

At 10 A.M. on Sunday, August 18, the Salomon board gathered to accept John Gutfreund's resignation and to elevate Warren Buffett to interim chairman and chief executive officer. As the meeting was about to convene, a Treasury official called to warn that the government would announce in just minutes that Salomon was suspended from bidding at Treasury auctions. The news was devastating. With $130 billion in short-term liabilities, Salomon had to roll over billions of dollars of debt every day, and any stampede of its already nervous customers and creditors for the exits would all but ensure the company's collapse. Other investment banks could also be toppled by the precipitous crash of confidence in Salomon. Its outside law firm, Wachtell Lipton Rosen & Katz, was put to work preparing a bankruptcy filing, which could leave nine thousand employees holding pink slips and tens of thousands of shareholders holding worthless shares. To Salomon's employees, the suspension of bidding—it was on the financial wires within minutes— looked like a death warrant.

Buffett immediately telephoned Treasury Secretary Nicholas F. Brady, pressing him to rescind the fatal decree or at least stay its execution. He warned of a domino effect and threatened to step out of Salomon if Brady did not step back. In a rash of frantic telephone exchanges that followed over the next several hours, Buffett placed his own credibility on the line, telling Brady at one point, "Nick, this is the most important day of my life." The SEC's Richard Breeden declared Salomon "rotten to the core," but the Fed's Gerald Corrigan and others were alarmed by the prospect of a Wall Street collapse, and at 2:30 P.M., just before a scheduled Salomon press conference, Brady agreed to back off on part of the suspension: Salomon would be permitted to bid at Treasury auctions but only on behalf of itself, not its customers. With half a loaf, Buffett believed, the firm could survive, and the board elevated him to chairman at an annual salary of $1. When asked a few minutes later at the press conference how he would simultaneously run both Salomon in New York and Berkshire Hathaway in Omaha, Buffett responded, "My mother has sewn my name in my underwear."

A week later the company formally admitted that it had violated Treasury auction rules, and the Federal Reserve began considering whether to terminate Salomon's status as a primary dealer. At its Open Market Committee meeting in October, John LaWare, a Fed governor, turned to Gerald Corrigan, head of the Federal Reserve Bank of New York, where the bidding violations had occurred, and asked, "Jerry, would the removal of the primary dealer status bring the firm down?" Corrigan replied that such was the prevailing view among both U.S. and foreign markets, and "we ourselves certainly think that is a possibility." Federal Reserve Chairman Alan Greenspan added that the Fed could not "suspend them temporarily as a primary dealer," for that would be "like executing somebody technically and then resuscitating them." The committee delayed any further action.

Simultaneously, Buffett was seeking to mend the inside of a badly damaged firm. Three days after taking over, he dispatched a memo to all Salomon officers, saying "You are each expected to report, instantaneously and directly to me, any legal violation or moral failure on behalf of any employee of Salomon." He listed his personal telephone number and added that among the only reporting exceptions would be parking tickets. A week later, in an address to all Salomon employees, he called for hard work along a straight and narrow path (see the box on the following page).

Buffett wrote shareholders on October 29 that "a few Salomon employees behaved egregiously." To avert a recurrence, he now assigned himself the role of "chief compliance officer," a task normally allotted lesser officers. He asked employees to measure their actions by a "newspaper test": Would they be prepared to see any behavior in question described by a "critical" reporter in a "local paper, there to be read by his spouse, children, and friends"? He asserted that the firm would achieve "superior returns [by] playing aggressively in the center of the court, without resorting to close-to-the line acrobatics."[1]

Gutfreund's delay of three months before reporting the bidding infractions "will prove costly," Buffett warned his shareholders, and indeed it did. Buffett and Salomon's new general

Warren Buffett's Comments to Salomon Employees, August 26, 1991

Now, the important thing is that we have the right view of ourselves. If we have the right view of ourselves, that will lead to deeds that will eventually give the world the right view of us. . . .

I don't think we can do any better than go back to J. P. Morgan, "First-class business in a first-class way." You know, if you have anything that you think about in the morning before you go to work, just repeat that: "First-class business in a first class way." . . .

Also, I expect you to get out and do a lot of business. The "first-class business in a first-class way" does not preclude in any way doing a lot of business; it does not preclude doing profitable business and it doesn't preclude gutsy business. It just means you keep the ball rolling down the middle of the court. . . .

If you lose money for the firm by bad decisions, like I've done plenty of times for Berkshire, I will be very understanding. If you lose reputation for the firm, I will be ruthless. . . .

What kind of a firm can come out of this? Well, in that regard I may have a loftier vision than virtually anyone, because I think great things can come out of this. . . . We have a chance to preserve all of the strengths of the past and have people look at us with a new eye. . . .

We want people basically to get rich around here, but we want them to get rich *through* the firm and not *off* the firm. We want them to get rich through the stock, frankly, and that message will eventually get out to investors and that's the kind of thing they want to hear. . . .

I think in the end we'll be more proud of this company than you've ever been before.

counsel, Robert Denham, reached an expensive settlement with the federal regulators: $122 million to the Treasury for violation of securities laws, $68 million to the Justice Department, and $100 million to a restitution fund for private damage claims that might result from fifty civil lawsuits. (Unclaimed funds were to revert to the government.) The $290 million settlement was the second largest ever for a financial institution, although significantly less than the $600 million Drexel Burnham Lambert had paid after its collapse in 1990. As a further penalty, Salomon was barred from bidding at the June and July 1992 auctions, resulting in an estimated $4 billion in lost trades.

For Salomon investors, the worst came as Salomon's own stock went into free fall. On August 8, 1991, the day before Gutfreund confessed his sins, company shares had sold for more than $36. Within six weeks they were selling below $21. In just thirty trading days, Salomon's shareholders lost $1.65 billion, more than half a billion dollars in one day alone.

The company also forfeited $400 million in potential business driven away by the scandal. Pacific Investment Management Company, the client whose name had been used in Mozer's "practical joke," dropped Salomon completely. The California Public Employees' Retirement System, Massachusetts State Teachers' Retirement System, State of Wisconsin Investment Board, and World Bank all suspended business with the company. So did Mercury Asset Management. The British Treasury removed Salomon as the lead manager for the U.S. sale of British Telecom stock, and Moody's Investors Service downgraded Salomon's credit rating. In the first half of 1991, Salomon had been the fifth largest stock underwriter on Wall Street, with an 8 percent market share. A year later, it was tenth with 2 percent. "There's nothing to teach you as much about how much something is worth," one of Salomon's new executives would later say, "than to almost lose it."

Betting the Company

"LIAR'S POKER" is a game of high-stakes bluff and bluster akin to the card game "I Doubt It." Two or more players hold a dollar bill against their chest, and as each makes claims about the bills' serial numbers, some true, some false, others decide whether to challenge the claims. Like I Doubt It, Liar's Poker can be played for the fun of it or make-believe stakes, but the Salomon tradition was to play the game for real. By company myth, Gutfreund had found Meriwether at his trading desk one day in 1986 and whispered, "One hand, one million dollars, no tears." Translation: For a single round of Liar's Poker, the stakes would be $1 million, with no whining permitted by the distraught loser. "No, John," Meriwether replied, "if we're going to play for those kinds of numbers, I'd rather play for real money. Ten million dollars. No tears."[2]

Looking at the $10 million bet, Gutfreund is said to have forced a smile and replied to Meriwether, "You're crazy." When his personal stakes were in the millions, he rejected Meriwether's challenge. Later, however, he would tolerate Mozer's challenge when his company's stakes were in the billions.

Betting the company was infrequent but not unknown. IBM wagered its future on developing the mainframe computer, and Boeing bet its existence on building a new jetliner, the 747. But these were grand strategic decisions, taken with planning and prudence. Gutfreund's small tactical decision to sit on the explosive information, by contrast, was evidently made with scant forethought. The delay might have been caused by nothing more than the increasing awkwardness that came with the passage of time, like an unwritten thank-you note that becomes harder to compose or a witness who fails to come forward in timely fashion.

Had Gutfreund been a midlevel manager, such a delay would have been troublesome but hardly fatal. There are other routes for bad news to reach the top, and a procrastinating midlevel manager can rarely bring a firm to its knees. But as Rosabeth Moss Kanter has found in her studies of company hierarchies, what she terms an "inverse law of uncertainty" is at work: the more responsible the position, the less predictable are its holder's actions. As a person moves up an organizational chart, the risks expand until, at the apex, they can become enormous. At that level, good decisions can lead to riches, bad ones to ruin. By delaying as long as he did at his level, John Gutfreund wagered the entire company.[3]

Even short of betting the enterprise, tolerance of improper behavior can generate costs that amount to many multiples of the ill-gotten gains. Salomon formed a task force after the debacle to identify which of its Treasury bids had been improper and how much the company had profited from them. Following a month's labor, the team identified eight improper bids, and it estimated their total profits at a mere $3.3 to $4.6 million. Because of the bids, Salomon later paid $290 million in government fines, making the ratio of penalty costs to illicit benefits better than 60 to 1.

Even Mozer's excessive February bid, which almost brought the house down, netted the firm little real profit. By submitting a 35 percent offer in Warburg's name, Mozer's offer had the effect of sharply reducing Salomon's own prorated share at the stop-out yield point. Without the improper Warburg bid, Salomon would have received its full 35 percent of the auction. With the Warburg bid, it acquired 38 percent, just 3 points more than it would have received with an above-the-board offer.

> *By implication:* At the top of the organizational chart, where the risks and uncertainties are greatest, decisions made or not made can have consequences that reach well beyond the organization to affect its very survival.

An Error of Judgment

DERYCK C. MAUGHAN, recruited by Warren Buffett to run Salomon Brothers, has termed the events a "billion-dollar error of judgment." Gutfreund had worked in municipal bonds and knew the government trading world well. As recently as 1987, Gutfreund—by then the firm's CEO—had been directly involved in finalizing the firm's bids for Treasury notes. In 1991,

Warren Buffett (front) and Deryck Maughan

he still maintained a desk on the bond-trading floor just feet from where the bogus bids were finalized. Though he himself had not traded Treasury bonds, he understood how federal auctions can be abused and customer names misused.

Gutfreund's acquaintances contended that he would have neither authorized nor allowed Mozer's transgressions, and no evidence indicated that he had. During the late 1980s, when other Wall Street institutions such as Drexel Burnham Lambert, Ivan F. Boesky Corporation, Kidder, Peabody & Company, and even Goldman, Sachs & Company had been tainted or brought down by insider trading, Salomon had remained unscathed. *Wall Street Journal* reporter James B. Stewart's chronicle of the industry's misdeeds, *Den of Thieves*, mentioned Salomon and Gutfreund only in passing, and only then for their discord with "hated rival" Drexel Burnham Lambert. Just after the scandal broke, Salomon managing director Richard Grand-Jean called Gutfreund "a person of great integrity."

Earlier in the year, Gutfreund himself had expressed pride in Salomon's record during an era when Wall Street behavior too often lived up to arbitrageur Ivan Boesky's famous line, "Greed is healthy. You can be greedy and still feel good about yourself." Gutfreund had been repulsed by the perversion of values. "What drove me bananas in the eighties was that all the existing rules—written and unwritten—were to be tested or violated." His own response had been "to try to run the business in as clean a fashion and as exemplary a fashion as I possibly could." He avoided junk bonds and hostile takeovers.[4]

Gutfreund's lapse in judgment, then, lay not in connivance nor in complicity but in an absence of alacrity. Other Salomon managers have compared the blunder to President Richard Nixon's inaction on first learning of the Watergate break-in: each was apprised early on of potentially explosive information; neither stepped forward. "Dick Nixon or John Gutfreund, it's the same thing," complained one Salomon executive. Offered another: "I think John went to sleep hoping it would just go away." Though a combative trader, Gutfreund admitted he was "not the most decisive" manager.

Had Gutfreund suspended or dismissed Mozer at the end of April, the May squeeze would not have transpired. Had he required immediate investigation, the later delays would not have occurred. Had he contacted the Fed's Gerald Corrigan in timely fashion, the impression of a cover-up would never have emerged.

By implication: Inaction can be as damaging to leadership as inept action.

A Management Style

IF THE SPECIFIC error of judgment was three months of silence, it was nonetheless an error consistent with a certain management style. During his watch—from his accession as top executive in 1978 until his resignation on August 18, 1991—Gutfreund carried ultimate responsibility for all that transpired below, and among his favorite management tools were secrecy and exclusion.

Nominally heading an executive committee of senior managing directors, Gutfreund often made decisions in private, informing committee and board members well after the fact. He oversaw a firm of both traders and investment bankers, but only the former graced his inner circle. He depended on prima donnas to deliver the results but was unwilling to rein in their excesses. He extolled performance and its rewards, but in 1990, when Salomon Brothers' profits plunged by $118 million, he increased the bonus pool by $120 million. He worried about risk management and legal compliance but ran both casually.

Like other stars in Salomon's galaxy, Gutfreund's personal mix of arrogance and bravado worked well in the company's cultural alloy of money and power. It served him less well, however, when more was needed; he has been quoted as telling a group of managing directors shortly before resigning, "No apologies to anyone for anything."

As the premier representative of one of Wall Street's great engines, Gutfreund assumed the role of "senior statesman and public spokesman" for the enterprise, especially in promoting its burgeoning global investment banking. His schedule was grueling. He had just returned from Japan in late April when he first learned of Mozer's February bid. Days after reviewing it with his top people on April 29, a meeting of less than thirty minutes, his focus had already returned to "statesmanship." Gutfreund understood from the meeting that the February action was improper but not unlawful, and he presumed others would warn Mozer that his past behavior was unacceptable and his future on notice.

During the week of April 29, Gutfreund presided over Salomon's annual shareholder meeting, ran a Salomon board meeting, and attended a meeting of the Chrysler Corporation board. The next week, he was a featured speaker at a World Bank event in Madrid and then traveled on Salomon business to London, Frankfurt, and back to London. The week of May 12, he hosted Salomon's managing directors' meeting in Orlando, visited its Tampa office, and attended his son's wedding. The week of May 19, he met with the chairman of Monsanto Company in St. Louis and the chairman of KeyCorp in Albany, flew to Paris for the weekend, and then traveled to Tokyo to meet clients and appear at functions honoring Deryck Maughan on his departure from Salomon's office there.

If Gutfreund's attention was focused elsewhere, his senior colleagues were equally unaware of the iceberg looming beneath the small tip Paul Mozer had admitted. Strauss, Feuerstein, and Meriwether accepted Mozer's claim that the February bid was an isolated mistake and recommended neither firing nor suspension. They decided that he should be admonished, and Meriwether informed Mozer that top management would make his misconduct known to the government.

Gutfreund and Strauss agreed at the April 29 meeting on Mozer's bid that they would manage the externals. Though in their view the firm had no legal duty to report the problem, together they would take the matter to Gerald Corrigan of the Federal Reserve. Arranging a joint visit to Corrigan's office, however, encountered practical barriers: blistering schedules placed Gutfreund and Strauss in New York at the same time for only six business days in May. Salomon's general counsel reminded them in passing to meet with Corrigan, and several times they reminded each other. Gutfreund anticipated that he would encounter Corrigan at a meeting or reception, where he would mention that he and Strauss had a concern to discuss. No Corrigan encounter materialized, however, and without an urgent note on the file, the Mozer problem soon fell through the cracks of running the giant enterprise. In June, as Salomon executives began to suspect wider malfeasance on Mozer's part following the May squeeze, Gutfreund decided to postpone further contact with Corrigan until he had all the facts.

Even when he learned the facts, Gutfreund did not share them with the individuals to whom he was directly responsible, the directors. When the Salomon board met on Wednesday, August 14, the directors debated the wording of what was about to be a devastating public admission in a second press release. But they were not informed by Gutfreund that he had received a letter from the Federal Reserve Bank of New York the day before, questioning the Fed's "continuing business relationship" with Salomon and demanding a detailed accounting within ten days. Chairman Gerald Corrigan had expected the letter to reach the board, since it implicitly questioned Gutfreund's future. The letter was not disclosed to the directors, however, and as Salomon's meltdown accelerated over the next several days with little apparent intervention from its directors, they seemed to have closed ranks with top management in defying the U.S. government. "Understandably," Buffett later recalled, "the Fed felt at this point that the directors had joined with management in spitting in its face."

The new head of Salomon Brothers, Deryck Maughan, would say in retrospect, "In a very complex, very large, diversified institution, somebody has to be looking after the shop, asking the questions, and providing direction and leadership." Warren Buffett would insist on reports of all legal misbehavior except parking tickets. But the challenge was also to ask questions and provide direction without veering toward the opposite danger of micromanaging, to create a cultural compass without overcontrol.

By implication: The perquisites of high office do not lessen the need for specific and consistent exercise of authority to ensure accountability inside an organization. Creation of a common understanding of preferred behavior may be especially important in harnessing the energies of those who are distant from or disdainful of the high office.

Installing New Leadership

WARREN BUFFETT'S investiture as Salomon CEO brought respite but not restitution. "The challenge facing Buffett," one news article reported in September 1991, "is to keep Salomon alive by reestablishing its credibility."[5] He drew on his reputation, his networks, his judgment, and his clout to right what was wrong before wrong overwhelmed what was still right. Known for his inner strength, coolness under fire, and ability to make difficult decisions, Buffett took his message of restoration to employees, customers, regulators, stockholders, and Congress. It was a calling: "You won't believe this—because I don't look that dumb—but I volunteered to take the job of interim chairman," he explained. "It's not what I want to be doing, but it will be what I will be doing until it gets done properly."

With Gutfreund resigning on Friday, August 16, Buffett devoted Saturday to identifying who will lead the firm with him. He privately asked each of the twelve remaining senior managers who should be designated, and all but two named the same individual: Deryck Maughan, then head of Salomon's investment banking. On Sunday afternoon, Maughan was on the New York trading floor, seeking to steady the Tokyo office, where the market was already open. Buffett stepped off an elevator on the floor, approached Maughan, a forty-three-year-old coal miner's son educated at the London School of Economics, and announced, "You're the guy." They moved to an auditorium, where they proclaimed to the five hundred reporters and employees gathered for a press conference that Maughan was the new chief operating officer of Salomon Brothers. Following the press parley, Buffett told a reconstituted executive committee that Maughan was unequivocally in charge. It was a decisive break, and in Salomon lore the two eras became "BC" and "AD," "before crisis" and "after Deryck."

The Wall Street Journal's headline the next day singled out the quality that Buffett most wanted: " 'Mr. Integrity' Is Promoted to Top Post."[6] Maughan's future was by no means assured, but Buffett repeatedly asserted that he himself was indeed only an *interim* chairman. Maughan had worked ten years in the United Kingdom's Treasury Department and four years in the London office of Goldman, Sachs, and he had been serving as chairman of Salomon Brothers Asia since 1986. Fellow managers viewed his elevation as inspired. William McIntosh, a managing director and thirty-year Salomon veteran, declared Maughan "destined to lead." Richard Grand-Jean, who had been Maughan's colleague in Japan, concurred: "When you talked to Deryck, you knew you were talking to the future chairman and CEO."

If Gutfreund's lethal weakness was indecision, Maughan's enduring strength was a willingness to take action. "He can grasp the complexities, determine what needs to be done, execute, and follow through," commented James Massey, a vice chairman. "Deryck is very decisive."

When Buffett had asked Salomon vice chairman and equity division head Stanley Shopkorn who should lead the firm, Shopkorn had named himself. Now Maughan forced Shopkorn out—his brash personality was too old-style. Maughan assigned profit and loss responsibilities to senior managers. He built up the firm's research capability, hiring a dozen new analysts. He also reshaped the equity trading unit: only three of the ten traders he inherited were still there a year later.

In his letter to shareholders several months after becoming chairman, Buffett concluded, "The best decision I have made since assuming my post was appointment of Deryck Maughan." Soon after Salomon's settlement with the U.S. government in May 1992, Buffett relinquished his interim roles. The board elevated Maughan to chairman and chief executive officer of Salomon Brothers and Robert Denham, Salomon's general counsel, to chairman and CEO of the parent, Salomon Inc. Maughan and Denham presided over the firm for another five years, until it was acquired by Travelers Group in 1997 for $9 billion; although the ride was turbulent, they gradually restored Salomon to relatively full financial health.

Forging a New Culture

SEEN FROM THE OUTSIDE, Paul Mozer's behavior appears remarkable, at least in part because on the inside it was treated as so unremarkable. Here was a key employee who had publicly denounced the Treasury, bilked the Federal Reserve, knowingly violated federal law, and repeated his offenses time and again. What's more, this broad swath of illicit behavior had been directed against what was arguably Salomon's biggest "customer," the U.S. government. In effect, Salomon was acting as the Treasury's investment bank, distributing its notes just as it would for a corporate customer seeking to issue new debt. How many red flags did Mozer have to fly?

In fact, all organizations run the risk of far-reaching damage by a rogue employee whose mind is on a personal windfall and whose hand is on a sensitive lever. Most construct systems of accounting, compliance, and control to protect themselves against the vagaries of human nature. But some foster cultures that nonetheless tolerate small excesses, indulge corner cutting, and sanction gray areas. Few executives ever ask outright, "How can we best circumvent the law?" But by both action and inaction, they can foster a code that permits forays into forbidden zones.

Cultural codes are like the air we breathe, life-sustaining yet rarely noticed. They shape the behavior of colleagues and senior managers and are shaped by it. By 1991, the cultural code of Salomon was well established for all to see. Gutfreund's proposal for a $1 million game of Liar's Poker became the grist of legend, and as it was told and retold, it also told newcomers and reminded old-timers that at Salomon extravagant, high-stakes risk taking was *the* way of life.

During the three years leading up to the 1991 debacle, Salomon reportedly rewarded Mozer with bonuses totaling $10 million. Mozer's 1990 performance—including his open feud with the Treasury—was implicitly sanctioned by Gutfreund's unwillingness to discipline or remove him. The firm's loose compliance policies sent much the same signal. When Mozer bid Warburg's name in the May auction, he instructed Thomas Murphy, another managing director working with him, to falsify the paperwork. No internal checks were in place to prevent it, then or later.

By contrast, the new Salomon executives declined to provide any bonuses, severances, health benefits, or legal expenses for any of the offending managers, except where obligated by prior contract. Under the leadership of Buffett, Denham, and Maughan, the firm

• Actively cooperated with federal regulators to uncover other improprieties

• Formed a board compliance committee among Salomon directors

• Appointed Buffet chief compliance officer

• Moved compliance officers out of their offices onto trading floors

• Made compliance self-policing, "building it in instead of inspecting it in"

• Extended risk analysis to regulatory, credit, operational, and environmental hazards

• Segregated trading functions to prevent perpetration and then concealment of improper acts

• Required review by legal staff of all correspondence with the Treasury and Federal Reserve

Restitution

IN LATE 1992, the Securities and Exchange Commission banned John Gutfreund for life from serving as a chairman or CEO of a securities firm and fined him $100,000. Thomas Strauss was suspended from the securities business and fined $75,000. Donald Feuerstein was not disciplined. The SEC found that John Meriwether had taken correct action in immediately reporting Mozer's breach but still held him liable for failing to insist that his superiors report the violation to the government; he was suspended from trading for three months and fined $50,000. The SEC censured the company's top executives for their failure "to take action to discipline Mozer or to limit his activities," which "constituted a serious breach of their supervisory obligation."

Paul Mozer served four months in prison after pleading guilty to lying to the Federal Reserve Bank of New York during its auction of February 21, 1991. He also paid a fine of $1.1 million and was barred from the securities industry for life. John Gutfreund would be denied his stock options and retirement benefits by the new Salomon.

The government did not bring criminal indictments against Salomon itself, a decision largely attributed to the preemptive cooperation by Buffett, Maughan, and Denham—and to Buffett's impeccable reputation. At Buffett's first press conference, he offered to remain until all questions were answered, a commitment that in the end kept him for three hours. He waived attorney-client privilege in giving the government the internal report of Salomon's wrongdoing prepared by outside counsel Wachtell Lipton, overriding its lawyers' strenuous objections. He hired no public relations firm, suspended the public affairs work of Salomon's Washington office, and fired its political consultants. He made a clean break with all those implicated in or even associated with the affair, including Wachtell Lipton. He was candid about Salomon's misdeeds with its varied constituencies. At a congressional hearing on September 4, 1991, the new Salomon chairman opened by saying "I would like to start by apologizing for the acts that have brought us here. The nation has a right to expect its rules and laws will be obeyed."

The day after his appointment as chairman, Buffett visited Chairman Richard Breeden of the SEC, which was leading the federal investigation. When Breeden, whose agency would eventually issue four hundred subpoenas in the case, warned that he would turn over every stone, Buffett responded, "Call us anytime someone doesn't give you what you want," and "you'll have a new person to deal with in twenty minutes."

The government's decision not to bring criminal action was decisive for Salomon's recovery. Many money managers are forbidden from dealing with admitted or convicted felons. Had Salomon been indicted or forced into a plea bargain, it might well have followed Drexel Burnham Lambert into Wall Street's dustbin. The Justice Department and SEC initially had their eye on a guilty plea or indictment and a $400 million penalty, but so well did Buffett cooperate throughout the investigations that prosecution now would seem more to penalize the good guys than deter wrongdoers. In the years that followed, Salomon's cooperation became a gold standard against which federal prosecutors would judge other companies' behavior.

By implication: Unequivocal cooperation, complete contrition, acceptance of responsibility, and a riveting focus on recovery are critical ingredients for restoring a beleaguered organization's reputation.

At the press conference on the afternoon of Sunday, August 18, just after the board's changing of the guard, Buffett was asked if he had read *Liar's Poker.* He had "a long time ago," he answered. When the reporter then asked if he has an opinion of the book, Buffett responded, "I want to make sure there is not a second edition." There has not been.

Warren Buffett, Robert Denham, and Deryck Maughan guided Salomon back to health. Yet, ironically, it was John Gutfreund who had ultimately paved the way for its recovery through an early but fateful decision. It was he who had convinced Buffett to invest, recruited him to the board, and sought his advice. Had Buffett not been a Salomon director, had he not been apprised of its operations, had he not been its primary investor, he would surely never have stepped forward. Just as Joshua Chamberlain's recruitment of the 2nd Maine helped turn the tide at Little Round Top, John Gutfreund's recruitment of Warren Buffett may have made the difference between the company's recovery and insolvency. Like Eugene Kranz's prior preparation of his flight teams for whatever dangers lay ahead, Gutfreund's frequent consultations with his most important investor and director ensured that Buffett could step into the breach when danger turned to catastrophe. If only Gutfreund had listened better to what Buffett was telling him, he might have saved his own career as well.

CHAPTER 8

❖

Nancy Barry Builds Women's World Banking

"I feel that my whole life has been preparing me to do this job."

IN 1987, NANCY M. BARRY was a high-flying, fast-moving executive at the World Bank. In only twelve years since receiving her MBA degree from Harvard, Barry had rocketed up the organizational chart and was now one of the bank's five highest-ranking women. As an agency of the United Nations, the World Bank could not pay the stratospheric salaries that many of Barry's Harvard classmates were commanding in management consulting and investment banking, but within the international development community, the World Bank was *the* high end. Its pay packages were generous, its managers flew first-class, and its actions mattered in tangible ways. Nancy Barry's decisions on where First World assistance should be spent in Third World projects affected tens of thousands of poverty-stricken lives. If her projects worked well, struggling families could catch their breath, start an enterprise, prolong their lives. If her schemes failed, the poor would stay mired in poverty.

Barry's programs took her to the far corners of the world and to the most consequential offices. While she was still in her twenties, she had found herself negotiating with those who

shaped their nations' destinies. In Mexico City she had bar-
gained with Pedro Aspe Armella, the minister of finance; in
India, with the governor of the Central Bank; in Colombia, with
the country's president.

Barry was chief of the World Bank's Industrial Development
Division, where she oversaw policy and research on programs
for which the bank was annually lending more than $4 billion.
Even more important, she had the chance to promote one of the
vastly underappreciated engines of modern development: tiny
but direct loans to poor people for expanding small enterprises.

Microfinance on a macro scale had been pioneered by
Women's World Banking and Grameen Bank in Bangladesh.
Grameen had opened in 1979 with $30 loans to forty-two poor
villagers. They had paid back the loans, and Grameen had gone
on to lend some $1 billion to 2 million low-income women in
35,000 villages. Virtually all of them—97 percent—had repaid
their debts, and hundreds of thousands of people below the
poverty line had miraculously climbed above it.

Under Barry's prodding, the World Bank had been moving in
the same direction. Long focused on "structural adjustment" to
make government a stimulus for growth rather than a drag on
it, the bank was now also investing in millions of low-income
families whose prosperity was driving the growth. Nevertheless,
as the decade came to a close, Barry found herself increasingly
plagued by doubts about the bank's ability to bring real prosperity to the poor.

While it was clear by the late 1980s that microfinance was a
powerful tool, senior bank officials were retreating from a
decade-long expansion of such assistance. Was there a future,
Barry worried, not only for building hydroelectric dams and
reducing national deficits but also for directly investing in poor
people? While she had risen high on the organizational pyramid, senior officials remained skeptical of her unorthodox
development strategies. Could she achieve what she wanted,
she wondered, within a bureaucratic cage? While the bank's

resources were unmatched in scale, their enormity also begot inertia. Would eradication of poverty in the years ahead, she asked, require more agility than the World Bank could ever hope to muster?

In the midst of this crisis of doubt, early in 1990, the directors of the tiny rival, Women's World Banking (WWB), asked Barry if she might be ready to cash in her fifteen years of World Bank experience. The founding president of WWB was stepping down, and the board's executive committee had decided that Barry should be the one to lead the organization into the century's end.

The opportunity was appealing, even compelling. Since its inception in 1975, WWB had lent to thousands of poor people in nearly fifty countries from India and Thailand to Botswana and Brazil. Barry knew the organization well, having served as a trustee since 1981. And the presidency offered welcome answers to Barry's nagging questions about the World Bank's strategy and capacity. WWB was dedicated to microcredit for the poor, it was offering her a position of unfettered leadership, and it was small enough to be nimble.

Still, compared to the World Bank, WWB barely registered on the radar screen of international development. By 1990, the World Bank was lending $15 billion annually; WWB presided over $2 million. A typical loan made by the World Bank was for $250 million; at WWB, $250. The World Bank's staff totaled 6,000; WWB's global staff numbered just 60.

While Barry would face only a modest income loss if she were to jump ship—a housing allowance would largely compensate for a smaller paycheck—she would suffer a radical decline in prestige and power: she would be resigning from a stellar career in the world's best-known, most influential development agency to face an uncertain future at a little-known boutique. When Barry told her bank associates that she was considering just such a move, the collective gasp was almost audible.

Nancy Barry

The Rise of a Development Manager

THE ELDEST OF five children, Nancy Barry had worked high school summers for a firm of consulting engineers built from scratch by her father. Three of her uncles had founded consulting companies of their own, and the confidence and optimism of successful entrepreneurship infused family gatherings. Another uncle had entered the Catholic priesthood and presided over a large parish and church social services for all of Los Angeles. Individual calling and collective cause permeated the family culture as well.

The success of the enterprise had brought affluence to the family, and in the early 1960s Barry vacationed with her parents in the seaside resort of Acapulco, Mexico. Her instincts, though, took her away from the glistening beaches and famed cliff divers. Instead, she wandered the nearby slums. Wretched housing, open sewers, and distressed lives so touched the teenager's curiosity that when she later traveled with her parents to New

York City, she found less appeal in the glitter of Broadway than in the culture of Harlem.

As a freshman at Stanford University in 1967–1968, Barry aspired to medicine, but when city riots, political assassinations, and Vietnam body counts overwhelmed student concerns, she turned instead to economics. Student body president David Harris achieved notoriety for destroying his draft card, and many Stanford students found themselves acquiring more from protest rallies than from classroom lectures. But Barry still thrived on coursework and learned from two of Stanford's outspoken faculty critics, Henry M. Levin and Martin Carnoy, that education can be oppressive or liberating, that institutions can obstruct or promote human development.

Upon graduating, Barry hopped a freighter to Peru with $400 in her pocket, twenty boxes of used auto parts for a friend's parents in Lima, and no job in store. Not long after arriving, she found what she was looking for: a government development project for helping small enterprises recover after a devastating earthquake. Barry leapt into the work, helping the government shift a $45 million grant from the United States for middle-class housing—there was no middle class—to lower-class enterprise. She learned that slum dwellers often possessed great industry but no credit to get going. She also learned that without good organization and management, virtuous projects cannot really reach the masses for which they are intended.

In 1973, to master what she saw as missing, Barry enrolled in the MBA program at the Harvard Business School. Near the end of her first year in the two-year program, McKinsey & Company partners visited the school to pitch their firm. McKinsey is one of the world's premier consulting services: its product is strategy; its customers, the Fortune 500; and its clients, CEOs. Some eight hundred students attended the briefing, but only two would be hired for a summer internship. Barry, one of the two, was recruited by the London office, a fateful decision since it involved her in managing McKinsey's contract with the government of Tanzania.

Established in 1964 by the merger of Tanganyika and the newly independent Zanzibar, Tanzania was led by Julius Nyerere, the charismatic president whose progressive vision and pragmatic attitude set him apart from his contemporaries across the African continent. To support the building of his nation, Nyerere hired McKinsey to plan its future. The McKinsey team rendered some of its service pro bono, no small contribution given that the firm's rates were among the highest in the world; even so, the McKinsey service contract was so large that it had become a line item in Tanzania's annual budget. At age twenty-four, Barry worked what seemed like twenty-four-hour days as a full-fledged member of a McKinsey team that was writing development history. She was hooked.

Upon returning to Harvard for her final year of the MBA program, Barry knew that her future lay more in development assistance than in consulting service. If McKinsey & Company was the apex of consulting, the World Bank was the pinnacle of development. Its Young Professional Program, a fast-track entry for high-potential managers, received eight thousand applications a year and selected the top twenty; again, Barry was one of the chosen few. The work looked ideal—a combination of analytical challenge, problem solving, and social purpose. When she joined the bank in 1976, Barry sought an assignment to assist small-scale start-ups among the poor, but she discovered there were no such programs. Undeterred, she persuaded the bank to dispatch her to India to devise a plan for investing in nascent enterprises, ranging from making manhole covers in Calcutta to weaving carpets in Kashmir. Soon she would be doing the same for nations in Africa and Latin America.

Barry rose to division chief for public sector management in Latin America and then, in 1987, to division chief for industrial development. She arranged and negotiated megaloans to nations around the world and in the course of that work forged personal ties with dozens of finance ministers and central bank directors. Within the World Bank, she found herself on virtually every major task force and the youngest person on most. Her candor and exuberance, combined with her instinct for calculated risk and insistence on tangible results, gave her special visibility within the bank's corridors of power.

Barry began spearheading the bank's policy planning in industry, trade, and finance. Armed with a mandate to examine and improve the bank's project strategy, she led a team of twenty-five professionals, and they found that the bank's drive for structural adjustment—wrenching changes in the ways governments raised taxes, subsidized crops, and regulated their economies—was not delivering the growth expected. Nor, she found, were large-scale industries repaying their loans under these programs: public sector development banks were getting back just over half of what they had lent.

Several senior managers whose programs had been chastised by Barry denounced her criticism. Turf protection and trench warfare were the warp and woof of organizational life, and Barry carried no illusions about their elimination. But she worried that parochial interests were undermining the bank's reason for being. On her scorecard, good guys put a nation's welfare first, the bank's welfare second, and personal welfare third. Too many of the bank's officials seemed to have those priorities reversed.

The bank's mission, in its own words, is to open markets and stimulate economies to "improve the quality of life and increase prosperity everywhere," especially among "the world's poorest." On paper, the match with Barry's personal goals could not have been better. When you "connect with a purpose greater than ourselves," she observes, "you are fearless, you think big, and you think beyond yourself." But when organizational purpose was eroded by bureaucratic infighting, the staff's energies were dissipated. Thus, when the board of Women's World Banking asked if Barry would consider leaving the World Bank, she was ready. In fact, WWB could not have caught Nancy Barry at a better time.

The Rise of Microfinance

THE WORLD BANK and other international organizations have long sponsored grand projects with multi-million-dollar price tags. The ultimate beneficiaries are struggling families, but the project executors are agency officials. They decide which investments are made and where they go, and they do much of the heavy lifting.

Microfinance, the raison d'être for Women's World Banking, inverts that paradigm. Its chief premise is that grassroots initiatives are the ultimate drivers of development. Small entrepreneurs create wealth where there is none, and when millions can be stimulated to do so in unison, much wealth follows. While railroad systems and banking regulations, for example, are essential to American commerce, the commerce itself is produced by Bill Gates, Sam Walton, and the thousands of other entrepreneurs who create new value and collectively do more for economic growth than all the structural adjustments and infrastructural projects put together. Vibrant economies have learned how to excite entrepreneurial initiative; stagnant economies have not.

For the tiniest of entrepreneurs, the biggest barrier is neither ideas nor energy but simply cash: for raw material to create a craft product, fertilizer for a cash crop, or payroll for an office staff. Conventional banks will not touch small start-ups since they require too little money and look too risky. Microfinance circumvents both barriers by combining nascent entrepreneurs into borrowing groups that make for larger loans and smaller risks.

The world's best-known practitioner of the art is Grameen Bank in Bangladesh. Its founder and director for the past two decades, Muhammad Yunus, formulated many of the concepts that are worldwide practice now, and hundreds of similar institutions have been founded in dozens of countries. In Bolivia, it is Banco Solidario. Its competitors distribute three quarters of their loans in blocks of $100,000 or more. Banco Sol, as it is known, writes loans a fraction that size, but its default rate beats the rest of Bolivian banking system by far, in large part because Banco Sol lends money to groups of at least three customers who jointly commit to repaying it and accept training on how to manage it. The formula works: just 0.04 percent of its accounts are more than thirty days in arrears—one hundredth the rate for the whole Bolivian banking system—and Banco Sol has become the country's largest commercial bank and one of its most profitable. What works in Bolivia and Bangladesh should work almost anywhere, but microfinancing still has far to go: by one U.N. estimate in the early 1990s, the world's poorest 20 percent draw only 0.2 percent of bank lending.

The Rise of Women's World Banking

WOMEN'S WORLD BANKING was conceived in 1975 during the United Nations' first world conference on women. Meeting in Mexico City, ten women from nearly as many countries devised a blueprint for an organization led by professional women to assist poor women. Four years later, they formalized their ideas as a Dutch nonprofit organization with the mission of expanding low-income women's "participation and power" by opening their "access to finance, information and markets."

Breaking with traditional welfare concepts, the new entity viewed poor women not as "passive beneficiaries of social services" but rather as "dynamic economic agents" in their own right. Instead of running projects with "top-down control from elsewhere," WWB's strategy has been to foster "self-determined local organizations" that will respond to "local needs" with "mutual accountability" and "lateral learning." Its first president, Michaela Walsh, came not from the world of development or welfare but from investment banking, relinquishing a lucrative partnership with Boettcher & Company, a Wall Street financial firm, to launch the fledgling enterprise.

By the time WWB offered its presidency to Nancy Barry, fifteen years after the Mexico City meeting, it had built a network of locally incorporated affiliates in thirty-five countries on five continents. In South Africa it was Women's Development Banking; in Nepal, Women's Entrepreneurial Association; in Ecuador, Corporación Femenina Ecuatoriana. Each has its own board, staff, and policies; all are committed to microfinance.

The worldwide affiliates dispense or insure thousands of tiny loans, and they do so in ways that make commercial bankers blanch. Personal jewelry often serves as collateral, as well it must since most loan recipients have little else worth pledging. WWB affiliates sometimes arrange for neighborhood groups to take responsibility for individual loans. It can be a potent preventive device: when one member is faltering, others are quick to render advice. It is also a powerful collection contrivance: if one member fails, others will repay the defaulter's share to preserve their own creditworthiness.

WWB affiliates do not subsidize their loans; though nonprofit, they are not welfare agencies. The affiliates charge more than commercial banks charge their prime customers but less than what informal lenders charge. (Some informal moneylenders demand as much as 10 percent *per day*.) The affiliates' interest rates are high enough to cover their costs, necessary for sustainability, but low enough to attract the poor, essential for practicality.

Before extending a $100,000 loan to a megaenterprise, a traditional bank insists on a thorough examination of its creditworthiness. Before issuing a $100 loan to a microenterprise, WWB can only hope it is guessing right. One auspicious sign is that the loan applicant already has a business under way, but it is still so pint-sized that its footprints are essentially nonexistent. Often the entrepreneur does not even view her business as a business; she is simply making ends meet by repeatedly producing some item of local value. But if she has been doing so for a while, it tells WWB that she is a self-starter and with a little credit and training she can do far better.

While WWB affiliates have only limited proven performance by which to weigh prospective borrowers, they more than make up for the missing due diligence through recurrent risk reassessment. WWB repayment schedules are often monthly, allowing loan officers to nip budding problems before they bloom, and borrowing periods are short, often six months. Moreover, since neither the amount nor the duration of the first investment is sufficient for takeoff, the women who succeed with their initial credit line typically come back for more. Of necessity, WWB bankers rely on a relationship based on repeated small loans to evaluate capacity rather than on a single all-out credit check before the big one. As a result, the default rate on their loans is less than 3 percent, on a par with the best of commercial banks. And the recurrent borrowing works: a study of Grameen Bank loan recipients found that after ten years of loans, 46 percent of the borrowers had risen out of poverty, compared with only 4 percent of nonborrowers. Grameen-served villages also evolved significantly higher wage rates than others, confirming the hypothesis that microcredit schemes enhance community as well as individual prosperity.

WWB affiliates use their own limited capital to underwrite some of their microcredit portfolio, but they also serve as matchmaker. An established lender may routinely make loans of $300,000 but balk at loans of $300 each for 1,000 people. "Most commercial bankers still think a guy in a three-piece suit, regardless of his credit rating, is a better credit risk than a poor black, brown, yellow, or white woman," Barry complains. If area banks cannot see a market among poor women or lack a staff to service so many loans, WWB affiliates make the market: they borrow $300,000 from the bank, slice it a thousand ways, and locate those craving a single slice. That way, commercial bankers see a return without also having to look at a thousand bedraggled women clogging their lobbies.

Loans can be as small as $50 or as large at $100,000—to a dairy cooperative in Thailand—but most are in the $500 range. One Gambian recipient illustrates the low end: she borrowed $50 to buy a barrel of toothpaste and profitably resold it to passersby by the spoonful.

Others have carved out slightly larger crannies, as seen in the prosperity of two Ghanians. Rejoice Grette Dekuku had raised enough money from family and friends to make and sell a limited number of batik fabrics that carry a message. "A lot of my work features scenes of women farming, cooking, and taking care of children," she explained. "Their hard work must never go underappreciated!" Yet her own hard work went unappreciated by local lenders, and she was forced to acquire her raw materials from suppliers at exorbitant interest rates. Two WWB loans and one training program later, Dekuku was prospering. Similarly, Janet Konadu had sold eggs at a truck stop for years, but her razor-thin margins had always prohibited stocking more than a few at a time. Local moneylenders demand interest payments of 100 percent or more for short periods, but a loan from a WWB affiliate in mid-1994 allowed Konadu to fill her shelves. Customers were drawn by the display, and within a year her sales were up by two thirds, enough to finance the building of a home for herself, her husband, and their seven children.

The Global Catalyst

THE GLUE WAS the New York office of Women's World Banking—a service center, communication hub, and program catalyst. From her president's office, Nancy Barry now supported an international network of more than a thousand affiliate staff members. She backed affiliate operations with cash from donors ranging from the Ford Foundation to the Dutch government. She trained their managers with two-week programs in balance sheets, income statements, and loan portfolios. And she cross-fertilized their managers by subsidizing mutual consultation: the directors of the Kenyan and Ugandan affiliates spent a week advising and learning from the other.

Like any franchise system, consistent performance is key. To qualify, a would-be affiliate must approach the New York office, not the other way around; bring at least $20,000 in local capital; commit to microfinance for poor women; and develop a business plan. That "separates the women from the girls," Barry

Janet Konadu, client of Women's World Banking, Ghana

reports. When an affiliate later falls short—as did one in the Caribbean that lent indiscriminately and another in Africa that was rent with conflict—New York withholds financing or even cancels the franchise. In all, it has voided thirteen affiliates during Nancy's seven-year reign, up from just four during the prior decade.

With New York backing, the WWB affiliates lobby local banks for more favorable treatment of poor women. At the urging of the Kenya affiliate, Britain's Barclays Bank, for example, no longer requires local women to obtain a husband's signature when acquiring a loan. At the suggestion of the Dominican Republic affiliate, local banks now issue credit cards to small-business women for the purchase of raw materials, recasting microfinancing into the more familiar consumer credit. An Indian affiliate is now training loan officers at a local bank in how to reach and work with poor women. At the instigation of a Colombian affiliate, WWB operations are finally recognized as bona fide banks, eligible for low interbank lending rates.

Underlying WWB's microfinance agenda is a development strategy transcending the banking system. WWB knows that men invest 40 percent of their income in their children's education and health, while women devote better than 90 percent. More disposable income in the hands of women now will translate into a smarter, healthier workforce later. "The object of our loan is not to help poor women survive," explains Barry, but to help poor women and their children "become less poor."

Matching Your Organization with Your Vision

FROM HER EARLY years in Tanzania and Peru, and even in Acapulco, Nancy Barry had been drawn to making right what is wrong. During her later years with the World Bank, she became convinced that microfinancing was *the* way to right the wrong. Millions of low-income women, she felt, were ready to solve their own problems if they could acquire the right resources. By the late 1980s, Barry would have seemed to be in a position to muster those resources, if only she could steer the World Bank's enormous talent pool and $15 billion budget in the right direction.

But Barry had also become persuaded that while the World Bank was committed to ending privation among the world's poor, it was just too top-down in design and too arm's-length in mentality to render the assistance the destitute require. The "future of the world," Barry concludes, "is not going to come out of the large, rigid, monolithic structures. It is going to come

Women's World Banking affiliate leaders meeting in Mexico City, 1994

from organizations, no matter how big they are, that act like small businesses: flexible, responsive, continuously learning."

WWB's New York operation was sure to act small because it was small. Instead of managing twenty-five professionals who oversee the investment of billions of dollars, Barry would be overseeing an office of four who shaped the investment of several million. "I knew there was almost no staff," she recalls, "and I had a gnawing worry that I would show up here and be managing air." It was not quite air: WWB had built a capital fund of $6 million. Yet from this Barry would have to guarantee affiliates' loans and cover all expenses. At the World Bank, she enjoyed abundant administrative support. At WWB, she knew, "If you don't buy your own pencils, you won't have pencils." The one secretary at WWB worked mainly on her nails, and when the newly arrived, hardworking Barry suggested that office work should be a priority, the secretary told her to "get a life." Working with WWB numbers, Barry later relates, often required removing six zeros from the figures she had managed at the World Bank.

Still, Barry's personal vision of where the world should be going fit far better with WWB's focus on microfinance. And her conception of the right organizational form fit far better with WWB as well. The World Bank had built its loan programs for small borrowers from zero to $3.3 billion during Barry's fifteen years there, but she had concluded that such programs would always be flawed by the bank's size and structure. "The only way to establish the right kinds of relationships, of lateral learning, of mutual accountability for results," she believes, is through institutions "that do not look like large corporate structures." Centralized program control is the problem; decentralized decision making, the solution. When it comes to targeting a loan recipient, it "has got to be people in the local banking and business community who have a relationship with that client, who can use their noses to make that kind of judgment," she argues. "Only they can decide for a set of poor women entrepreneurs what is the mix of credit, savings, training, and commercial links that will allow them to get beyond survival to growth."

Since Barry's choice had become a matter of principled change versus practical contentment, and since her comfort and security at the World Bank were growing with age, the change, she decided, had better come now. "If I didn't do it at the age of forty," she confesses, "I probably never would." It was the moment to "put my mind and spirit where my mouth is." One colleague asked, "Why are you leaving when you have such a great career?" Another told her that her decision was "nuts." Happily, a third colleague counseled her that WWB was the future, the World Bank the past. And her father, self-made entrepreneur that he was, reassured her that finally she would have a real job.

For Barry, though, the fit with WWB was two-way. WWB was poised to grow and needed to expand if its mission of serving millions were ever to be realized. Doing so would require as much verve from the affiliates as from the hub. It would also require enlisting hundreds of established institutions into the cause. Barry's experience in promoting decentralization from above and empowerment from below would serve the firm well. So, too, would her missionary's zeal to spread the gospel and her personal reputation with leading financiers around the world. WWB required Nancy Barry's personal and organizational commitments as much as she sought its.

For both Nancy Barry and WWB, the moment might seem propitious, but for Barry the transition still seemed fraught with danger. The landscape of American corporate life is filled with examples of those who, like Barry, made the right leap at the right time for the right reasons; but it is equally littered with examples of those who didn't.

When Alex Mandl, then the number two executive at AT&T, announced in 1996 that he was abandoning America's largest telecommunications company for Associated Communications (later to be renamed Teligent Corporation), a start-up firm that was focusing on small-business services, many in big business wondered how he possibly could relinquish staff, perks, and corporate jets, not to mention a clear shot at AT&T's top slot. Today, Mandl says of his new work, "I hardly see it as a job. I see it as something that's now mine, my life, my future. It is something that is much more me, much more built by me, in the context of my principles and agendas and perspectives of how a business should grow."[1]

By contrast, Michael A. Miles rose to the apex of Philip Morris Companies in 1991 through its Kraft General Foods subsidiary. Tobacco, however, was both Philip Morris's biggest cash cow and its gravest political problem, as legislators and litigators increasingly challenged the maker of Marlboro cigarettes, and by 1994, Miles's decisions on tobacco pricing, capital lobbying, and company restructuring put him at odds with both directors and investors. His track record up the food side of the company had been stellar, but he had moved into the top suite at a time when another set of strategic skills was required, including a stomach for aggressive counterattacks against the escalating assault on smoking. After just three years at the helm, the board replaced him with Geoffrey C. Bible, a smoker and seasoned veteran of the tobacco business.[2]

By implication: Realizing your leadership potential depends on making a match between your vision and an organization. The challenge is to find the right opportunity, pick the right moment, and make the right move.

Finding an Engine That Works

THE FACTORS THAT make poverty and welfare so perpetual—no capital, no capacity, no skills—are precisely what microfinance promises to overcome. Best of all, microfinance is a perpetual-motion machine, a self-sustaining construct that balances the interests of lender and client. WWB affiliates do not merely root for the poor; they have a built-in incentive to make sure the poor succeed because it is only with high repayment rates and repeated borrowing by its clients that an affiliate can pay its own bills and expand its coverage. The clients have equal incentive to make the affiliate succeed: only with solvency and growth by the affiliate can their future loans be assured. Adding to the cash of one adds to the cash of the other. Rarely are the interests of the poor and nonpoor so well aligned to ensure that the success of each depends on that of the other.

Entomologist Peter Kenmore has brought much the same perpetual-motion reasoning into play in his fine-tuning of the "green revolution" that swept across the rice paddies of Southeast Asia. Thanks to the revolution and its fourfold approach—improved seed, better irrigation, more fertilizer, and stronger pesticides—rice farmers have doubled their yield in millions of paddies from India to Indonesia. Yet such short-term success has come at a disastrous long-term cost. Pesticides destroy indiscriminately: both rice-devouring pests and their natural enemies. Inevitably, a few of the most genetically favored pests survive, and with the field cleared of enemies, their ranks grow back far stronger than ever, and farmers must lay down ever more toxic levels of pesticides to combat them.

To fight this cycle, Kenmore promotes what has become known as "integrated pest management," or IPM. Instead of pesticides, farmers fight bad bugs with good ones. The program trains farmers in the principles of field biology, entomology, and hydrology. Given that millions lack even the rudiments of literacy and numeracy, the task is daunting, but there is no other way since the ecology of each rice field is different. Once expert, farmers can accomplish without pesticides what they could achieve before only with them. The results, like those from microenterprise, are tangible: by eliminating the need to purchase pesticides—some 30 percent of the cost of rice growing—IPM farmers effectively increase their disposable income by the same amount. Once hooked, they become natural recruiters of others: their success depends on other growers adopting the same methods since they are all part of the same ecosystem.[3]

Defying the principles of physics, both Kenmore and Barry have created machines that require little more than an initial prodding from the outside. Once in motion, the machines are self-propelling. The challenge is to supply a small nudge to large numbers, and that is the essence of the punch delivered by the IPM and microcredit programs. Both have created world-wide vehicles for jump-starting the initiative of millions—and then getting out of the way as the poor work to overcome their own poverty.

By implication: In serving others—whether low-income women, rice-growing farmers, or dividend-hungry investors—finding a self-sustaining engine that works is an essential step in delivering value to them.

Unifying Opposites

COMMERCIAL BANKERS SEE no value in marketing to the insolvent; social workers see no value in commercializing assistance to the poor. Conservative and liberal, self-help versus state aid, the two worlds operate on the basis of clashing gestalts and opposing rules; growth and profit for one, uplift and equity for the second. Nancy Barry's message to each side is to learn from the other if results are to be achieved. At a 1996 forum for mainstream bankers sponsored by the U.S. comptroller of the currency, for example, she reminded them that they were forgoing a rich profit stream by ignoring low-income borrowers. At the 1995 Beijing forum for women, she reminded them that they were forgoing a self-sustaining engine by subsidizing low-income borrowers.

Mamphela Ramphele advocates much the same tactics in bringing black students into white universities. With Steven Biko, Ramphele had helped found South Africa's black consciousness movement in the 1960s. After a tumultuous career as a physician and antiapartheid activist, Ramphele earned her doctorate in anthropology in 1991 and joined the faculty of the University of Cape Town, arguably the nation's leading university. Four years later, with apartheid ended, Ramphele became a candidate for the institution's highest post, vice chancellor, but her status as a national heroine appeared to count for little. With her candidacy pending before the largely white faculty senate, a convocation of mostly black students—in a school now nearly half black—gathered to hear her views, and few offered comfort. One speaker denounced her candidacy as "insidious and insincere," little more than a personal pursuit of prestige and pay. Others accused her of doing too little to assist them, especially in moderating the elite standards that had long defined the university's operations.

In the face of such attacks, Ramphele remained unrelenting, rejecting the "culture of entitlement" and insisting that blacks and whites meet the same professional standards. By the end, she had won over much of the student audience and, more important, enough of the university faculty. Several weeks later, faculty members narrowly approved her elevation to become the institution's first female head and first black leader. Ramphele's views remained unequivocal throughout: "Contrary to popular myth, poor people did not struggle in order to have equal access to mediocrity."[4]

By implication: Bound by no convention, combine what works best from even the most opposed traditions.

Thinking Big for Becoming Big

IN 1994, Women's World Banking estimated that microcredit from all sources was reaching just a fraction of those who needed it—8 million out of an estimated 500 million people who run micro- or small businesses worldwide. WWB's goal, Nancy Barry decided, should be universal credit access, not welfare charity, for all. But getting there would require a delivery capacity far beyond what she had inherited, local affiliates far stronger than those she had acquired, and a worldwide movement far greater than what she saw.

Expansion of WWB thus became a priority, and in Barry's first seven years at the helm, she increased its capital assets from $6 million to $30 million, its New York staff from 6 to 30, and its worldwide affiliate staff from 100 to 1,000. Strengthening the WWB affiliates was also a priority; to do so, she pressed for sovereignty in place of dependence. Affiliates had expected New York to provide 80 percent of their direction and service. Now they knew only 20 percent would come from the hub; the rest would have to come from themselves.

The microcredit movement also required radical expansion since WWB could never shoulder more than a fraction of the load. Yet WWB could play a role in stimulating outside interest, and Barry was determined to make that happen. In 1991, the World Bank formed a Donor's Committee on Small Enterprise Development, and Barry joined it. In 1994, the United Nations formed an Expert Group on Women and Finance, and she chaired that. And when still another vehicle was needed, she created it, enlisting fifty leaders from finance ministries, central banks, and microcredit agencies into a Global Policy Forum to foster financing for the poor.

At the first U.N. Conference on Women, held in Mexico City in 1975, microfinancing was barely discussed, and then mainly by the ten women who would subsequently form WWB. The final communiqué from Mexico City contained but a single sentence on women and credit. By the Fourth World Conference on Women in Beijing in 1995, credit had become a leading issue, and the final communiqué called for economic empowerment of women and wide access to credit. Barry associated the microcredit agenda with history's great tides. The "movement is comparable to the abolition of slavery," she argued. "It really is an economic revolution."

Barry also works to redirect the priorities of national and international development agencies. "We want to reallocate existing aid to microfinance schemes," she asserts, since, in her view, they are more efficient than government spending and far more durable. Once the poor have incomes of their own, she argues, "they can look out for themselves." The giants of the development community have been listening. In 1995, the U.S. Agency for International Development tripled its budget for small-scale lending to $140 million, and the World Bank announced a new $200 million microfinancing program for the poor.

In 1997, the movement's momentum reached the White House. With Nancy Barry among the organizers, Hillary Clinton cohosted a microfinance conference that drew 2,900 people from 137 countries. "Whether we are talking about a rural area in south Asia or an inner city in the United States," Clinton proclaimed, "microcredit is an invaluable tool in alleviating poverty, promoting self-sufficiency, and stimulating economic activity in some of the world's most destitute and disadvantaged communities." Nancy Barry could not have said it better. The Microcredit Summit launched a global campaign to reach 100 million of the poorest families by 2005.

The goals of the campaign seem staggering. To add another 92 million people to the rolls of those already receiving microcredit will require $22 billion in new grants, low-interest loans, and commercial lending. The individual loans will be nearly infinitesimal by the normal standards of banking: 88 million Third World recipients are targeted for loans averaging only $200 each, while 4 million recipients in the industrialized nations will gets loans averaging $1,000 each. Collectively, the campaign aims to extend microcredit to a fifth of all the people on the face of the earth who presently lack it. Nancy Barry, though, does not want to stop there. Just as Roy Vagelos is determined to distribute Mectizan to all 20 million people across the globe who are threatened with river blindness, so Barry is determined to expand microcredit to *everyone* who needs it. "If sometimes we sound evangelical," Barry told the summit, "it is because we are trying to change the world." And the world was already changing. James D. Wolfensohn, president of the World Bank, offered at the Microcredit Summit what his predecessors during Barry's time at the bank would never have said: "I am personally, absolutely, and totally committed to this activity."

By implication: If big is the only way to achieve your mission, thinking big no matter how small you start is the only way to reach it.

Connectedness

"THE CONNECTEDNESS OF who we are and what we do," Barry reflects, "is totally related to our effectiveness." At WWB she has found an effectiveness that has eluded her in the past. Despite Barry's abundant success at the World Bank, for her it was not the right place; WWB is. Undergirding Barry's vision of where she is going is an underlying conception of what she should be. "I believe that we were put on Earth for a purpose," she confides. "For me, that purpose is most simply put in the word 'connectedness.' Connectedness, first, to the power that is greater than ourselves; secondly, connectedness to purpose, which in my case, given my destiny, is a connectedness with poor people and opening up access so that poor people can change their own destinies and realize their own God-given talents."

As a favored speaker at development forums around the world, she uses her opportunities to press the cause, even among those least likely to embrace it. After a 1994 presentation at the World Bank, Barry was asked how it should change, and she bluntly urged:

• *New policies:* The World Bank now "specializes in what governments should not do."

• *More responsibility:* The bank is repaid even when projects fail, undermining its "accountability for results."

• *Revived culture:* The bank should be cultivating integrity and openness, yet both had been more evident when she joined the bank than when she left it.

• *Clients first:* Private discussion obsesses on getting ahead instead of helping the poor get ahead.

*Nancy Barry and Chandra Jagaria, a used-clothing vendor and
microcredit borrower in India*

• *Less bureaucracy:* The bank should break its monolithic
structure into a lattice of "small, strong, and purposeful organizations."

• *More innovation:* The bank needs "not another reshuffling
of the boxes" but fresh air from the outside.

• *Narrowed gap:* The bank should close the breach between
"who you are" and "what you do."

At the 1996 biennial meeting for WWB affiliates in Nairobi,
Kenya, Barry reminded herself and affiliate leaders why they
were there: "What we are trying to do in the WWB is one of
the most important things on earth because through one simple
measure—opening up low-income women entrepreneurs'
access to financial information and markets—everything else
changes."

As a speaker at the 1997 Microcredit Summit shortly after her father had passed away, she told the audience of several thousand, "He was a very spiritual man, he recognized that we cannot do it alone, and he put his beliefs into action." He, too, had a calling: "He lived a life of small actions, with big ripple effects, and ended up fulfilling the purpose of his life." Like father, like daughter.

CHAPTER 9

❖

Alfredo Cristiani Ends
El Salvador's Civil War

"I looked at the country the way I looked at my business."

REBELS HAD INVADED El Salvador's capital, San Salvador, seizing entire neighborhoods. Residents were stunned to see masked guerrillas brandishing Soviet-made AK-47 assault rifles on their streets and U.S.-made A-37 attack jets flying overhead, unloading explosives on their homes. President Alfredo F. Cristiani, only five months in office, was horrified. The city was being overrun in what threatened to become El Salvador's own Tet offensive, a turning point in a protracted struggle that might signal the beginning of the end.

Four nations in Central America—El Salvador, Guatemala, Honduras, and Nicaragua—had long been convulsed with civil strife. The toll in destroyed lives and wrecked economies had been devastating, and El Salvador's struggle had been as costly as any. By 1989, as Cristiani took his oath of office, 70,000 Salvadorans had lost their lives—and this in a population of only 6 million. An equivalent percentage of the United States population today would amount to 3 million dead; an equal percentage in 1860 would have amounted to 360,000 people, close to the total number of deaths among Union and Confederate soldiers combined. Proportionally, the Salvadoran conflict had become as bloody as America's own Civil War.

The struggle, in fact, was three-sided. The guerrillas, who called themselves the Farabundo Martí National Liberation Front (FMLN) were an amalgam of five insurgent groups functioning under a unified command but with separate armies. The government of El Salvador itself was ruled by the Nationalist Republican Alliance (ARENA), a right-wing political party brought to power by its charismatic founder, ex–army major Roberto d'Aubuisson. And the Salvadoran military, nominally an arm of the government, operated as a force unto itself, a separate power in the struggle for supremacy.

The FMLN presided over much of the country's north and northeast and was encroaching elsewhere. D'Aubuisson, whose association with "death squads" had made him unpalatable both to the international community and to many at home, had picked Alfredo Cristiani, a businessman without a political record, to serve as ARENA's presidential candidate. During the campaign, Cristiani promised "permanent dialogue" with the FMLN, and the voters elected him to a five-year presidency.

But events just before and after Cristiani's inauguration were hardly auspicious for dialogue. El Salvador's attorney general, Roberto García Alvarado, was killed by a bomb placed under the roof of his jeep, and just nine days into the new administration, the minister of the presidency, José Antonio Rodríguez Porth, was assassinated.

The government and FMLN held desultory discussions in Mexico City in September and one month later in Costa Rica. As the talks in Costa Rica were ending, the daughter of a powerful army colonel was slain outside her San Salvador home. A few days later, the residence of a prominent opposition politician was blown up, and the headquarters of a trade union was soon bombed, killing ten. The FMLN called Cristiani's rejection of its peace terms a "virtual declaration of war."

The rebels launched a general offensive on November 11, tying up major areas of the capital city and other urban centers. In the early-morning hours of November 16, with much of the city under siege, an army commando unit slipped through the

President Alfredo Cristiani

gates of the University of Central America. The soldiers roused five Jesuit priests from their beds, including the rector of the university, Ignacio Ellacuría; forced them to the ground in a nearby courtyard; and shot them in the back of the head. A sixth priest and a groundskeeper and her daughter, accidental witnesses to the massacre, were murdered as well.

The international community was in an uproar. Many suspected—correctly, as would later become evident—that senior army officers had ordered the killings. The U.S. Congress condemned the violence in El Salvador, and Connecticut Senator Christopher Dodd warned that Cristiani would have to demonstrate that he was "in control of his government." The stakes were great: the United States had already donated $4 billion to the government and was now supporting it at a rate of $1.4 million a day.

Alfredo Cristiani had held office for less than six months. A former coffee grower, he was now president of a country facing disintegration after years of bitter struggle. His air force wanted to bomb the neighborhoods where the guerrillas were ensconced.

His armed opponents wanted to wipe him and his government from the face of the earth.

The Conflict

EL SALVADOR HAD been home to one of Latin America's longest and bloodiest civil wars, a product of endemic conflict between wealthy landowners and impoverished peasants, between military corps and civilian elites, between the doctrines of capitalism and socialism.

In October 1979, when reform-minded army officers staged—with the blessing of the United States—a coup d'état, they sought to curb the influence of the most conservative military circles, and they pushed a two-pronged program of land reform and guerrilla suppression. But none of the initiatives proved successful. A proposed agrarian redistribution would have affected 60 percent of the coffee-growing land, but most of the plan was shelved. Steps to rein in the army and check the rebels achieved little. Concluding that an entrenched military was thwarting all reform, progressive groups were increasingly drawn to the insurgents. Convinced that an empowered peasantry would surely transform modest change into socialist revolution, conservative circles moved further to the right.

Roberto d'Aubuisson was among those cashiered from the armed services by the junta reformers, and he gathered around him disgruntled elements of the right, both military and civilian. D'Aubuisson had served as a ranking official in the Salvadoran National Security Agency, the army's intelligence arm. Now, with files taken from its offices, he compiled a list of those suspected of collaborating with the left and encouraged the "death squads" to do their job.

On March 24, 1980, the Catholic archbishop of El Salvador, Oscar Arnulfo Romero, was saying mass in the chapel at San Salvador's Divine Providence Hospital, where he was also a resident. The day before, he had concluded a homily by condemning the rising violence: "Before an order to kill given by man,

FMLN members in northern El Salvador, 1984

the law of God must prevail that says, 'Thou shalt not kill.' " He had appealed to troops on the front line: "No soldier is obliged to obey an order that is against the law of God." To military officers it was a call to mutiny. A sniper slipped inside the chapel, fired a single shot, and fled.

Archbishop Romero's funeral resulted in further tragedy. As a representative of Pope John Paul II neared the end of his eulogy in Metropolitan Cathedral, a bomb exploded among the 30,000 people who had gathered on the steps. More bombs burst, shooting erupted, and as mourners surged into the cathedral, forty were crushed to death or shot in the melee.

By this time, assassinations were averaging a staggering 750 per month. The Sandinista overthrow of Nicaraguan dictator Anastasio Somoza Debayle on July 19, 1979, added to the growing sense of crisis. The Sandinista government became a shining symbol and ally for the Salvadoran insurgents—and a warning of what Salvadoran and U.S. governing circles were desperate to avoid. Members of the defeated Nicaraguan

Soldiers on patrol in San Salvador, 1988

National Guard fled through El Salvador, and their loss of property, prosperity, and homeland made an indelible impression on the Salvadoran National Guard. Nicaragua is closer to Miami than Miami is to Washington, warned President Ronald Reagan, and El Salvador is nearer Texas than Texas is to Massachusetts.

The FMLN's combatant strength was estimated at 10,000 or more, and in the aftermath of a dramatic 1983 FMLN attack on an army encampment, it seemed that the insurgents might have battled their way to a draw, or better. Prominent families and executives sought refuge abroad. One business leader commuted daily by air between Guatemala City and San Salvador, unable to run his business from abroad but afraid to spend the night in his hometown. "There were days," U.S. Ambassador Thomas Pickering would later say, "when we wondered whether we would make it through the next two or three months."

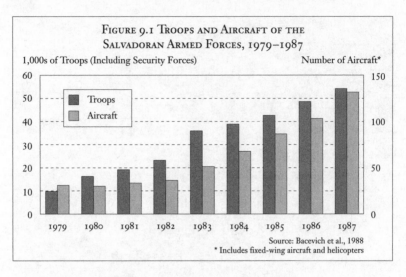

FIGURE 9.1 TROOPS AND AIRCRAFT OF THE
SALVADORAN ARMED FORCES, 1979–1987

1,000s of Troops (Including Security Forces)   Number of Aircraft*

Source: Bacevich et al., 1988
* Includes fixed-wing aircraft and helicopters

With generous U.S. backing, the Salvadoran military rapidly expanded its numbers and munitions during the next several years (see Figure 9.1). At the same time, efforts were made to open negotiations, but neither side embraced the concept since each still saw victory at the end of the tunnel.

Roberto d'Aubuisson campaigned for the national presidency as the ARENA candidate in 1984, and he was almost as harsh on political reformers as he was on the FMLN. To him, the similarities outweighed the differences. He was fond of calling the main centrist group—the Christian Democratic Party—a "watermelon," green on the outside and red on the inside.[1]

Despite such harsh rhetoric, centrist candidate José Napoleón Duarte decisively defeated d'Aubuisson, and his victory impressed U.S. policy makers. In accord with the 1984 recommendations of the U.S. National Bipartisan Commission on Central America—the "Kissinger Commission"—the Reagan administration further expanded economic assistance to bolster the government, doubling its 1984 contribution of $216 million to $434 million in 1985 (see Figure 9.2)

The FMLN responded by intensifying its use of economic

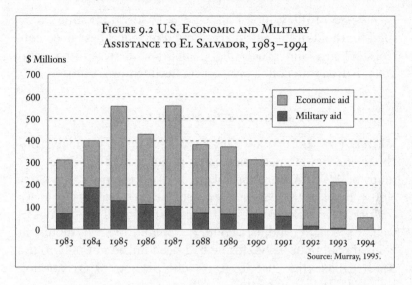

FIGURE 9.2 U.S. ECONOMIC AND MILITARY
ASSISTANCE TO EL SALVADOR, 1983–1994

$ Millions

Economic aid
Military aid

Source: Murray, 1995.

sabotage, destroying railroads, auto bridges, public buses, and electrical lines (see Figure 9.3). Nothing was sacred: guerrillas seized a cattle farm and used machine guns and grenades to slaughter 204 milk cows. The FMLN also targeted the nation's number one cash crop, coffee. In 1978, coffee had accounted for

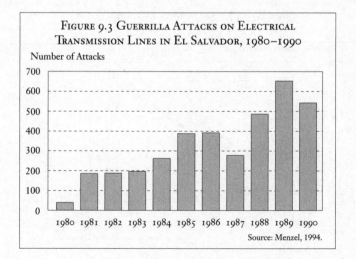

FIGURE 9.3 GUERRILLA ATTACKS ON ELECTRICAL
TRANSMISSION LINES IN EL SALVADOR, 1980–1990

Number of Attacks

Source: Menzel, 1994.

241

53 percent of the value of all exports; it was the nation's only solid foothold in the world economy. But rebels destroyed coffee stockpiles and processing plants, and between 1980 and 1989, Salvadoran coffee production declined by a third.

Cristiani's Ascent to Office

WHILE THE RELATIVE strengths of the military and FMLN ebbed and flowed, near the end of the decade the political fortunes of ARENA were ascendant. In 1988 elections, the party won control of the national legislature and a majority of mayoralties. The 1989 presidential election could fall to ARENA as well, if the right candidate could be found. Robert d'Aubuisson knew it could not be he, for he had been linked not only to the death squads but also to the 1980 slaying of Archbishop Romero. He looked instead to Alfredo Cristiani.

Until the 1980s, Cristiani had prospered as a coffee grower in El Salvador's flourishing economy. Like so many others, he was appalled by the escalating violence, and he was aghast to see the economy in reverse. By 1989, the gross domestic product per

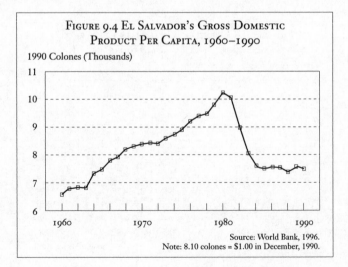

FIGURE 9.4 EL SALVADOR'S GROSS DOMESTIC
PRODUCT PER CAPITA, 1960–1990

1990 Colones (Thousands)

Source: World Bank, 1996.
Note: 8.10 colones = $1.00 in December, 1990.

capita had declined to levels not seen for two decades (see Figure 9.4). As a conservative businessman, he also feared the growing success of radical movements in Central and South America. The Sandinista victory in Nicaragua had ominous portents both for his nation and for his own livelihood.

Cristiani's father was of Italian heritage, his mother Swiss. The family table had featured spaghetti one night, sauerkraut the next. He had attended the American School in San Salvador, and in 1968 he graduated with a business major from Georgetown University in Washington, D.C., where he had been a classmate of another future president, Bill Clinton. Cristiani was a good student, but he also relished sports: he had played on the Salvadoran National Basketball Team and had won a national squash championship.

Cristiani valued friendship and from his early years had built a diverse network of loyal acquaintants. They knew "Freddy" as relaxed and convivial, but they also recognized an enterprising side that was organized and competitive. From his father he acquired a habit of hearing before deciding and of remaining tranquil in adversity. From his mother came a relentless energy and drive for achievement.

A family pharmacy in San Salvador generated a modest but respectable income during Cristiani's childhood, enough for his parents in 1955 to purchase a coffee farm perched on the fertile slopes of a dormant volcano just two hours by car from San Salvador. His mother came to oversee the plantation, while his father exported its produce and managed the pharmacy. Cristiani worked on the family farm during school vacations, and as he associated with the rural workers and their children, he acquired an appreciation for those of diverse stations.

Upon graduation from Georgetown, Cristiani applied his management studies to coffee growing. By then the farm was employing two hundred year-round and seven hundred at harvesttime, and work assignments, employee payrolls, and balance sheets filled Cristiani's twentysomething years. So did decisions about fertilizer costs, pruning techniques, and labor productivity. By convention, each worker carried a saw, shears, and machete for trimming the trees, but Cristiani created teams of three, each working with a different tool, for faster pruning during the short growing season.

Cristiani also discovered the value of hands-on management. He worked with the rank and file to mulch the unproductive coffee leaves, and after a day's harvest, he frequently joined his work crew in the national pastime, a game of soccer. He appreciated the merit of walking around well before it became a publicized virtue in Tom Peters and Robert Waterman's *In Search of Excellence*.

A decade of growing family prosperity, however, was about to be undone by events far beyond the family's control. Cristiani's brother had purchased his own farm, but it had been expropriated after the 1979 army coup and he had resettled in Guatemala. Cristiani's farm was near a growing FMLN stronghold, and in 1980 local guerrilla leaders told him that they would soon be taking over. When he pleaded for a delay to allow harvesting of the nearly ripe crop, his peasant workers passed word that he was not to be harmed and the harvesting was to be permitted. But the rebels set up a regional headquarters on the property soon thereafter, and Cristiani fled to the capital.

Two years later the army recaptured the farm, and Cristiani flew the forty miles from San Salvador to have his first look. As his helicopter landed, he was appalled to see bomb craters and bullet marks everywhere. The coffee trees were overgrown with tropical brush. The home where he had spent so much of his youth was gone; only the cement foundation remained. He stayed only two hours, not to return until after the peace settlement a decade later.

Until now, Cristiani had shown scant interest in politics, but when ARENA friends asked him to help monitor ballot counting on national election day in 1984, he volunteered. "In trying to become a politician," Cristiani recalls, "I had no interest whatsoever." But he was available: even his coffee mill, five miles from the farm and one of the few family enterprises remaining, came under repeated FMLN assault. "We had a lot of time to spare," he recalls.

Within a year, d'Aubuisson asked if Cristiani would move up to general party secretary, succeeding d'Aubuisson himself. The hard-driving, forty-five-year-old party architect and evangelist remained the kingmaker, and he decided that Cristiani best represented the party's future. When Cristiani returned from a business trip to the United States in mid-1988, he was surprised to find d'Aubuisson and other party officials waiting for him in his home. He first guessed that they must have come to discuss ARENA's candidate for the 1989 presidential election. He was right about the topic, but they had already done the discussing: it was to be he. "You ought to get somebody with more political experience," he objected. But d'Aubuisson answered, "The people are not going to vote for a politician. They are tired of politicians. What they want is somebody who can do things and solve problems."

Cristiani's past was respectable to many voters, party faithful, and Washington officials. His vision was settlement, his style pragmatic. During a presidential debate among the four leading candidates, he concluded by confirming his agreement with 85 percent of what had been said, adding that he was ready for dialogue with ARENA's archenemy, the FMLN. On June 1, 1989, Cristiani accepted the presidential sash from the outgoing Duarte and pledged a government based on the principles of "liberty, honesty, legality, and security." He was forty-one years old, and all hell was about to break lose.

Descent into Chaos

ON OCTOBER 31, 1989, a massive bomb exploded in a trade union office, triggering an event that would set into motion the beginning of the end. The office was the headquarters of the National Trade Union Federation of Salvadoran Workers. With a leadership associated with an insurgent group fond of kidnapping businessmen, it was not an unnatural target for the extreme right. But the explosion killed the union's general secretary, Febé Elizabeth Velázquez, a twenty-seven-year-old mother of three young children, and nine others. In its anger, the FMLN leadership broke off its dialogue with the Cristiani government and prepared to launch a long-planned general uprising.

The rebels named their insurrection "Long Live Febé Elizabeth" and set a goal of seizing and holding major sections of the capital and five other cities for at least three days. Some leaders even envisioned toppling Cristiani's government. Commencing at dusk on Saturday, November 11, four thousand FMLN guerrillas attacked police stations, army barracks, and air bases across the country. The offensive had been widely anticipated—army leaves had already been canceled—but the scale of the attack came as a shock. The security officer for the U.S. Embassy had concluded just a day before that the season's main social event, the Marine Ball, should not be postponed.

Fighting erupted in twenty separate areas of San Salvador, and residents dived for cover as bullets ricocheted off walls and shrapnel sprayed streets. Christopher Babcock, a twenty-five-year-old native of Spokane, Washington, and a social studies and English teacher at the American School, was driving home just a few doors from Cristiani's private residence when a grenade fragment fatally shattered his skull. Power was off in many neighborhoods, and explosions and Gatling guns were heard across the city throughout the night.

Guerrilla cadres with instructions to kill Cristiani infiltrated the areas around his private and presidential residences and fired handheld rockets at both, but the president and his wife were dining with friends on the shores of Lake Coatepeque, a scenic crater lake forty miles west of San Salvador. Other cadres attacked the residence of the president of the legislative assembly. Though he and his family were at home, they escaped injury.

Late that evening, several FMLN guerrillas on the run from government soldiers cut through the grounds of the University of Central America, dynamiting a gate, passing by the Jesuit residence, and vanishing into the night. The next morning, Sunday, an army unit inspected the damage and cordoned off the university, controlling who came and went. Cristiani declared in a radio broadcast at 10:30 A.M. that "the army will triumph," and later in the day he announced a suspension of constitutional guarantees and a nationwide curfew from 6 P.M. to 6 A.M.

On Wednesday evening, Colonel Guillermo Alfredo Benavides attended an emergency meeting of the armed forces' twenty-five most senior commanders at Estado Major, the fortified general staff headquarters in central San Salvador. Benavides was director of the military academy, to which a mobile brigade from the Atlacatl base had been reassigned to combat the offensive, and he was responsible for a security zone that included the university, just half a mile to the south. With much of San Salvador in enemy hands and defeat of the army possible, Benavides instructed Lieutenant José Ricardo Espinoza, commander of the Atlacatl brigade, to find the university rector and other "delinquent terrorists," who were deemed the "intellectual leaders" of the revolt. Benavides was only partially right: the rector and his charges were sympathetic to the plight of the poor, but the FMLN's intellectual capital lay elsewhere. In the heat of the moment, however, such distinctions counted for little.

The brigade already knew the campus because it had carried out the earlier inspection. "This is a situation in which it is them or us," Benavides told Espinoza. "We're going to begin at the top. . . . You did the search, and your men know the site." The rector, he added, "must be eliminated—I don't want any witnesses."

By 2 A.M. on Thursday, November 16, the assignment had been carried out with AK-47s and M-16s. The rector, five other Jesuits, and two witnesses were all dead or dying. As the Atlacatl soldiers exited the university's front gate, they replaced a sign reading "No classes today" with their own: "The FMLN executed the enemy spies. Victory or death, FMLN."

The battle for San Salvador raged for two more weeks. One of Cristiani's most difficult decisions was taken on the evening of the fourth day: his generals were asking for permission to use bombs, tanks, and artillery against neighborhoods held by the guerrillas. "Look, isn't there some other alternative?" demanded the president. The Red Cross was pleading for a cease-fire to allow noncombatants to move out of the way. Cristiani and his commanders debated the options from 6 to 10 P.M. Fearing a Beirut solution if he did not approve the counterattack, Cristiani gave the go-ahead at midnight.

A prominent business executive, Archie Baldocchi, managed to reach his downtown office every day during the offensive, but, he recalled, "it felt like you really were in Vietnam." The military and insurgents would each suffer the loss of more than 400 dead and 1,000 injured. Some 3,000 homes would be damaged in aerial and artillery attacks, 70,000 residents displaced by the fighting, and 1,000 civilians killed in the cross fire.

A Peace Accord

THE FMLN MORE than achieved its first objective of holding ground for at least seventy-two hours. But it never came close to overthrowing the Cristiani regime, and, like the military, the insurgents were sobered by the carnage.

Spurred by what was being compared with Vietnam's Tet offensive, the Salvadoran armed forces had to face a heretofore forbidden course: compromise with the enemy. The Cristiani government was ready as well. Whole sections of San Salvador were in ruins, and half of El Salvador's municipalities no longer had functioning authorities. "The intensity and duration of the offensive," wrote Richard Boudreaux and Marjorie Miller of the *Los Angeles Times*, "has mocked all official predictions and sent Cristiani's elected right-wing government reeling."

But the offensive's intensity and duration also presented an opportunity for resolution. The military was as exhausted as the

FMLN. For both, anything like a decisive victory on the battlefield seemed a faint glimmer at best. Half of the government's spending was going into prosecution of the war. Cristiani and his pragmatic allies, in the words of one diplomatic observer, just "want[ed] to get it over with." And with impeccable rightwing credentials, Cristiani was in a far better position to bring along recalcitrant military officers. The time had come for the president to make it happen.

In January 1990, Cristiani announced that Colonel Benavides and two lieutenants and six soldiers of the Atlacatl brigade were suspects in the Jesuit murders. The investigation continued for months, marked by continuous military cover-up. But the stonewalling undermined domestic and international confidence in the military and thus constrained the ability of even the hardest of the hard-liners to resist Cristiani's strategy openly.

He quickly moved to seize the advantage. On April 4, 1990, in Geneva, the Salvadoran government and the FMLN agreed to start negotiating. On May 21, in Caracas, they fixed a negotiation schedule. Two months later, on July 26, they concluded a human rights accord in Costa Rica.

When further negotiations on the future role of the Salvadoran armed forces and FMLN armed rebels floundered, both sides sought military advantage to bolster their bargaining position. The army moved to dislodge the FMLN from its long-standing rural control in the north and northeast. The FMLN, in turn, launched still more urban offensives in May, June, September, and November. With both sides jockeying for leverage, 1990 proved almost as bloody as 1989.

Finally, in September 1991, the government and FMLN agreed in New York, under U.N. auspices, to create an institution to oversee and enforce a peace agreement. They created a commission to vet members of the armed forces with an eye to removing those with a record of human rights abuses. They also established a new police force, its ranks to be a blend of the old and the new: a fifth would come from the former national police, a fifth from the FMLN cadre, the remainder from fresh recruitment. The armed forces, purged of their most abusive officers and downsized from 63,000 to 32,000 troops, would no longer be used for internal security. The FMLN was legalized.

The final peace accord was signed at the Castle of Chapultepec in Mexico City on January 16, 1992. ARENA hard-liners urged Cristiani to let his negotiators initial the accord, and he announced that he would attend but not sign. But after the agreement was signed by his six negotiators, five FMLN negotiators, and five guerrilla commanders, it was carried over to Cristiani, who added his own name in a preplanned act that few had known about in advance. In his speech to the assembled dignitaries, Cristiani called for building a "truly democratic form of life" in El Salvador. He then departed from the script and, to the pleasant amazement of those observing, walked over to the guerrillas and shook the hand of each. The room of several hundred witnesses erupted in ovation, and many viewers of the live broadcast in El Salvador would remember that moment best. "The long night of El Salvador is coming to its end," declared U.N. Secretary-General Boutros Boutros-Ghali. Huge crowds gathered in San Salvador's Plaza Cívica and Plaza Libertad to celebrate the accord. When Cristiani flew home that evening on a Boeing 737, he joined the pilot in the cockpit, and they announced his return by buzzing the rooftops around the plazas.

Conviction

FROM THE MOMENT Cristiani found the ARENA party members waiting for him in his home, he was sure that an historic opportunity was at hand, and he was committed above all else to making it happen. "You have to be totally convinced of what you are doing," Cristiani reflects. "If you try to fake it, there will come a time when you are tested, and you will fail." U.S. Ambassador William Walker described his impression of

Cristiani in a September 1989 cable to Washington: "Cristiani's motives include what I firmly believe is a personal commitment to a negotiated, constitutional solution: a conviction that further political and economic progress requires peace."

ARENA and army voices were demanding a "military solution" in the wake of the November offensive; had Cristiani escalated the armed struggle, it would have proven popular. When a three-month search for peace stretched into a three-year pursuit, the alternatives became tempting. But he remained, in the words of the chief military negotiator, a "man of coherence in a world of incoherence," an unwavering proponent of peace.

By implication: The conviction of your vision is the sine qua non for its achievement. Without a clear-minded fix on where you want to get, the opportunities and pressures for diverting from it will ensure you will not arrive there.

An Outsider's Eyes

CRISTIANI SAW THE presidency in part through the spectacles of the family-business manager that he is. "I looked at the country the way I looked at my business," he said after leaving office. "Only now I have six million shareholders, and each has one vote." Moreover, "seeing the country as a business enterprise rather than a political enterprise—in which you have to make decisions and produce results—gave me a framework and a confidence to get things done." His unpolitical past served to transform permanent "obstacles" into solvable "problems" and public cynicism into national confidence. "In politics you always tell half the truth," he says, but solving problems and building confidence requires more than that.

The negotiations between the government and FMLN were akin to the labor-management negotiations that Cristiani had once overseen. Intensity was added because the two sides wanted to destroy each other, but the perspective was informative nonetheless since it reminded him to look beyond zero-sum solutions to areas of mutual gain. "Defining a problem is key to solving a problem," he says. "What you have to learn is that the other guy has a different definition of the problem." The FMLN placed military and land reform at the top of its problem list; Cristiani singled out judicial and electoral reform. He selected as his chief negotiator an attorney who had long represented a business association in collective bargaining.

As Cristiani was preparing for the start of talks with the FMLN in the fall of 1989, he arranged for Roger Fisher, a prominent negotiator and coauthor of *Getting to Yes*, to offer a two-day seminar in San Salvador on the art of bargaining and compromise. "Our team was not a negotiating expert," Cristiani recalls, and "we had to understand what they want, what we want, and how it is possible to come together." Knowing that it takes two to settle, Cristiani also supported a subsequent Fisher seminar for the FMLN negotiators in Nicaragua. If the two negotiating teams were "going to become skilled at 'dancing' together," Fisher warned in a memo to both, "it may help to have them learn the same steps," and Cristiani prodded both sides to do so.

By implication: Viewing political challenges, as unique as they are, through the eyes of management experience can transform the seemingly intractable into the prospectively solvable.

Becoming a Leader

INITIALLY, CRISTIANI'S DEMEANOR, his presentations, his speeches were, in a word, bland. He had served as head of the country's coffee exporters' association and was not new to holding an audience's attention, but kissing babies and electrifying rallies were not among his proven talents. To some, his bearing was shy; to others, his elocution was boring. At mass gatherings during the campaign and even after his election, he sometimes began speaking only to be drowned out by rhythmic chants of "D'Aubuisson, d'Aubuisson, d'Aubuisson."

Cristiani was also a relative newcomer to a political mine-field whose major figures were already seasoned players. D'Aubuisson had led the party for nearly a decade and had served as president of the legislative assembly in the early 1980s. FMLN leaders such as Joaquín Villalobos and Ana Guadalupe Martínez had been active for years—in arms and in politics, of course, but also in diplomacy. In August 1981, France and Mexico had recognized the FMLN as a "representative political force." Cristiani's predecessor, Duarte, had served as mayor of San Salvador before becoming president; so too would Cristiani's successor, Armando Calderón Sol.

Political experience as limited as Cristiani's can sometimes give rise to naive hopes and limited understandings. One participant in the early policy deliberations of the Cristiani government recalled that the president at first had expected the guerrillas to accept a negotiated settlement within three months. Ignacio Ellacuría, rector of the University of Central America, met with Cristiani during the early months of his administration and later confided that Cristiani had seemed out of his depth in comprehending the engines of the civil war that he was committed to shutting down.

But if personal charisma and political experience were notable by their absence, Cristiani brought other qualities that served him in their stead. His elocution broke from past presidencies, in which the occupant sometimes acquired, or insisted on receiving, a prominence greater than the office itself. President Duarte spoke in the first person singular; President Cristiani, in the first person plural. So fond was Duarte of the word "I"—*yo*—that his style of presidency came to be known as *yoismo*. The term *nosotrismo*—from *nosotros*, or "we"—was never applied to Cristiani's governing style, but the shared sense of duty he created was vital to his success. When Cristiani's military chief of staff reminded him on taking office that he was the nation's commander in chief, the president responded that he had not really earned the title but hoped to do so by the end of his term.

During the November 1989 offensive, Cristiani's persona remained that of the unruffled executive. He had much to be stressed about, including the FMLN's assault on his home and the prospect of San Salvador becoming a Central American Beirut. The armed forces were pressing to bomb the guerrillas out of San Salvador. Journalists, diplomats, and the Vatican were clamoring for swift justice in the Jesuit murders. He and his wife changed homes every night as a security measure.

Nor was Cristiani necessarily safe even among his own supporters. ARENA contained a wing of strident anti-Communists who viewed violence against their opponents as one weapon in a just cause. "El Salvador will be the tomb where the Reds are buried," declared the party anthem. And Cristiani worried that extreme elements in ARENA viewed his call for negotiations as a sellout. When Cristiani and a handful of party reformers met with several moderate outsiders, an ARENA member asked, "Do you know what they call us?" Answering his own question, he reported that inside the party they were known as "the ARENA Communists." An associate warned Cristiani that some in his party even saw his assassination as a legitimate way to elevate his far-right vice president to the presidency.

Though threats persisted, Cristiani displayed a demeanor that was composed and in control, even during the darkest days of the November offensive. He would achieve an oratorical style that would retain a crowd; he would develop a personal style that would soothe the nation. He would learn what is required to be presidential.

By implication: Such leadership skills as persuasive speaking, persistence in achieving one's agendas, and personal confidence can be developed in office; much of leadership is a learned capacity that need not be limited by birthright or prior experience.

Delegating Authority

FOR CRISTIANI, economic reform could not await a political settlement, yet the latter became his full-time calling. During the FMLN offensives, his bunker hours were endless. During negotiations rounds, the strategy discussions were incessant. He would take telephone calls from President George Bush of the United States, Secretary General Javier Pérez de Cuéllar of the United Nations, President Oscar Arias Sánchez of Costa Rica, and dozens of others; and he would make numerous trips to the United States, Europe, Asia, and Latin America in search of support. Of necessity, he would turn much of what occupies most presidents over to his advisers. Critics would assert that he had deputized the rule of the country to others, but, Cristiani retorts, "I had to delegate."

In delegating responsibility for both day-to-day operations and economic restructuring, Cristiani risked ceding control to less qualified hands. Here his solution was what so many executives of U.S. corporations have learned to do when decentralizing. "I picked good ministers," he later said, and "I told them to do the job without my interference."[2]

The Salvadoran Foundation for Social and Economic Development was Cristiani's Heritage Foundation, a private center for dialogue among those committed to a free-market economy. One of its principals, Mirna Liévano de Marques, had organized seminars for five years for Cristiani and those who would become his economic brain trust. This, Cristiani remembers, "is where we built a team."[3]

Liévano de Marques herself became Cristiani's minister of planning, responsible for coordinating all cabinet-level economic and social policies. She orchestrated food and housing relief during the November offensive and guided liberalization while the president was preoccupied with negotiations. "You are the minister of planning," Cristiani told her as his administration took power. "Please never come to me for answers. You are enough of an adult to solve all the problems."

In the first days of Cristiani's administration, the minister of finance visited the president's office to secure his approval for major decisions. After several meetings, Cristiani informed him that such meetings were no longer necessary—he should just take the actions he deemed appropriate.

Even the government's negotiation team enjoyed substantial autonomy. Cristiani received an incessant flow of demands to instruct the team one way or the other, even to replace some of its members. But he buffered the team against the demands and urged the improbable assemblage—a colonel, lawyer, and poet were on the team—to work with mutual respect and collective confidence. With Cristiani's encouragement, the team adopted a policy of building consensus rather than voting. In nightly conversations with the chief negotiator, Oscar Santamaría, the president served as counselor and coach, not commanding general. As he had learned in the coffee groves, "A good manager works with his team; you roll up your sleeves."

Colonel Mauricio Vargas had been wounded three times in combat against the FMLN, and many of his army associates had been disabled or killed. Now he was serving as the military's representative at the bargaining table. When he early on complained that the FMLN were "provocative and conspiratorial," Cristiani responded, "Mauricio, let them be provocative and conspiratorial, but don't you become provocative and conspiratorial."

The bargaining was personally trying, recalls Oscar Santamaría: FMLN negotiators were "trying to get at the table what they wanted by war" and threatened more. The FMLN demanded complete demilitarization, but any hint of such demobilization at the table spawned talk of a coup d'état at home. Cristiani "motivated us to keep going" by repeatedly voicing his support for the team, Santamaría remembers. The president reminded the team of its "historic" mission on behalf of "future generations" and reaffirmed its need to remain composed.

By implication: Pick your associates well, back them fully, empower them with both accountability and responsibility, and they will produce far more than you ever will achieve on your own.

Negotiating Agreement

GETTING TO MEXICO CITY required reconciliation of the often violently opposed opinions of Alfredo Cristiani's personal advisers, party officials, and army officers, not to mention the FMLN. While he would not meet with the guerrilla negotiators himself until the Chapultepec signing, he orchestrated the negotiations throughout. He was known to be a careful listener, open to feedback and suggestion but alert to parochial lobbying and self-pleading. He insisted on reliable information and looked at it with an analytic eye. He had a keen sense for issues that deserved attention and solutions that were workable. All this and more would be needed to overcome the enormous opposition even on his own side. "I would say that 0.2 percent supported" settlement, recalled David Escobar Galindo, one of the government's negotiators, "and 99.8 percent opposed it."

With the armed forces and the FMLN fighting to a draw yet both averse to compromise, Cristiani unrelentingly pressed for a solution. Soon after his election, he sent an intermediary to tell the FMLN that he genuinely sought a dialogue; the go-between reported back that the guerrillas were thinking more about insurrection than about negotiation. Cristiani sent word that "this is no longer possible," but he understood their need to find out for themselves, as they would in the November offensive.

When the FMLN finally consented to renewed talks, even sitting with the insurgents seemed to legitimate a "criminal" organization in the eyes of many military officers. Some asked why they were talking after defeating the guerrillas in November. Others feared—correctly, as they would learn—that a settlement would end their military careers. "We are the rivals," confided one army general, "so it is difficult for us to believe it is best to negotiate." But Cristiani explained that the U.S. Congress was losing patience and his own had diminished as well with the discovery that an army colonel had ordered the Jesuit murders.

Once negotiations were under way, Cristiani incorporated the officer corps into the process. Even while grumbling persisted that a military coup d'état would be better than a civilian sellout, the president met monthly with his forty top commanders. He reaffirmed an earlier commitment that dissolution of the armed forces would never be an option at any negotiating table. He detailed what was happening at the talks and solicited their counsel. He also established eight standing groups of soldiers from all ranks. One focused on constitutional reform, another on the future of the armed forces, a third on education. At each step in the bargaining, Cristiani asked, "What do you think of the FMLN demands? What should we tell our negotiating team?"

The negotiations, which restarted in the spring of 1990, approached their finale in December 1991. The secretary-general of the United Nations, Javier Pérez de Cuéllar, would be retiring on New Year's Eve, and both sides feared that the informal gains might unravel if not formally ratified under his dominion. The negotiating teams reconvened in New York on December 16 and gradually whittled away at the still-divisive issues in the composition of the police, reduction of the army, and supervision of the cease-fire. Still, large gaps remained as New Year's approached, and on December 28 Cristiani flew to New York with Defense Minister General René Emilio Ponce.

On the evening of December 30, Cristiani was closeted with his team. They knew they would now have to make concessions if a deal was to be reached. Remaining on the table were the organization of the national police and the security of FMLN guerrillas. Near midnight, with twenty-four hours remaining, Cristiani moved to a corner of the room. "I looked around and saw his face," remembered one participant, "serene, calm, deep in thought." General Ponce quietly warned that it was not a time for anybody to disturb the president. The FMLN was demanding training and financing for its ex-combatants to build small businesses; Cristiani decided to accede. He wanted the ex-guerrillas concentrated in three regions for disarming, but the FMLN wanted thirty; he decided to compromise at eight.

As New Year's Eve revelers gathered in New York's Times Square on December 31, Cristiani and the FMLN were approaching their midnight deadline at the United Nations without a deal. At 5 P.M., Cristiani walked into the secretary-general's office and asked that he press the FMLN. Pérez de Cuéllar replied that he and his wife would shortly be leaving for a long-planned Caribbean vacation. Cristiani threatened, "If you leave, I'm leaving too." Later that evening, the negotiators agreed to stop the hands of the clock just before the New Year's ball dropped in Times Square, the moment when Pérez de Cuéllar was to step down. At 12:20 A.M., the clock still stopped, they reached final agreement.

By implication: Consistent, unrelenting efforts to hear and reconcile diverse positions, even when rooted in deeply entrenched and immensely powerful interests, are prerequisite to overcoming any conflict and mobilizing the resources that the contending parties are withholding.

A Negotiated Revolution

BEFORE THE NEGOTIATIONS seminar in the fall of 1989, Roger Fisher had told President Cristiani and his team that it was "difficult to conceive of a comprehensive peace document that each side could sell to its constituents. It has been said of El Salvador that God Himself could not put a draft on the table that each side could sign and persuade its constituents to respect." But the two sides did sign with the support of their constituencies. The National Guard and special security forces were abolished, along with the National Intelligence Directorate, the elite infantry battalions, and all paramilitary groups. The FMLN guerrillas were disarmed and demobilized, its leaders welcomed as legitimate politicians.

Radio Venceremos, FMLN's clandestine voice during the civil war, had often broadcast from portable transmitters on the backs of guerrillas. Now it became a nationwide FM station based in San Salvador. For a while, it and companion station Radio Farabundo Martí aired protest songs and alternative news, but economic realities led both to accept commercial advertising and U.S. rock music.

The chief intermediary for the United Nations termed the final agreement a "negotiated revolution." The U.S. House of Representatives voted 414–0 to "express its admiration for President Cristiani for his unflagging service to the cause of peace and democracy in El Salvador." The U.S. Senate voted 96–0 to extend "particular praise to President Cristiani for the courage and determination of his personal efforts to bring peace to El Salvador." Minnesota Senator David Durenburger added that the peace "proves beyond any doubt that one person can make all the difference in the world." Bernard Aronson, the American diplomat on the front line, entitled a 1994 article in *The Washington Post* "The Man Who Saved El Salvador."[4]

The 1994 national elections in El Salvador pitted Armando Calderón Sol of ARENA against Rubén Zamora of the Democratic Convergence and FMLN. Calderón Sol defeated Zamora in a runoff by roughly two to one—68 to 32 percent— but FMLN candidates and those the FMLN supports won a quarter of the legislative assembly seats, making it the main opposition party. In 1997 elections, the FMLN increased its share of the legislative assembly's 82 seats from 14 to 27 and its share of the nation's 262 mayoral offices from 13 to 54, including San Salvador and its blue-collar suburbs. The FMLN pulled even in popular voting as well, carrying 32 percent of all ballots to ARENA's 33 percent.[5]

Economic growth was restored. The gross domestic product

President Alfredo Cristiani and the peace accord

per capita, in decline throughout the 1980s, rose again, hitting 3 percent growth in 1992 and 1993, 4 percent in 1994, and 5 percent in 1995, among the highest expansion rates in the Western Hemisphere. After reviewing the growth numbers in 1996, the World Bank concluded that El Salvador's economic performance "is a remarkable success story."[6]

Alfredo Cristiani left office with a 70 percent approval rating and, though a private citizen, remains El Salvador's most celebrated public figure. When asked after his presidency in what he took greatest satisfaction, he replied that it was his ability not only to avoid having to go into exile but also to drive freely anywhere in the country.

In 1994, Salvadoran business leaders created Escuela Superior de Economía y Negocios, a four-year business school, to educate a new generation for the reconstruction ahead. Its mission is to develop "the future business leaders of El Salvador

and Central America." One of its driving energies and first rector was Ricardo Poma, whose brother, Roberto, had died at the
hands of an FMLN faction. Its first director was Mirna Liévano
de Marques, President Cristiani's minister of planning. Its student ranks included the son of Cristiani's minister of defense,
the son of the army officer who served on Cristiani's negotiating team, the son of the candidate of the Christian Democratic
Party defeated by Cristiani, and the daughter of the leader of
the Salvadoran Communist Party.[7]

As I was leaving the Cristiani residence at dusk in early June
1997 after interviewing him, our conversation turned to his
evening plans. The bleak days of the FMLN offensive had dominated our earlier discussion, but struggle of a distinctly more
pleasant sort was on tap for that night. His son was soon to
arrive with a friend to watch a television broadcast of the third
game of the National Basketball Association championship
series. During the civil war, government intelligence had uncov-
ered a plot to kidnap Cristiani's son. Now the young man's main
concern, his father reported, was whether the Chicago Bulls'
Michael Jordan could repeat his performance in the first game
of this NBA title series, when he had scored a last-second, tie-
breaking shot against the Utah Jazz. Cristiani's son was for the
Bulls, his friend for the Jazz. Cristiani was for a good game.

Conclusion: Vision plus Action

EXAMINING WHAT OTHERS have done when businesses, lives, even the fate of nations are on the line does more than pitch us into the middle of high drama; it also teaches us to think more strategically and act more decisively. By watching those who lead the way—as well as those who go astray—we can see what works and what fails, what hastens our cause or subverts our purpose.

Remembering what Roy Vagelos did for Mectizan, what Arlene Blum attained on Annapurna, and what Joshua Lawrence Chamberlain achieved at Gettysburg can instruct our own decisions when the moment demands. Alfredo Cristiani's courage of his convictions, Eugene Kranz's unflinching determination, and Nancy Barry's inner calling provide graphic examples by which to measure and model our own life's course, just as John Gutfreund's hesitation and Wagner Dodge's retreat warn us that when time counts, delay can mean disaster. And Clifton Wharton's restructuring of TIAA-CREF reminds us what leadership is all about: improving and perhaps even transforming what we have inherited from others without subverting the organization's mission or making the organization the slave of our egos.

Destination and Delivery

THE SINGLE MOST important lesson from these moments is the overwhelming significance of vision and action. Without a clear sense of destination, we are apt to flounder about, and without knowing how to get to that destination, we will never reach it even when we see it.

In the absence of vision and action, Little Round Top might not have held and Salvadoran strife might still be rampant. River blindness would remain widespread, Teachers Insurance might remain a monopoly. Apollo 13 would not have returned, nor would a woman's place have been on top. Had there been more vision and action, Salomon might never have faced a near-death experience and Mann Gulch might never have become the final resting place for thirteen smoke jumpers.

In the leadership course that I offer for midcareer managers in Wharton's executive MBA program, I ask each student for an assessment of a person who best exemplifies his or her ideals of leadership. Some managers choose a public figure such as Colin Powell, Margaret Thatcher, or Warren Buffett; a few profile a fictional character such as *Star Trek*'s Captain Kirk; but most focus on winning executives in their own firms. Whoever is chosen, the qualities that most often distinguish them from others are the same ones that make the difference in the nine accounts in this book: their exceptional capacity to articulate a plan and lay out a way of achieving it.

One manager's account of Captain Kirk illustrates in a small way the larger point. Bones McCoy, the physician on the starship *Enterprise* under Kirk's command, objected to assisting a wounded alien that looks more mineral than animal. He complained, "I'm a doctor, not a bricklayer," but Captain Kirk insisted that his doctor aid the injured alien. Forced to solve the problem he would not have otherwise resolved on his own, McCoy finally found an effective, nonprescriptive antidote: cement.

In kindred fashion, the Apollo 13 engineers told Eugene Kranz that their calculations revealed no way of returning the three astronauts safely to earth. But Kranz insisted that they find one anyway. "We will never surrender," Kranz declared. "This crew is coming home." Forced back to the drawing board, the engineers devised a lifesaving solution.

The critical focus in both cases: a determination to fix what seems irreversibly broken. The essential ingredient: unswerving support for and pressure on those who can solve the problem.

Sharing the Lessons

EPISODES OF LEADERSHIP are almost always rich with surface action, but each such moment—whether that leadership succeeds or fails—illustrates embedded and enduring principles. So it is with the nine accounts detailed in this book and summarized below. By remembering not just what these nine people achieved but also what principles guided—or failed to guide—their actions, we can better understand what we ourselves should do.

In remembering these principles, it is vital to recall the experiences from which they arise. If the stakes are not tangibly sensed, if we do not feel that we were almost there, the moment's value is lost. To use the lessons, we have to perceive, if only momentarily, that we too are charging down Little Round Top, that we too are authorizing a miracle drug that no one who needs it can ever afford, that we too are witnessing killer avalanches obliterate our tracks, that we too are hearing a transmission from the heavens; "Houston, we've had a problem."

Increasing our store of vivid leadership encounters is only half the challenge, though. Such accounts can direct and inform our own actions, but they become all the more powerful when they are shared with and shape the actions of others. By reliving Wagner Dodge's disastrous end in Mann Gulch with your associates or Eugene Kranz's final triumph with Apollo 13, you and they can gain a greater appreciation of the value of flawless teamwork. By considering again why Roy Vagelos decided to commit his company to giving away a product forever, your colleagues may be emboldened to transcend a short-term calculus. Once conveyed within an organization, such stories constitute a common ground. Widely understood, they become an implicit framework for guiding and judging a firm's leadership.

NINE LEADERSHIP MOMENTS, NINE LEADERSHIP PRINCIPLES

Roy Vagelos at Merck	***Know yourself:*** Understanding your values and where you want to go will assure that you know which paths to take.
Wagner Dodge in Mann Gulch	***Explain yourself:*** Only then can your associates understand where you want to go and whether they want to accompany you.
Eugene Kranz and Apollo 13	***Expect much:*** Demanding the best is a prerequisite for obtaining it.
Arlene Blum on Annapurna	***Gain commitment:*** Obtaining consensus before a decision will mobilize those you are counting upon after the decision.
Joshua Lawrence Chamberlain at Gettysburg	***Build now:*** Acquiring support today is indispensable if you plan to draw upon it tomorrow.
Clifton Wharton at TIAA-CREF	***Prepare yourself:*** Seeking varied and challenging assignments now develops the confidence and skills required for later.
John Gutfreund at Salomon	***Move fast:*** Inaction can often prove as disastrous as inept action.
Nancy Barry at Women's World Banking	***Find yourself:*** Liberating your leadership potential requires matching your goals and talents to the right organization.
Alfredo Cristiani in El Salvador	***Remain steadfast:*** Faith in your vision will ensure that you and your followers remain unswerving in pursuit of it.

Recalling these accounts—their triumphs and their disasters—with your colleagues is a way of fostering their leadership and that of those around them.

It is for this reason that those who become great leaders have often been great storytellers. This is evident in *Leading Minds,*

Howard Gardner's study of such commanding world figures as George C. Marshall, Margaret Mead, and Mahatma Gandhi. Gardner discovered that tales were the mobilizing medium for all these leaders. They gave persuasive accounts, Gardner observes, "about where they were coming from and where they were headed, about what was to be feared, struggled against, and dreamed about." Whether informal dialogue or formal speeches, the mobilizing power of their rhetoric came less from telling numbers and more from compelling narratives.[1]

Martin Luther King delivered more than 350 speeches in 1963 alone, including the most enduring of all, his stirring oratory on the steps of the Lincoln Memorial in Washington, D.C., before the more than 200,000 people who had joined the March on Washington for civil rights. "I say to you today, my friends, that in spite of the difficulties and frustrations of the moment I still have a dream. It is a dream deeply rooted in the American dream." The organizers had allocated King a mere eight minutes, and that was all he needed to deliver a speech that few can forget: "I have a dream that one day this nation will rise up and live out the true meaning of its creed. . . . I have a dream that my four little children will one day live in a nation where they will not be judged by the color of their skin but the content of their character." Powerfully turned accounts, concludes Gardner, attract the followers who create leaders.

We know from experience that managers learn leadership best from example and communicate leadership best through example. Many organizations publish management guides suggesting, for example, a dozen steps to more effective leadership, but most people will recall and act on such lists only when they are tinged with tension and rooted in accounts of mission and accomplishment, reason and passion, courage and cowardice.

Research on learning supports this conclusion: when broad concepts and generic principles are formally acquired without reference to the actions or decisions in which they are embedded, the knowledge remains inert. When managers are asked what company programs have been most important for their development, they cite confrontation with novel problems for which their existing capacities are inadequate and to which they must apply new skills. Learning to lead is most often a combination of experimenting and witnessing, of experiencing and watching.[2]

A Leadership Trek

A STORE OF leadership accounts is an invaluable foundation for decision making when it really counts, and the sources for expanding our repertoire of such instances are rich and varied. Examples of leadership are well chronicled, for instance, in *Profiles of Courage*, John F. Kennedy's account of eight U.S. senators facing their moments of truth. Such examples also abound in *Essence of Decision*, Graham Allison's chronicle of President Kennedy's own moment when facing down Soviet missiles in Cuba. And they can be found in almost any organization whose managers are making decisions that count.

To increase the store of vivid leadership encounters and to provide a forum for sharing with others, I organized a "leadership trek," a two-week walk in the shadow of Mount Everest. With colleague Edwin Bernbaum and a team of midcareer managers, we explored the legendary valleys and passes of the high Himalayas. Surrounded by the mountain's lore and mysteries and using mountaineering as a metaphor for the mental lands we inhabit, we drew on the region's triumphs and disasters to reflect on our own preparation for decision making.

As we walked the trails, we asked ourselves how expeditions to Everest, Annapurna, and other Himalayan peaks build the leadership required to reach their summits. And we pondered larger issues as well: Can the mysterious hidden valleys of Tibet, some resembling the fictional Shangri-La of James Hilton's *Lost Horizon*, offer fresh insight into our own leadership potential? And what does it mean to attain a summit? What have we achieved once we arrive? Arlene Blum has offered one reply:

"You never conquer a mountain. You stand on the summit a few brief minutes, and then the wind blows your footsteps away."

On the trek's second day we moved through forests of rhododendron, magnolia trees, and giant firs, and by late afternoon we reached Namche, a trading crossroads nestled among stupendous peaks all around. Our discussion that evening centered on Maurice Herzog, the French mountaineer who had first reached the summit of Annapurna, and on Arlene Blum, whose climbing team reached the summit later. Herzog's climb had been unusual: unlike most expedition leaders, he reached the top himself, but exhausted and frostbitten, he and a ropemate faced near disaster on the way down. Would they have been better off if Herzog had remained below, as Blum chose to do in leading her own Annapurna expedition? There, he might have better coordinated the Herculean evacuation that followed. Or was Herzog's decision to lead from the front critical to getting his team on top? Arlene Blum's decision not to go for the summit herself would seem to have been vindicated when the four climbers under her leadership did reach the top of Annapurna, yet when two other climbers set out for what would prove a disastrous second ascent, Blum was unable to keep them from going. Would she have been able to prevent the twosome's fatal climb if she had led from the front?

On the trek's fifth day, we entered one of the highest inhabited valleys of the Himalayas. There, we crossed a tributary from Mount Everest's Khumbu Glacier and hiked into the village of Dingboche, perched on a hillside at more than 14,000 feet. Our subject for the evening was the first American ascent of Everest in 1963 and the first-ever ascent of its precipitous West Ridge by others on the same expedition. Here we saw two climbing objectives and two kinds of leadership: one pair of U.S. climbers chose to go for the unclimbed and more difficult West Ridge route, while a second pair set out to ascend the previously climbed and less dangerous South Col route. The first pair opted for an "alpine" style of ascent, in which they climbed on their own without Sherpas or backup, the second for a "siege" style with ample assistance. Why did they decide on such different approaches? we asked. How did that choice affect their prospects of success? And what distinctive leadership styles did each require?

Later that evening, our own party of nineteen divided into two groups. One was to climb a spectacular point at more than 18,000 feet on one of the largest walls in the world, the famed southern face of Lhotse, rising to a 27,923-foot summit; the other was to climb an overlook of the Imja Khola Valley and Island Peak, whose summit towers more than 20,000 feet. We considered our goals for the next day: How and why would each of us choose one destination over the other?

The following evening, with the two groups back from their high points, we asked what had gone right—and what wrong—both today and on the fateful afternoon of May 10, 1996, when two climbing groups, simultaneously nearing the summit of Mount Everest, had been hit by a violent storm. Drawing on Jon Krakauer's *Into Thin Air*, we examined the decisions and actions of the two teams' leaders as they desperately sought safe haven for all. Eight climbers—including both leaders—never found it. We asked where their decisions might have been different, how their leadership had mattered, and what we might do better for safely reaching our own summits in the future.

Building Leadership

ONE OF THE ironic discoveries of recent restructuring in private companies, medical centers, and government agencies has been that giving away power judiciously sometimes makes one more powerful. By granting work associates more authority to get the job done and tools to make it happen, a manager becomes more authoritative. With their relationships to customers, patients, and the public more clearly established, one's associates acquire a greater incentive to respond. With responsibility for decisions more clearly delegated, everyone on the management tree acquires a stronger wherewithal to act. With accountability more clearly pinpointed, they also acquire a better reason to perform. And with the results delivered and reputation enhanced, one places oneself in a position to acquire more power to get an even bigger job done.[3]

The same is true for leadership. It is not just how many followers one has; it is also how many leaders one has created among them. The more leadership in the ranks, the more effective is one's own.

Widespread restructuring has also ushered in an era of teamwork and network, driving out command and control. A manager's ability to lead a team is now a function of the team members' capacity to lead as well. Spreading leadership is thus not just a matter of working down. Fostering more leadership among peers and the powers that be is a prerequisite for effectively exercising one's own. Put differently, giving away power makes one more powerful, while creating more leaders all around oneself can make one all the more a leader. And as we have seen, from the outer limits on Mount Everest to the inner workings of company life, from Joshua Lawrence Chamberlain to Alfredo Cristiani, from Eugene Kranz and Nancy Barry to John Gutfreund and Clifton Wharton, from Arlene Blum to Wagner Dodge and Roy Vagelos, it is leadership large and small that makes all the difference.

A Leader's Guide

Roy Vagelos at Merck

• Clearheaded thinking about why you have been appointed to an office and what those who have placed you there expect of you is prerequisite to clear-minded, if not predictable, decision making.

• Identifying ways of bolstering long-term investor and public interest, even if they momentarily reduce shareholder returns, can foster a favorable culture, build a company cadre, and establish a public reputation that can more than compensate for any temporary shortfalls in investor value.

• Achieving an organization's imperative is a leader's calling, but sometimes we confront moments when we must do other-

273

wise. Such moments must be relatively unique, otherwise the inconsistency in our organizational leadership will be evident for all to see; but if they are unthinkingly bypassed, our value as a leader may be doubted by everyone, including ourselves.

• Knowing where you want go and what your values are can be essential to getting there, to ensuring that all of your interests and concerns are factored into fast-moving decisions, and to avoiding later regrets about being less than clear-minded. Building that understanding into any organization's culture can help all employees be clear-minded and fast-acting as well.

R. Wagner Dodge and Mann Gulch

• If you have made several problematic decisions in a row, be prepared to have your leadership questioned. It may be a moment of personal trial, a point when the cooperation of others is most needed but least forthcoming.

• If you want trust and compliance when the need for them cannot be fully explained, explain yourself early. If you need information on which you must soon act, ask for it soon. Being a person of few words may be fine in a technical position, but it is a prescription for disaster in a position of leadership.

• If you expect those who work for you to exercise their own judgment, provide them with the decision-making experience now. If you count on them to understand the conditions as best they can, share your past experience with them now. If your leadership depends on theirs, devolving responsibility and sharing stories is a foundation upon which it will reside. Thinking strategically when confronted with a crisis or challenge is a learned skill that requires sustained seasoning.

• If you have difficult decisions to make and insufficient time to explain them, a key to implementation may be loyal allies who are sure to execute them through thick or thin. Establishing those allies now is the only way to ensure that their support will be at the ready when needed, and it will sometimes be needed when it is far too late to be created.

• In periods of anxiety and stress, it is your least experienced associates who will reach the panic zone first. Providing newcomers with as much early training and mentoring as possible is one way of moving their panic point well to the right when the heat is on.

• If your organization is facing a period of uncertainty, change, or stress, now is the time to build a strong culture with good lines of interior communication, mutual understanding, and shared obligation. A clear sense of common purpose and a well-formed camaraderie are essential ingredients to ensure that your team, your organization, or your company will perform to its utmost when it is most needed.

Eugene Kranz and Apollo 13

• Expecting high performance is prerequisite to its achievement among those who work with you. Your high standards and optimistic anticipations will not guarantee a favorable outcome, but their absence will assuredly create the opposite.

• When both speed and precision count, sharing information and keeping everybody's eye on *both goals simultaneously* are essential for achieving both.

• Construct decision-making teams and procedures for intensive problem solving before they are needed. Bringing to the fore those most qualified to make the decisions, regardless of background or obligation, will aid decision making.

• Developing teams and teams of teams through training and exercise can create the implicit understandings that make for fast and accurate decision making when the teams are under duress but must act.

Arlene Blum on Annapurna

• A new position of leadership will engender the experience you lack on arrival, and seeking feedback on your performance in the position will ensure that you take advantage of the experience.

• Recognizing people's diverse motives for participating is an essential first step in mobilizing their contributions. Creating an opportunity for all to succeed—whatever their motives—is an essential second step in harnessing their contributions even when the room at the top is not big enough for all.

• When a summit, product, or project seems well within reach, dampening overconfidence can ensure that energy remains focused on achieving it; when it appears almost out of reach, encouraging greater confidence can ensure that the motivation remains focused on achieving it as well.

• Infusing collective action with transcendent meaning can add greater reward to successful completion of a task, but it can also add greater risk to those involved. When a broader purpose is aimed for, crafting an appropriate balance between expectations on the outside and risk taking on the inside is the challenge.

Joshua Lawrence Chamberlain at Gettysburg

• If you are appealing for the support of a critical group, make your ultimate, shared objectives the platform. Convince its members that the cause is just, the calling noble, the course collective, the challenge critical; remind them that the goal cannot be reached without their energetic engagement.

• Winning the confidence of your people now may well be indispensable in a yet-unforseen time when you face your ultimate test. No one can know when that day will come or even if it will. But if it does, early investments in winning support among even your most stalwart opponents may make the difference between success and defeat when it counts most.

• Some of today's small actions in mobilizing others may prove of little value, but others may have great results. Since you often cannot know which will later become critical, you cannot afford to avoid or ignore any now.

• Authority systems help ensure that our decisions contribute to an organization's mission, but they can also get in the way. Recognizing when autonomous action is the right course—and learning to act on that recognition—can be essential, both for yourself and for those upon whom you depend.

• When you are thrust into a responsible position with scant warning and even less preparation, ask what actions are called for in the position, what strategies have worked in the past, and how others have previously responded to the challenges you now face.

Clifton R. Wharton Jr. at TIAA-CREF

• Moving yourself through varied and increasingly responsible management experiences develops the personal confidence and diverse skills required to master different, more ambitious arrays of tasks; moving yourself across varied organizations fosters the capacities essential to leading still different institutions.

• Buy-in by all those affected by an organization's change hastens its achievement. Consultation with them, engagement of them, and appeals to them are the critical steps for building acceptance of the change.

• Leading change is like riding a bucking bronco: if you are not finding satisfaction, you may want to switch the horse or even change the event.

• The qualities that make a difference are the special province of no racial, gender, or national group; the opportunity to apply them is the prerequisite for developing them, whatever the group.

John Gutfreund at Salomon

• At the top of the organizational chart, where the risks and uncertainties are greatest, decisions made or not made can have consequences that reach well beyond the organization to affect its very survival.

• Inaction can be as damaging to leadership as inept action.

• The perquisites of high office do not lessen the need for specific and consistent exercise of authority to ensure accountability inside an organization. Creation of a common understanding of preferred behavior may be especially important in harnessing the energies of those who are distant from or disdainful of the high office.

• Unequivocal cooperation, complete contrition, acceptance of responsibility, and a riveting focus on recovery are critical ingredients for restoring a beleaguered organization's reputation.

Nancy Barry at Women's World Banking

• Realizing your leadership potential depends on making a match between your vision and an organization. The challenge is to find the right opportunity, pick the right moment, and make the right move.

• In serving others—whether low-income women, rice-growing farmers, or dividend-hungry investors—finding a self-sustaining engine that works is an essential step in delivering value to them.

• Bound by no convention, combine what works best from even the most opposed traditions.

• If big is the only way to achieve your mission, thinking big no matter how small you start is the only way to reach it.

• The conviction of your vision is the sine qua non for its achievement. Without a clear-minded fix on where you want to

Alfredo Cristiani in El Salvador

get, the opportunities and pressures for diverting from it will ensure you will not arrive there.

• Viewing political challenges, as unique as they are, through the eyes of management experience can transform the seemingly intractable into the prospectively solvable.

• Such leadership skills as persuasive speaking, persistence in achieving one's agendas, and personal confidence can be developed in office; much of leadership is a learned capacity that need not be limited by birthright or prior experience.

• Pick your associates well, back them fully, empower them with both accountability and responsibility, and they will produce far more than you ever will achieve on your own.

• Consistent, unrelenting efforts to hear and reconcile diverse positions, even when rooted in deeply entrenched and immensely powerful interests, are prerequisite to overcoming any conflict and mobilizing the resources that the contending parties are withholding.

Notes

Introduction: Leaders Under Fire

The opening quote is from John F. Kennedy, 1956, p. 258.

1. Burns, 1978; Drucker, 1996; Phillips, 1992; Dietel, 1996.
2. Hillary, 1996.
3. Raymond Smith, presentation in Philadelphia, 1993.
4. Gibson, 1996.
5. Waldman, Ramirez, and House, 1996.

Chapter 1: Roy Vagelos Attacks River Blindness

The opening quote is from a 1987 announcement by Merck & Company, with P. Roy Vagelos serving as chief executive (Wigg, 1993, p. 29). The account draws primarily on Eckholm, 1989; Friedland, 1989; *MSDI Newsletter*, 1989; Weiss, 1991; Campbell, 1992; Lynn, 1992; Wigg, 1993; Zimmer, 1995; Musa, 1996; *River Blindness News* of the Global 2000 River Blindness Program of the Carter Center; presentations by P. Roy Vagelos at the Wharton School, University of Pennsylvania, on November 13, 1996, and November 5 and 7, 1997; and interviews conducted by the author with William C. Campbell (June 18 and 19, 1997) and P. Roy Vagelos (July 2, 1997).

1. Taylor, Pacque, and Munoz, 1990.
2. Friedman, 1970.
3. J. Shapiro, 1996; Dunlap, 1996.

4. Merck & Co., Inc., 1993.
5. Huebner, 1996.
6. Waddock and Graves, 1997.
7. Lynn, 1992, p. 237; *Financial Times*, 1993.
8. McCoy, 1997a, b.
9. Foster, 1983; Lipton and Raymond, 1984.
10. Harrington et al., 1996.
11. Carter, 1993.
12. Leary, 1995.
13. Eckholm, 1989; World Bank, 1995; Agence France Presse, 1993.
14. Carter, 1993; Merck & Co., Inc., 1996; presentation by P. Roy Vagelos, Wharton School, University of Pennsylvania, November 13, 1996.

Chapter 2: Wagner Dodge Retreats in Mann Gulch

The opening quote is from Robert Sallee, cited in Maclean, 1992. The account is primarily drawn from Maclean, 1992, and also from *Life*, 1949, and Weick, 1993.

1. This was the lifesaving solution adopted by residents of the hills above Oakland, California, when an explosive fire in October 1991 raced through their neighborhood. Several terrified residents survived by plunging into their swimming pools. Twenty-four others were not so fortunate as the wind-driven flames leveled everything in their path.
2. Drucker, 1996, p. xiv.
3. Ginnett, 1993.
4. Weick, 1990.
5. Fiedler, 1992.
6. Katzenbach and Smith, 1993.

Chapter 3: Eugene Kranz Returns Apollo 13 to Earth

The opening quote is by Eugene Kranz soon after the explosion on Apollo 13. The account draws primarily on Lovell and Kluger, 1994; Cooper, 1972; Shepard and Slayton, 1994; WGBH Educational Foundation, 1994; and interviews with Eugene Kranz conducted by Jeffrey Kluger (May 29, 1992, and January 7, 1993) and by the author (February 17, 1997).

1. Wilford, 1997, pp. 32, 1.
2. Eden, 1992.
3. Mintzberg, 1973, 1990.
4. *The New York Times*, 1970.

Chapter 4: Arlene Blum Ascends Annapurna

The opening quote is from Blum, 1980, p. 36. The account draws primarily on Ullman, 1964a; Blum, 1979, 1980, 1992; Bernbaum, 1990; Komarkova, 1979; Miller and Komarkova, 1979; Frison-Roche and Jouty, 1996; Thomas, 1997; and the author's interviews with Arlene Blum (March 25, 1997) and Irene Miller (April 7, 1997).

1. Thomas, 1997.
2. Herzog, 1953.
3. LaChapelle, 1966.
4. Smith, 1994.
5. Krakauer, 1997.
6. Ullman, 1964b; Hornbein, 1966; Emerson, 1964.
7. Brodmann and Curry, 1978.
8. Brodmann and Curry, 1978.
9. McCain, 1988; Herzog, 1980.
10. Society of Woman Geographers, 1992; Crowley, 1979.
11. McCain, 1988.
12. Gilbert, 1996.

Chapter 5: Joshua Lawrence Chamberlain Defends Little Round Top

The opening quote is from Joshua Lawrence Chamberlain's address at the dedication of the Twentieth Maine Monument at Gettysburg on October 3, 1889, cited in Trulock, 1992, p. 143. The account draws primarily on Wallace, 1960; Coddington, 1979; Tucker, 1983; Trulock, 1992; Chamberlain, 1994; Golay, 1994; and Perry, 1997.

1. Shaara, 1974.
2. Shaara, 1974, p. 24.
3. Shaara, 1974, pp. 28–31.
4. Text of speech furnished by Lotus Development Corporation; see also Bulkeley and Putka, 1995.
5. Trulock, 1992, pp. 154–155, 446; the official history was published in 1896.

Chapter 6: Clifton Wharton Restructures TIAA-CREF

The opening quote is from Clifton Wharton during an interview with the author (August 29, 1997). The account draws primarily on *The New York Times*, 1969; Drucker, 1976; Heller, 1987; Mangan, 1987; Sebastian, 1987; TIAA-CREF, 1987, 1992, 1993; Davis, 1988; Feinberg, 1988; Zigas, 1988; Rosenberg, 1989; *Chief Executive*, 1990; Greenough, 1990; Levinson, 1993; Vise, 1993; Mercer, 1997; Sass, 1997; interviews conducted by the author with Clifton R. Wharton Jr. (August 29, 1997); Elizabeth E. Bailey (July 28, 1997); John H. Biggs (October 24, 1997); David Alexander (October 27, 1997); Father Theodore Hesburgh (October 28, 1997); and William H. Waltrip (October 29, 1997); and information available through TIAA-CREF's Web page at <http://www.tiaa-cref.org>.

1. Bodie and Crane, 1997.

Chapter 7: John Gutfreund Loses Salomon Inc.

The opening quote is by John Gutfreund in Bartlett, 1991. The account draws primarily on Bianco, 1985; Lewis, 1989; Buffett, 1991a, b; Kaplan, 1991; Hansell, Selby and Sender, 1991; Salomon Inc., 1991; Cavanaugh and Fenster, 1992; Grant, 1992; Hansell, 1992; Howard, Darby & Levin, 1992; Moreton, 1992; Moreton and Crane, 1992; Paine and Santoro, 1994a, b, c; Lowenstein, 1995; Connor, 1997; Loomis, 1997; and an interview with Philip Howard conducted by the author (April 9, 1997).

1. Buffett, 1991a, b.
2. The story may be no more than apocryphal. Both Gutfreund and Meriwether have denied the incident occurred.
3. Kanter, 1977.
4. Stewart, 1991, p. 223.
5. Hansell, Selby, and Sender, 1991.
6. Power and Siconolfi, 1991.

Chapter 8: Nancy Barry Builds Women's World Banking

The opening quote is by Nancy Barry in Austin, 1991, p. 12. The account draws primarily on Women's World Banking, 1994, 1995a, b, c, 1996a, b, c, 1997; documents available on or through Web sites for Women's World Banking, <http://titsoc.soc.titech.ac.jp/titsoc/higuchi-lab/icm/wind/wwb-info.html>; World Bank, <http://www.worldbank.org/html/extdr/toc.html>; and Microcredit Summit, <http://www.microcreditsummit.org>; Fong, 1990; Gorman, 1990; Austin, 1991; Larson, 1991; Cadot, Milway, and Milway, 1993; Howells, 1993; Barry, 1994, 1996; Carrington, 1994; Spodek, 1994; Khandker, Khalily, and Khan, 1995; Tefft, 1995; Walker and Boulton, 1995; Bornstein, 1996; Kuper, 1997; Microcredit Summit, 1997; Packer-Tursman, 1997; and interviews conducted by the author with Nancy Barry (April 8, June 28, and August 26, 1997); Deanna Rosenswig (former vice-chair of Women's World Banking, September 8, 1997); Jan Piercy (U.S. Executive Director, World Bank, September 10, 1997); James E. Austin (Harvard Business School, September 8, 1997); Robert Picciotto (Director General, Operations Evaluation, World Bank, September 10, 1997); and Mohini Malhotra (Manager, Secretariat, Consultative Group to Assist the Poorest—A Micro-Finance Program, World Bank, September 11, 1997).

1. Kupfer, 1996.
2. Henriques, 1994; E. Shapiro, 1994a, b.
3. Useem, Setti, and Pincus, 1992.
4. Daley, 1997; Ramphele, 1995; Woods, 1987.

Chapter 9: Alfredo Christiani Ends El Salvador's Civil War

The opening quote is from Alfredo Cristiani during an interview
with the author (July 20, 1996). The account draws primarily on
Falcoff and Royal, 1987; LeoGrande, 1990; Menzel, 1994;
Montgomery, 1995; Murray, 1995; Whitfield, 1995; Byrne, 1996;
World Bank, 1996; and interviews conducted by the author with
Alfredo Cristiani (July 20, 1996; June 6 and 7, 1997); Oscar Arias
(March 1, 1997); Archie Baldocchi (June 6, 1997); Ricardo
Castaneda (April 8, 1997); Ricardo Poma (February 21, 1997); Fidel
Chávez Mena (June 7, 1997); Rodolfo Parker (June 6, 1997); René
Emilio Ponce Torres (June 7, 1997); Oscar Alfredo Santamaría
(June 6, 1997); Francisco R. R. de Sola (June 6, 1997); Mirna
Liévano de Marques (June 7, 1997); and Mauricio Ernesto Vargas
(June 7, 1997).

1. Christian, 1991.
2. Useem, 1993.
3. Finkelstein and Hambrick, 1996.
4. *Congressional Record*, May 11, May 25, and October 4, 1994;
   Aronson, 1994; Stanley and Call, 1997.
5. Rohter, 1997.
6. World Bank, 1996, pp. 1–2.
7. Mission statement of Escuela Superior de Economía y
   Negocios, 1997.

Conclusion: Vision plus Action

1. H. Gardner, 1995, p. 14.
2. Druckman and Bjork, 1994, pp. 36–56; Fiedler, 1994; McCall,
   Lombardo, and Morrison, 1988; Davies and Easterby-Smith,
   1984.
3. Gore, 1993; Useem, 1993.

Sources

Agence France Presse. 1993. "Explosion in African River Illness: WHO." December 9.

Allison, Graham T. 1971. *Essence of Decision: Explaining the Cuban Missile Crisis*. New York: HarperCollins.

Aronson, Bernard. 1994. "The Man Who Saved El Salvador." *The Washington Post*, May 11, A21.

Austin, James E. 1991. *Women's World Banking*. Boston: Harvard Business School.

Barry, Nancy. 1994. "Women Making a Difference: The World Bank and Women's World Banking." Washington, D.C.: Speech at the World Bank, March.

Barry, Nancy. 1996. "Ethics and Spiritual Values and the Promotion of Environmentally Sustainable Development." Washington, D.C.: Speech at the World Bank, October 3.

Bartlett, S. 1991. "Changing of the Guard at Salomon," *The New York Times*, August 17, D1.

Bernbaum, Edwin. 1990. *Sacred Mountains of the World*. San Francisco: Sierra Club Books.

Bianco, Anthony. 1985. "The King of Wall Street." *Business Week*, December 9.

Blum, Arlene. 1979. "Triumph and Tragedy on Annapurna." *National Geographic*, March, 295–311.

Blum, Arlene. 1980. *Annapurna: A Woman's Place*. San Francisco: Sierra Club Books.

Blum, Arlene. 1992. "Preface." In *Leading Out: Women Climbers Reaching for the Top*, Rachel da Silva, ed. Seattle: Seal Press.

Bodie, Zvi, and Dwight B. Crane. 1997. *Personal Investing: Advice, Theory, and Evidence from a Sample of TIAA-CREF Participants.* Boston: Global Financial System Project, Harvard Business School.

Bornstein, David. 1996. *The Price of a Dream: The Story of the Grameen Bank and the Idea That Is Helping the Poor to Change Their Lives.* New York: Simon & Schuster.

Boudreaux, Richard, and Marjorie Miller. 1989. "Offensive Pushed Salvador War to New, Bloodier Level." *Los Angeles Times.* November 30, 1.

Brodmann, Ron, and Bill Curry. 1978. "Personalities." *The Washington Post*, May 3, D3.

Buffett, Warren. 1991a. Letter of August 21 to Salomon Inc. and others. New York: Salomon Inc.

Buffett, Warren. 1991b. "A Report by the Chairman on the Company's Standing and Outlook," October 29. New York: Salomon Inc.

Bulkeley, William M., and Gary Putka. 1995. "IBM Chairman Gives Lotus Workers Pep Talk Day After Pact to Buy Firm." *The Wall Street Journal*, June 13, B5.

Burns, James MacGregor. 1978. *Leadership.* New York: Harper & Row.

Byrne, Hugh. 1996. *El Salvador's Civil War: A Study of Revolution.* Boulder, Colo.: Lynne Rienner Publishers.

Cadot, Olivier, Katie Smith Milway, and Michael Milway, eds. 1993. "Transforming Enterprise." In *Future Value: Enterprise and Sustainable Development.* Fountainbleau, France: INSEAD (European Institute of Business Administration).

Campbell, William C. 1992. "The Genesis of the Antiparasitic Drug Ivermectin." In *Inventing Minds: Creativity in Technology*, Robert J. Weber and David N. Perkins, eds. New York: Oxford University Press.

Carrington, Tim. 1994. "In Developing World, International Lenders Are Targeting Women." *The Wall Street Journal*, June 21, A1, 6.

Carter, Jimmy. 1993. "Foreword" to David Wigg, *And They Forgot to Tell Us Why: A Look at the Campaign Against River Blindness in West Africa.* Washington, D.C.: World Bank.

Cavanaugh, Shelia C., and Steven R. Fenster. 1992. *Salomon Inc.* Cambridge, Mass.: Harvard Business School.

Chamberlain, Joshua Lawrence. 1994 (republished). *Bayonet! Forward: My Civil War Reminiscences.* Gettysburg, Pa.: Sam Clark Military Books.

Chief Executive. 1990. "Not So Silent Partner." November–December, 40–43.

Christian, Shirley. 1991. "Salvadoran Far-Right Leader Ill with Cancer." *The New York Times*, July 22, A4.

Coddington, Edwin B. 1979. *The Gettysburg Campaign: A Study in Command.* New York: Macmillan.

Connor, John. 1997. "Salomon Status Weighed by Fed After Scandal." *The Wall Street Journal*, January 10, B5A.

Cooper, Henry S. F., Jr. 1972. *Thirteen: The Apollo Flight That Failed.* Baltimore: Johns Hopkins Press.

Crowley, Susan. 1979. "Despite Ban on Tris, Consumers Confused over Safety of Sleepwear." *The Washington Post*, July 12, District Weekly, p. 2.

Daley, Suzanne. 1997. "The Standards Bearer." *The New York Times Magazine*, April 13, 35–37.

Davies, Julia, and Mark Easterby-Smith. 1984. "Learning and Developing from Managerial Work Experiences." *Journal of Management Studies* 21: 169–183.

Davis, L. J. 1988. "$60 Billion in the Balance." *The New York Times Magazine*, March 27, 16 ff.

Dietel, J. Edwin. 1996. *Leaders' Digest: A Review of the Best Books on Leadership.* Chicago: American Bar Association.

Drucker, Peter F. 1976. *The Unseen Revolution: How Pension Fund Socialism Came to America.* New York: Harper & Row.

Drucker, Peter F. 1996. "Not Enough Generals Were Killed." In *The Leader of the Future*, Frances Hesselbein, Marshall Goldsmith, and Richard Beckhard, eds. San Francisco: Jossey-Bass.

Druckman, Daniel, and Robert A. Bjork, eds. 1994. *Learning, Remembering, Believing: Enhancing Human Performance.* Washington, D.C.: National Academy Press.

Dunlap, Albert J. 1996. *Mean Business: How I Save Bad Companies and Make Good Companies Great.* New York: Times Books.

Eckholm, Erik. 1989. "River Blindness: Conquering an Ancient Scourge." *The New York Times Magazine*, January 8.

Eden, Dov. 1992. "Leadership and Expectations: Pygmalion Effects and Other Self-Fulfilling Prophecies in Organizations." *Leadership Quarterly*, Winter, 271–305.

Emerson, Richard M. 1964. "Sociology," in *Americans on Everest*, James Ramsey Ullman and Other Members of the Expedition. Philadelphia: Lippincott.

Falcoff, Mark, and Robert Royal, eds. 1987. *The Continuing Crisis: U.S. Policy in Central America and the Caribbean.* Lanham, Md.: University Press of America.

Fiedler, Fred E. 1992. "Time-based Measures of Leadership Experience and Organizational Performance: A Review of Research and a Preliminary Model." *Leadership Quarterly* 3 (Spring): 4–23.

Fiedler, Fred E. 1994. *Leadership Experience and Leadership Performance.* Alexandria, Va.: U.S. Army Research Institute for the Behavioral and Social Sciences.

Feinberg, Phyllis. 1988. "TIAA-CREF's First Outside Chairman Steers Steady Course of Change." *Pension World*, September.

Financial Times. 1993. "The Changing Image of Glaxo." July 26.

Finkelstein, Sydney, and Donald C. Hambrick. 1996. *Strategic Leadership: Top Executives and Their Effects on Organizations.* Minneapolis–St. Paul: West.

Fisher, Roger, and William Ury. 1992. *Getting to Yes: Negotiating Agreement Without Giving In.* Boston: Houghton Mifflin.

Fong, Pang Yin. 1990. "Big Move to a Smaller Institution." *New Straits Times.*

Foster, Lawrence G. 1983. "The Johnson & Johnson Credo and the Tylenol Crisis." *New Jersey Bell Journal* 6: 1–7.

Friedland, Sandra. 1989. "Pharmaceutical Company Shares Its Harvest of Achievements." *The New York Times*, Section 12 NJ: 1.

Friedman, Milton. 1970. "The Social Responsibility of Business Is to Increase Its Profits." *The New York Times Magazine*, September 13.

Frison-Roche, Roger, and Sylvain Jouty. 1996. *A History of Mountain Climbing.* Deke Dusinberre, trans. New York: Flammarion.

Gardner, Howard. 1995. *Leading Minds: An Anatomy of Leadership.* New York: Basic Books.

Gardner, John. 1993. *On Leadership.* New York: Free Press.

Gibson, Richard. 1996. "McDonald's Accelerates Store Openings in U.S. and Abroad, Pressuring Rivals." *The Wall Street Journal,* January 16.

Gilbert, Shirley. 1996. "Leading the Climb" (interview with Arlene Blum). *Measure.* Palo Alto: Hewlett-Packard Company.

Ginnett, Robert C. 1993. "Crews as Groups: Their Formation and Their Leadership." In *Cockpit Resource Management,* Earl L. Wiener, Barbara G. Kank, and Robert L. Helmreich, eds. San Diego: Academic Press.

Golay, Michael. 1994. *To Gettysburg and Beyond: The Parallel Lives of Joshua Lawrence Chamberlain and Edward Porter Alexander.* New York: Crown.

Gore, Albert. 1993. *Creating a Government That Works Better and Costs Less.* New York: Random House.

Gorman, Christine. 1990. "Women Start Taking Credit: An Unusual Institution Helps Third World Entrepreneurs." *Time,* June 4.

Grant, Linda. 1992. "Taming the Bond Buccaneers at Salomon Brothers." *Los Angeles Times Magazine,* February 16.

Greenough, William C. 1990. *It's My Retirement Money, Take Good Care of It: The TIAA-CREF Story.* Homewood, Ill.: Irwin.

Hansell, Saul. 1992. "Deryck Maughan's All-Volunteer Army." *Institutional Investor,* August, 27–39.

Hansell, Saul, Beth Selby, and Henny Sender. 1991. "Who Should Run Salomon Brothers?" *Institutional Investor,* September, 11–14.

Harrington, David, Heather Miles, Alison Watkins, Anne Williamson, and Diane Grady. 1996. "Putting People Values to Work." *McKinsey Quarterly* 3: 163–167.

Heller, Scott. 1987. "TIAA Chief to Tell Colleges Employees Deserve Choice in Pension Investments." *Chronicle of Higher Education,* August 12.

Henriques, Diana B. 1994. "Philip Morris's Chief Executive Abruptly Quits." *The New York Times,* June 20, D1.

Herzog, Maurice. 1953. *Annapurna: First Conquest of an 8000-Meter Peak.* Nea Morin and Janet Adam Smith, trans. New York: Dutton.

Herzog, Maurice. 1980. "Foreword," in Arlene Blum, *Annapurna: A Woman's Place*. San Francisco: Sierra Club Books.

Hunt, Sir John. 1960. "Foreword," in *The Last Blue Mountain: The True and Moving Story of the Ill-Starred Expedition Against Mount Haramosh*. New York: Doubleday & Company.

Hillary, Peter. 1996. "Everest Is Mighty, We Are Fragile." *The New York Times*, May 25, 19.

Hornbein, Thomas F. 1966. *Everest: The West Ridge*. San Francisco: Sierra Club.

Howard, Darby & Levin. 1992. "Memorandum on Behalf of John H. Gutfreund," submitted to the U.S. Securities and Exchange Commission, June 17. New York: Howard, Darby & Levin.

Howells, Cynthia. 1993. "Women's World Banking: An Interview with Nancy Barry." *Columbia Journal of World Business*, Fall, 20–32.

Huebner, Tasha. 1996. "Merck—The Company with a Conscience." *The Wharton Journal*, November 18, 1, 6.

Kanter, Rosabeth Moss. 1977. *Men and Women of the Corporation*. New York: Basic Books.

Kaplan, Gilbert. 1991. "True Confessions" (interview with John Gutfreund). *Institutional Investor*, February, 51–62.

Katzenbach, Jon R., and Douglas K. Smith. 1993. *The Wisdom of Teams: Creating the High-Performance Organization*. Boston: Harvard Business School Press.

Katzenbach, Jon R., et al. 1996. *Real Change Leaders: How You Can Create Growth and High Performance at Your Company*. New York: Random House.

Kennedy, John F. 1956. *Profiles in Courage*. New York: Harper & Row.

Khandker, Shahidur R., Baqui Khalily, and Zahed Khan. 1995. *Grameen Bank: Performance and Sustainability*. Washington, D.C.: World Bank.

Komarkova, Vera. 1979. "American Women's Expedition, Annapurna I." *American Alpine Journal* 22: 45–58.

Krakauer, Jon. 1997. *Into Thin Air: A Personal Account of the Mt. Everest Disaster*. New York: Villard.

Kuper, Simon. 1997. "A Leap in the Dark with Microloans." *Financial Times*, January 31.

Kupfer, Andrew. 1996. "What, Me Worry?" *Fortune*, September 30, 121–124.

LaChapelle, Edward B. 1966. "The Control of Snow Avalanches." *Scientific American*, February, 92–102.

Lanker, Brian. 1989. *I Dream a World: Portraits of Black Women Who Changed America*. New York: Stewart, Tabori & Chang.

Larson, Andrea. 1991. *Women's World Banking: The Early Years*. Charlottesville, Va.: Darden Graduate School of Business Administration, University of Virginia.

Leary, Warren E. 1995. "With One Disease Nearly Erased, Assault Is Planned on Another." *The New York Times*, December 6.

LeoGrande, William M. 1990. "After the Battle of El Salvador." *World Policy Journal* 7: 331–356.

Levinson, Marc. 1993. "The Old College Try." *Newsweek*, January 11, 46–47.

Lewis, Michael. 1989. *Liar's Poker: Rising Through the Wreckage on Wall Street*. New York: W. W. Norton & Co.

Life. 1949. "Smokejumpers Suffer Ordeal by Fire." August 22, 17–22.

Lipton, Elisabeth Ament, and Thomas J. C. Raymond. 1984. *Tylenol*. Boston: Harvard Business School.

Loomis, Carol J. 1997. "Warren Buffett's Wild Ride at Salomon." *Fortune*, October 27, 114–132.

Lovell, Jim, and Jeffrey Kluger. 1994. *Lost Moon: The Perilous Voyage of Apollo 13*. Boston: Houghton Mifflin.

Lowenstein, Roger. 1995. *Buffett: The Making of an American Capitalist*. New York: Random House.

Lynn, Matthew. 1992. *The Billion Dollar Battle: Merck v. Glaxo*. London: Mandarin.

Maclean, Norman. 1992. *Young Men and Fire*. Chicago: University of Chicago Press.

Mangan, Katherine S. 1987. "Debate over Faculty Pension-Plan Policies Heats Up; Critics Await Report from TIAA-CREF Trustees." *Chronicle of Higher Education*, September 23.

McCain, Nina. 1988. "At Home on Top of the Mountains." *The Boston Globe*, Living Section, November 21, 49.

McCall, Morgan W., Jr., Michael M. Lombardo, and Ann M. Morrison. 1988. *The Lessons of Experience: How Successful*

Executives Develop on the Job. Lexington, Mass.: Lexington Books.

McCoy, Bowen H. 1997a. "The Parable of the Sadhu." *Harvard Business Review*, May–June, 54–64.

McCoy, Bowen H. 1997b. "When Do We Take a Stand?" *Harvard Business Review*, May–June, 60.

Menzel, Sewall H. 1994. *Bullets Versus Ballots: Political Violence and Revolutionary War in El Salvador, 1979–1991.* New Brunswick, N.J.: Transaction Publishers.

Mercer, Joye. 1997. "TIAA-CREF Expands Its Offerings as Competitors Attract New Business." *Chronicle of Higher Education*, July 25, A35–36.

Merck & Co., Inc. 1993. "Declaration of Strategic Intent." Princeton, N.J.: Merck & Co., Inc.

Merck & Co., Inc. 1996. "1995 Report: Corporate Responsibility." Princeton, N.J.: Merck & Co., Inc.

Microcredit Summit. 1997. *Declaration and Plan of Action.* Washington, D.C.: Results Education Fund.

Miller, Irene, and Vera Komarkova, 1979. "On the Summit." *National Geographic*, March, 312–313.

Mintzberg, Henry. 1973. *The Nature of Managerial Work.* New York: Harper & Row.

Mintzberg, Henry. 1990. "The Manager's Job: Folklore and Fact." *Harvard Business Review*, March–April, 163–176.

Montgomery, Tommie Sue. 1995. *Revolution in El Salvador: From Civil Strife to Civil Peace.* Boulder, Colo.: Westview.

Moreton, Patrick. 1992. *Salomon and the Treasury Securities Auction: 1992 Update.* Cambridge, Mass.: Harvard Business School.

Moreton, Patrick, and Dwight Crane. 1992. *Salomon and the Treasury Securities Auction.* Cambridge, Mass.: Harvard Business School.

MSDI Newsletter. 1989. "Journey: A Scientist's Dream Comes True." West Point, Pa.: Merck Sharp & Dohme International.

Murray, Kevin (with Tom Berry). 1995. *Inside El Salvador.* Albuquerque, N.M.: Resource Center Press.

Musa, Tansa. 1996. "Cameroon-Health: NGO Coalition Brings Hope to the Blind." Inter Press Service, October 6.

Nadler, David A., and Michael L. Tushman. 1990. "Beyond the Charismatic Leader: Leadership and Organizational Change," *California Management Review*, Winter, 77–97.

The New York Times. 1969. "Michigan State Chief: Clifton Reginald Wharton Jr." October 18.

The New York Times. 1970. "Safe Return" (editorial). April 18, 28.

Packer-Tursman, Judy. 1997. "Benefits Seen in Tiny Loans to World's Poorest." *Pittsburgh Post-Gazette*, February 4.

Paine, Lynn Sharp, and Michael A. Santoro. 1994a. *Leadership Problems at Salomon*. Cambridge, Mass.: Harvard Business School.

Paine, Lynn Sharp, and Michael A. Santoro. 1994b. *Leadership Problems at Salomon (A)*. Cambridge, Mass.: Harvard Business School.

Paine, Lynn Sharp, and Michael A. Santoro. 1994c. *Leadership Problems at Salomon (B)*. Cambridge, Mass.: Harvard Business School.

Perry, Mark. 1997. *Conceived in Liberty: Joshua Chamberlain, William Oates, and the American Civil War*. New York: Viking.

Phillips, Donald T. 1992. *Lincoln on Leadership*. New York: Warner Books.

Power, William, and Michael Siconolfi. 1991. " 'Mr. Integrity' Is Promoted to a Top Post." *Wall Street Journal*, August 19, A5.

Ramphele, Mamphela. 1995. *Across Boundaries: The Journey of a South African Woman Leader*. New York: Feminist Press.

Rohter, Larry. 1997. "Former Rebels Make Impressive Advances in Salvador Elections." *The New York Times*, March 26, A5.

Rosenberg, Hilary. 1989. "The Education of TIAA-CREF." *Institutional Investor*, April, 68–77.

Rosenthal, A. M. 1993. "On My Mind: The Wharton Case." *The New York Times*, December 3, A33.

Salomon Inc. 1991. Statement of Salomon Inc. Submitted in Conjunction with the Testimony of Warren E. Buffett, Chairman and Chief Executive Officer of Salomon Inc., Before the Securities Subcommittee, Committee on Banking, Housing and Urban Affairs, U.S. Senate, September 10. New York: Salomon Inc.

Sass, Steven A. 1997. *The Promise of Private Pensions: The First Hundred Years.* Cambridge, Mass.: Harvard University Press.

Sebastian, Pamela. 1987. "Some Academics Move to Widen Choices." *The Wall Street Journal,* August 31.

Shaara, Michael. 1974. *The Killer Angels.* New York: Random House.

Shapiro, Eben. 1994a. "Philip Morris CEO Resigns Under Pressure." *The New York Times,* June 20, A3.

Shapiro, Eben. 1994b. "Philip Morris Plans an Attack on EPA Report." *The New York Times,* June 24, B1.

Shapiro, Joshua. 1996. *Sky,* January, 68–74.

Shepard, Alan, and Deke Slayton. 1994. *Moon Shot: The Inside Story of America's Race to the Moon.* Atlanta: Turner Publishing.

Smith, Gary. 1994. "An Exclusive Club." *Sports Illustrated,* June 27, 72–84.

Society of Woman Geographers. 1992. *Honors Winners and Flag Carriers.* Washington, D.C.: Society of Woman Geographers.

Spodek, Howard. 1994. "The Self-Employed Women's Association (SEWA) in India: Feminist, Gandhian Power in Development." *Economic Development and Cultural Change* 43: 193–202.

Stanley, William, and Charles T. Call. 1997. "Building a New Civilian Police Force in El Salvador." In *Rebuilding Societies After Civil War: Critical Roles for International Assistance,* Krishna Kumar, ed. Boulder, Colo.: Lynne Rienner Publishers.

Stewart, James B. 1991. *Den of Thieves.* New York: Simon & Schuster.

Taylor, Hugh R., Michel Pacque, and Beatriz Munoz. 1990. "Impact of Mass Treatment of Onchocerciasis with Ivermectin on the Transmission of Infection." *Science,* October 5, 116–118.

Tefft, Sheila. 1995. "Give a Poor Woman a Fish? No. A Fishing Pole? No. A Loan? Yes." *The Christian Science Monitor,* September 13, 1, 5.

Thomas, Robert M. 1997. "Raymond Lambert, 82, Dies; Paved the Way on Mt. Everest." *The New York Times,* March 3, B10.

TIAA-CREF. 1987. *The Future Agenda: Report of the Special Trustee Joint Committee.* New York: TIAA-CREF.

TIAA-CREF. 1992. *TIAA-CREF Executive Compensation Policy and Practice: An Overview.* New York: TIAA-CREF.

TIAA-CREF. 1993. "TIAA-CREF Celebrates Its 75th Anniversary." *The Participant: Quarterly News for TIAA-CREF Participants*, April, 2–3.

Trulock, Alice Rains. 1992. *In the Hands of Providence: Joshua L. Chamberlain and the American Civil War*. Chapel Hill, N.C.: University of North Carolina Press.

Tucker, Glenn. 1983. *High Tide at Gettysburg*. Dayton, Ohio: Morningside House.

Ullman, James Ramsey. 1964a. *The Age of Mountaineering*. Philadelphia: Lippincott.

Ullman, James Ramsey. 1964b. *Americans on Everest*. Philadelphia: Lippincott

Useem, Michael. 1993. *Executive Defense: Shareholder Power and Corporate Reorganization*. Cambridge, Mass.: Harvard University Press.

Useem, Michael. 1996. *Investor Capitalism: How Money Managers Are Changing the Face of Corporate America*. New York: Basic Books.

Useem, Michael, Louis Setti, and Jonathan Pincus. 1992. "The Science of Javanese Management: Organizational Alignment in an Indonesian Development Program." *Public Administration and Development* 12: 447–471.

Vise, David A. 1993. "Strong Manager, Soft Market: TIAA-CREF's Wharton Leaves Fund Solid Despite Some Problems." *The Washington Post*, January 22.

Waddock, Sandra A., and Samuel B. Graves. 1997. "The Corporate Social Performance–Financial Performance Link." *Strategic Management Journal* 18: 303–319.

Waldman, David A., Gabriel G. Ramirez, and Robert J. House. 1996. "CEO Charisma and Profitability: Under Conditions of Perceived Environmental Certainty and Uncertainty." Philadelphia: Jones Center for Management Policy, Strategy, and Organization, Wharton School, University of Pennsylvania.

Walker, Tony, and Leyla Boulton. 1995. "Micro-Lending Offers Power to World's Poor." *Financial Times*, September 5.

Wallace, Willard M. 1960. *Soul of the Lion: A Biography of General Joshua L. Chamberlain*. Gettysburg, Pa.: Stan Clark Military Books.

Weick, Karl E. 1990. "The Vulnerable System: An Analysis of the Tenerife Air Disaster." *Journal of Management* 16: 571–593.

Weick, Karl E. 1993. "The Collapse of Sensemaking in Organizations: The Mann Gulch Disaster." *Administrative Science Quarterly* 38: 628–652.

Weiss, Stephanie. 1991. "Merck & Co., Inc." Stanford: Business Enterprise Trust.

WGBH Educational Foundation. 1994. *Apollo 13: To the Edge and Back* (video). Boston: WGBH Educational Foundation.

Whitfield, Teresa. 1995. *Paying the Price: Ignacio Ellacuría and the Murdered Jesuits of El Salvador.* Philadelphia: Temple University Press.

Wigg, David. 1993. *And Then They Forgot to Tell Us Why: A Look at the Campaign Against River Blindness in West Africa.* Washington, D.C.: World Bank.

Wilford, John Noble. 1970. "Power Failure Imperils Astronauts; Apollo Will Head Back to Earth," *The New York Times*, April 14, 1, 32.

Wills, Garry. 1994. *Certain Trumpets: The Call of Leaders.* New York: Simon & Schuster.

Women's World Banking. 1994. *United Nations Expert Group on Women and Finance.* New York: Women's World Banking.

Women's World Banking. 1995a. "Client Success Stories." *What's New*, July, 1–14.

Women's World Banking. 1995b. *The Missing Links: Financial Systems That Work for the Majority.* New York: Women's World Banking.

Women's World Banking. 1995c. *Report from the U.S. Banking Innovation Council Meeting.* New York: Women's World Banking.

Women's World Banking. 1996a. *Report of the Workshop of African Microfinance Practitioners.* New York: Women's World Banking.

Women's World Banking. 1996b. *Institution Building in Microfinance: Lessons from Funders and Practitioners.* New York: Women's World Banking.

Women's World Banking. 1996c. *Expanding Our Reach and Effectiveness.* New York: Women's World Banking.

Women's World Banking. 1997. *Women's World Banking: Strategy Statement, 1997 to 1999.* New York: Women's World Banking.

Woods, Donald. 1987. *Biko.* New York: Henry Holt.

World Bank. 1995. "From Girls' Schools in Balochistan—To Health in Zimbabwe: World Bank Reports from the Field," February 28. Washington, D.C.: World Bank.

World Bank. 1996. *El Salvador: Meeting the Challenge of Globalization.* Washington, D.C.: World Bank.

Zigas, David. 1988. "Forcing an Old Pension Fund to Learn a Few New Tricks." *Business Week,* July 18: 122–123.

Zimmer, Jeff. 1995. "City of Medicine Award Winners Honored 3 Researchers." *Herald-Sun* (Durham, N.C.), October 12, A1.

Acknowledgments

When possible, I have sought to interview those personally familiar with the events chronicled here, and many have provided invaluable firsthand accounts and primary documents. They are identified in the endnotes for each of the chapters, and their generous gift of time and information is greatly appreciated.

Others rendered special assistance in reaching the principals or documenting their moments, including Edwin Bernbaum of Berkeley, California; Mauricio Borgonovo of Miami, Florida; Judith Dobrzynski of *The New York Times;* Susan Eckstein of Boston University; Thomas Gilmore of the Center for Applied Research, Philadelphia; Ute Jokisch de Goens of San Salvador, El Salvador; Jeffrey Kluger of *Time* magazine; Rene Molina Angel and Alexis Sermeno of Escuela Superior de Economía y Negocios, San Salvador, El Salvador; Patricia Sellers of *Fortune* magazine; and the staff of NASA's Lyndon B. Johnson Space Center.

I have greatly benefited from the fine editorial guidance of four individuals with whom I have worked extensively in preparing these accounts. They are Peter Cowen of Boston, John Mahaney of Times Books/Random House, Howard Means of *The Washingtonian* magazine, and Raphael Sagalyn of Sagalyn Literary Agency. From first blueprint to final copy, they have assisted virtually every aspect of this endeavor, and I am very grateful for their excellent counsel throughout.

Friends and relatives—Julia Bell, Tarleton Cowen, Joseph Rosenbloom, Susan Rosenbloom, Andrea Useem, Bert Useem, Elizabeth Useem, Howard Useem, Jerry Useem, John Useem, Ruth

Useem, and Susan Useem—have contributed invaluable ideas for the book's focus and framing.

These nine accounts and their leadership implications have been developed and refined in numerous courses and programs during the past several years. The most extended venue has been the Wharton Executive MBA Program, and I would like to express deep appreciation to the more than five hundred students who have participated in my leadership courses for the program. Their reactions and writings have been a critical factor in my decision to focus on learning from leaders on the line. "When things go according to plan," advised one of the participants, "leading is relatively easy. It is those times when they don't that leadership is at its most challenging." For the unstinting support rendered by the program's directors—Diane Harvey, Howard Kaufold, Catherine Molony, and David Stewart—I am most grateful.

Other venues, too, have been essential to the development of the stories and ideas found in this book. For those opportunities, I extend special thanks to Jeff Barta, Jane Hiller Farran, Scott Koerwer, Robert Mittelstaedt, Alison McGrath Peirce, Sheldon Rovin, Sherrill Rosoff, Patricia Steele, Michael Seitchik, and Yumi Wakayama of the Wharton Executive Education Program; and to Bruce Allen, Michael Baker, Michael Baltes, Janice Bellace, Geoffrey Brooks, Peter Cappelli, Thomas Donaldson, Thomas Dunfee, Stewart Friedman, Thomas Gerrity, Timothy Habbershon, Joseph Harder, Chris Hardwick, Marti Harrington, Robert House, Anjani Jain, John Kimberly, Steven Kobrin, Bruce Kogut, Peter Linneman, Leonard Lodish, Ian Macmillan, Thomas Malnight, Annie McKee, Jerry Rosenbloom, Greg Shea, Jeffrey Sheehan, Jitendra Singh, Harbir Singh, Paul Tiffany, and Ross Webber of the Wharton School of the University of Pennsylvania.

For similar reasons, I would like to thank Charles Dwyer, Judith Rodin, Stephen Steinberg, and Robert Zemsky of the University of Pennsylvania; Suthi Ekahitanonda, Toemsakdi Krishnamra, and Patcharaphorn Phantarathorn of Sasin Graduate School of Business Administration, Chulalongkorn University, Bangkok, Thailand; Shinichi Ichimura of the International Centre for the Study of East Asian Development, Kitakyushu, Japan; Ann De Jaeger of Video Management, Brussels, Belgium; Dipak Jain, Kellogg Graduate School of Management, Northwestern University; Mirna Liévano de Marques and Ricardo Poma of Escuela Superior de Economía y Negocios, San Salvador, El Salvador; David Morrison, Thomas Scherer, and Klaus Schwab of the World Economic Forum, Geneva, Switzerland; Anita Orellana and Rafael Rodriguez of Seminarium, Santiago, Chile; Manuel Robleda G. de Castilla and David Konzevik of the Mexican Stock Exchange, Mexico City; William Ross of Temple University; and Injay Tai and William Wang of SMEC Media & Entertainment Corporation, Taipei, Taiwan.

We all have our own leadership moments to look back upon and new ones surely await us. If you would care to share your own moments, please forward them to <lead@ wharton.upenn.edu>. An updated "Leader's Guide" and other leadership development information are posted at <http://leadership.wharton.upenn.edu/leaders/digest/current.shtml>.

In introducing a collection of women's mountaineering stories, Arlene Blum has written: "Knowledge of the extraordinary deeds of these women can help each of us to climb our own metaphorical mountains and to live our lives with strength and confidence." In a similar vein, Sir John Hunt, leader of the 1953 British expedition that first ascended Mount Everest, once said: "The true result of endeavor, whether on a mountain or in any other context, may be found rather in its lasting effects than in the few moments during which a summit is trampled by mountain boots. The real measure is the success or failure of the climber to triumph, not over a lifeless mountain, but over himself: the true value of the enterprise lies in the example to others of human motive and human conduct." It is through such deeds and endeavors that we can better appreciate our own leadership within and how best to bring it out, and it is thus the nine people whose informative experiences we have recounted here to whom the ultimate acknowledgment must be extended.*

*Blum, 1990; Hunt, 1960.

Index

See also Chamberlain, Joshua
Lawrence
Mallory, George, 95
Management style. *See specific person*
Mandl, Alex, 224–25
Mann Gulch fire
Board of Review concerning,
55–56, 57
crew's background/experience at,
44–46, 57–58, 61
Dodge's credibility at, 53–56
Dodge's failures at, 57–58
Dodge's solution at, 51–52, 53,
56–57
and Dodge's style, 55–56, 57–58
fatalities at, 52–53
fire at, 43–58
legacy of Dodge's decisions at, 64
options at, 50
panic of team at, 56, 59–62, 63
and team building, 62
team spirit at, 48
terrible discoveries at, 49–50
Manufacturing plants, productivity
in, 83–84
Manzi, Jim P., 142–43
Marshall, George C., 267
Martínez, Ana Guadalupe, 253
Massachusetts State Teachers'
Retirement System, 193
Massey, James, 202
Mattingly, Ken, 78, 87
Maughan, Deryck C., 195, 199,
200, 201–2, 204, 205, 206
Mead, Margaret, 267
Meade, George G., 128, 130, 131,
132, 135–37, 140, 150
Mectizan
Africans' response to, 24
approval of, 22, 33
development of, 12–13, 16–21

and ending of River Blindness,
21, 39
financial support for, 23–24,
37–39
giving away of, 22–23, 33, 35,
40, 230
impact of decision about, 30,
41–42
limitations of, 24
lost income from, 25
manufacture and distribution of,
22–24, 25, 33, 37–38, 39
as medical triumph, 39
and shareholders, 25–32, 33–34,
40
See also Ivermectin; Vagelos, P.
Roy
Mentors, 62, 69, 91–92, 149
Merck & Company
culture at, 19, 22, 23, 29–30, 35,
37
employee commitment/pride at,
30, 35, 37
"The Gift of Sight" statue at,
39–40, 42
history of, 21–22
Japan's relationship with, 29–30
mission statement of, 29
product development at, 16–17
reputation of, 29–30, 41
shareholders of, 12, 25–32,
33–34, 40
See also Mectizan; Vagelos, P.
Roy
Merck, George W., 21, 29
Merck Sharp & Dohme Research
Laboratories, 16
Mercury Asset Management,
184–85, 193
Meriwether, John W., 178, 179,
185, 195, 199, 204–5

Photographs

Several organizations and individuals have kindly consented to the use of their photographs. Eugene Richards of Magnum provided the first image in Chapter One, and Merck & Company provided the others. In Chapter Two, Peter Stackpole (Time Warner) is responsible for the first and third images, and the U.S. Department of Agriculture for the other two. Chapter Three images are from the National Aeronautics and Space Administration. Arlene Blum, the subject of Chapter Four, provided the second, third, sixth, and seventh images for that chapter; Vera Komarkova furnished the first, Irene Miller the fourth, and Marie Ashton the fifth. Chapter Five photos are from the Library of Congress. The first image in Chapter Six is courtesy of William Coupon, and the second of TIAA-CREF. For Chapter Seven, the photo credit goes to, respectively, John Abbott, Associated Press, and Claudio Edinger of Gamma/Liaison. Women's World Banking provided images for Chapter Eight. For Chapter Nine, the author is responsible for the first and last images, and Tommie Sue Montgomery and Corinne Dufka for the second and third, respectively.

About the Author

MICHAEL USEEM is the director of the Center for Leadership and Change Management at the Wharton School, University of Pennsylvania, where he is also the William and Jacalyn Egan Professor of Management. He has worked with many organizations in both the public and private sector, including Bell Atlantic, Hewlett-Packard, the U.S. Agency for International Development, and the United Nations. His previous books include *Investor Capitalism* and *Executive Defense*. He regularly leads Wharton graduates on leadership treks to the Himalayas.

ALSO BY MICHAEL USEEM

When the consequences are big and the pressure is on, making the right decision is harder than ever—and it matters the most. From using small steps to make hard choices to developing a circle of advisors, Michael Useem's practical guide is invaluable for business and for life.

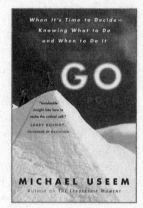

THE GO POINT
$14.95 paperback (Canada: $16.95)
978-1-4000-8299-5

Today's best leaders know how to lead up, a necessary strategy when a supervisor is micromanaging rather than macrothinking, or when investors demand instant gain but need long-term growth. Through vivid, compelling stories, Michael Useem reveals how upward leadership can transform incipient disaster into hard-won triumph.

LEADING UP
$15.95 paperback (Canada: $23.00)
978-1-4000-4700-0